GOOD&NIGHT
GOD&BLESS

Paratus press
AUSTRALIA

GOOD
GOD

MacKillop
Foundation

Part of the proceeds of the sale of this book goes to
THE MARY MACKILLOP FOUNDATION
(founded by the Sisters of St Joseph)
Mount Street, North Sydney, NSW 2060, Australia
The Mary MacKillop Foundation helps those without a
choices, without hope, without a voice.
www.marymackillopfoundation.org.au

NIGHT BLESS

A GUIDE TO **CONVENT**
AND **MONASTERY**
ACCOMMODATION
IN EUROPE

VOLUME ONE
AUSTRIA
CZECH REPUBLIC
ITALY

BY TRISH CLARK

GOOD NIGHT GOD BLESS

goodnightandgodbless.com
info@goodnightandgodbless.com

Paratus Press
PO Box 539, Roseville NSW 2069, Australia
info@paratuspress.com

AUTHOR Trish Clark
CONSULTANT EDITOR Gabiann Marin for Script and Story
EDITOR Janet Hutchinson
PROOFREADER Annabel Adair
INDEXER Tricia Waters
DESIGNERS Stuart Gibson and Nathan Wong for Book Design Australia Pty Ltd
ORIGINAL ILLUSTRATIONS Nathan Wong
MAPS Amanda Haes for Cowgirl Graphics
AUTHOR IMAGE Ian Barnes Photography
ADDITIONAL IMAGES *courtesy of* iStockPhoto
PRODUCTION Roger Ng and Xuan Luo for Midas Printing, China

Paratus press
AUSTRALIA

NOTE ❧ While every care has been taken to provide accurate information in this book, it's inevitable that in some cases prices, the availability and style of accommodation, directions, opening times, transport times and routes and other details will have changed by the time you travel. It's essential that you check all important details before travelling. Please help us prepare future editions by emailing your advice to *update@goodnightandgodbless.com*
❧ Similar accommodations are available throughout Europe—upcoming titles in the *Good Night and God Bless* series will cover France, England, Ireland, Germany, Spain and Eastern Europe.

National Library of Australia
Cataloguing-in-Publication Entry

Clark, Patricia Maureen, 1946–
Good Night and God Bless: a guide to convent and monastery accommodation in Europe
Volume One: Austria, Czech Republic & Italy
Abbeys—Guest accommodations—
    Europe—Guidebooks
Convents—Guest accommodations—
    Europe—Guidebooks.
Monasteries—Guest accommodations—
    Europe—Guidebooks.
Spiritual retreat centers—
    Europe—Guidebooks.
Processions, Religious—
    Europe—Guidebooks.
Rites and ceremonies—
    Europe—Guidebooks.
206.502540
ISBN 978-0-646-48520-1

Contents

Foreword

I T'S JUNE 1970 and my working holiday has finally landed me in Rome. Here I am with my backpack, ready to begin my adventure. Upon my arrival in the Eternal City, I find my much-preferred youth hostel fully booked. The manager kindly directs me to a convent nearby which he cheerfully informs me accommodates paying guests. I am alarmed at this suggestion that I stay in a religious guesthouse. I have never even heard of such a type of accommodation and am more than a little unsettled, anxious at the idea of spending even one night of my overseas adventure under the same roof as nuns. I imagine dour-faced sisters, rigid rules, an uncomfortable bed in an austere room, being woken early, and maybe even obligatory prayer times for guests. However, being on a limited budget, I have little choice and so glumly head off.

❡ The convent is run by an order of nuns on the Via Sistina, very near the Spanish Steps and nestled within the walls of a palace which is centuries old.

❡ I am warmly welcomed, although I immediately discover that the nuns don't speak any English and I must rely on my own 'bible', a run-down Italian dictionary from which I struggle to string together a few sentences in hesitant, basic Italian. The kind sisters earnestly respond to my questions, struggling with broken English and sign language.

❡ Still feeling apprehensive, I am escorted to my room, which was once a nun's cell. Having been taught by nuns in my Australian schooldays, the realisation I am about to sleep in one's bed is a little unnerving. The room is only small but spotlessly clean and, thankfully, the mattress quite comfortable.

❡ Each morning, I wake just in time for breakfast to the sound of song. The nuns are celebrating early morning Mass. Breakfast is served in the dining room at tables set with polished silver on crisply starched white tablecloths. Eager young postulants serve fresh bread rolls and home-made jam and from generous silver jugs pour delicious, steaming hot milky coffee. Before I head out for the day's sightseeing, the nuns give me a list of the best places to eat in the local area.

❡ Each night, my otherwise peaceful sleep is interrupted by opera arias, wafting into my window from across the narrow cobblestone street. A buxom, pyjama-clad woman with dark, unruly hair exuberantly throws open her shutters to deliver intense renditions to a starry audience, them slams them shut again. Her performances are always accompanied by frantic appeals from the darkness. *Silenzio, silenzio.*

❡ Fast forward and here I am, more than 30 years later, back on the Via Sistina and checking in to that very same convent. I am pleasantly relieved to discover little has changed. En suite bathrooms have been added to most of the guestrooms and if the nuns and their guests wish to avoid climbing the grand marble staircase there's now a tiny, 2-person lift. The sisters still don't speak much English, and the breakfast menu hasn't been updated at all. But the milky coffee is as delicious and plentiful as I remember it, and the nuns still seem to know where all the best restaurants are.

❡ There's a constant flow of travellers through the dining room now—a far cry from the mere handful of passers-by of yesteryear who, like me, were blessed to find out about this gem of a place by word of mouth. Still, even now the convent and monastery guesthouses of Europe are secrets for those 'in the know'.

❡ While this may partly be required to keep this religious accommodation safe from too much exploitation, ironically, without the support of the wider public many of these unique places of prayer and lodging will eventually be sold— most likely to hotel groups with the intention of retaining the 'religious theme' while inflating the prices.

❡ So why not try something different and unique next time you travel to Europe? Sleep in a convent, monastery or Christian hotel that caters specifically for tourists and holidaymakers. Or, if it's a soul-cleansing experience or spiritual sanctuary that you seek select a suitable retreat or take a religious pilgrimage.

❡ These days, with information more freely available and the web taking the hassles out of booking overnight stays, it's easy for travellers to include a unique experience in their holiday itinerary.

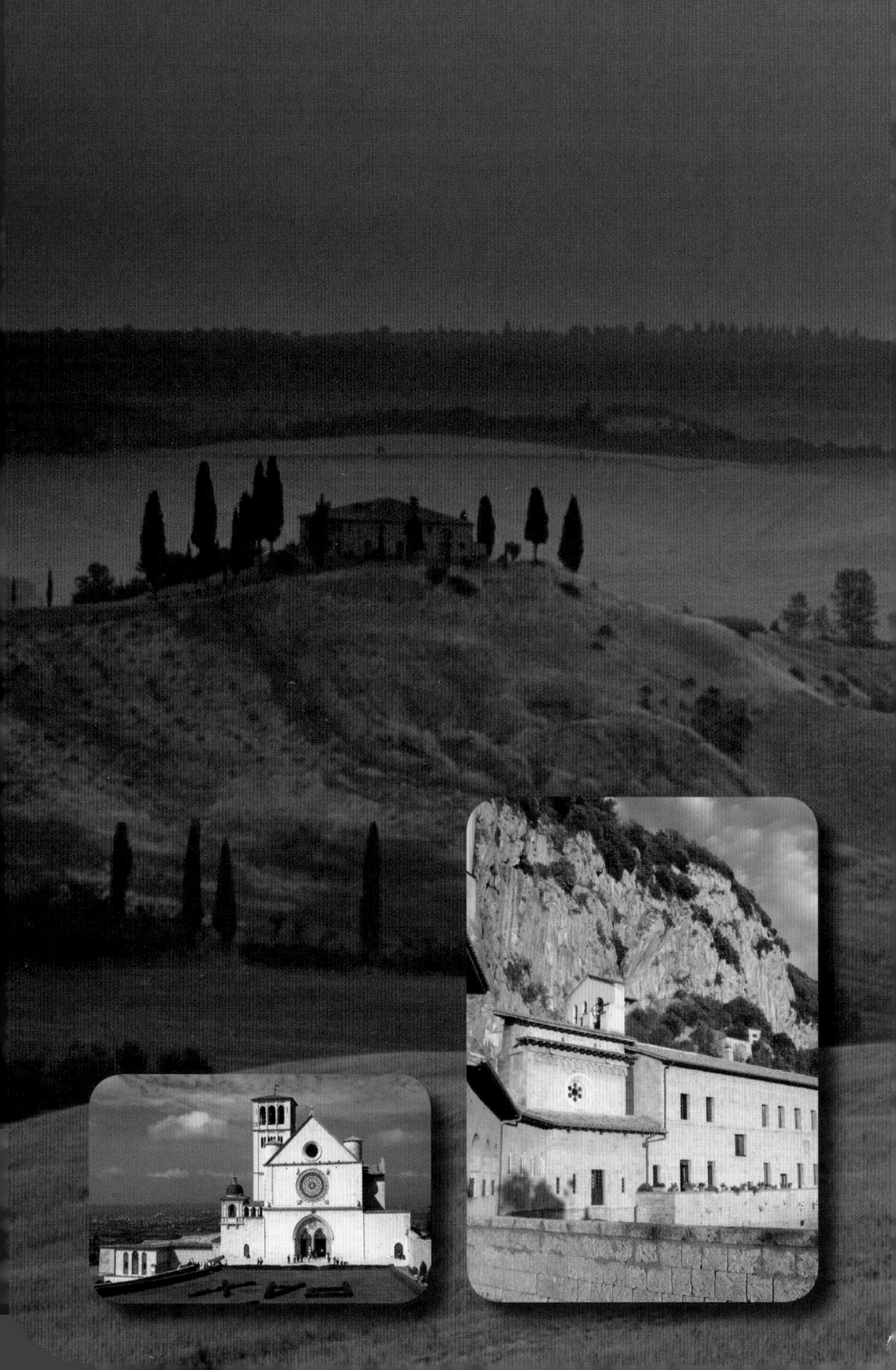

Post your own photos
of convents and
monasteries in Europe
on our website for
other readers to share,
and see all the places
pictured in this book
in detail, by visiting
*goodnightandgodbless.
com/photos*

All images courtesy
of iStockPhoto and
Lucy, Tom and Trish
Clark, *except* Göttweig
Monastery (back cover,
top right), Monastery
of Heiligenkreuz (this
page, bottom left) and
The Abbey of St Gerold,
Vorarlberg (this page,
top right); © Copyright
Österreich Werbung/
Trumler (Austrian
National Tourist Office).

Introduction

 **_GOODNIGHT AND GOD BLESS_** is a guide to alternative tourist accommodation in convents, monasteries, abbeys and Christian hotels in **Italy**, **Austria** and the **Czech Republic**, run by various mainstream Christian religious denominations.

As a result of a shortage of religious personnel, coupled with the increasingly high financial overheads in maintaining their ancient buildings, some religious orders have been forced to meet costs by offering tourist accommodation. Many convent and monastery buildings have been restored, with renovations often including en suite bathrooms, lifts and dining rooms. Others have share bathrooms and simple facilities. Single rooms are generally available at single prices.

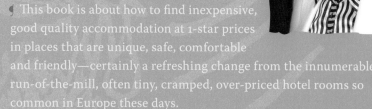

This book is about how to find inexpensive, good quality accommodation at 1-star prices in places that are unique, safe, comfortable and friendly—certainly a refreshing change from the innumerable run-of-the-mill, often tiny, cramped, over-priced hotel rooms so common in Europe these days.

Despite the usual view of religious accommodations, staying in a religious establishment does not necessarily mean adopting austerity. Pleasure does not necessarily go out the window the minute you book in. Wine is often served at lunch and dinner. Meals are sometimes prepared using the monastery's home-grown herbs and vegetables and some convent dining rooms are popular with the locals.

❡ A string of health spas have been established by an order of sisters in Austria, taking advantage of the thermal springs on the convent estates. Some sisters have even trained as beauticians and can offer facials that equal—if not better—those at your local salon. Other orders have converted deteriorating buildings into first-class meeting and business centres, fitted with state-of-the-art video and conferencing facilities. Unused monks' and nuns' cells have been transformed into modern guestrooms with hotel-style amenities.

❡ They are located in diverse places: in medieval palaces perhaps, or fronting onto grand piazzas; in the centre of bustling towns and cities, in charming rural villages, or in the countryside surrounded by lavender fields, vineyards and olive groves. But all warmly welcome overnight guests.

❡ Country monasteries are often working establishments where, as well as housing guests, the monks and nuns work in the vineyards, orchards or olive groves, on the farm, or in the fields tending lavender, vegetables, hops and other crops. Guests are more than welcome to lend a helping hand.

❡ Not all the nuns and monks may speak your language, but that never seems to be a handicap. Indeed, while many hotel guests are inclined to keep to themselves, the friendly, sociable atmosphere of a convent dining room encourages people to mix, talk and share their experiences.

LISTINGS ❧ The listings include **convents** and **monasteries** that are **open to tourists and holidaymakers**, as well as accommodation for those seeking a **spiritual experience** or wishing to make a **pilgrimage** or **retreat**. There is a difference to the type of experience you can expect from these two different types and that needs to be considered before you undertake to stay in these styles of accommodation.

OPEN HOUSES ❧ **Open Houses** are those religious orders that open their doors to **tourists**. They have a relaxed, informal atmosphere where guests are able to enjoy their holiday in a casual manner. Although there are no strict rules and regimes, basic respect for Christian tenets and the religious people living there is understandably expected.

SPIRITUAL RETREATS ❧ **Spiritual Retreats** are convents and monasteries accepting **guests for spiritual activities** and are usually quiet, sober establishments with a prevailing air of peacefulness and piety. Often there is a strict rule of **silence**. Such places are only appropriate for those who are serious about making a retreat or engaging in spiritual activities and definitely are not suitable for people looking for a hotel kind of experience. Nevertheless, both types have one thing in common: *the hospitality is indisputably genuine.*

❡ Staying in a monastery or convent, either for relaxation or spiritual purposes, is a unique experience which has its own flavour, no matter how relaxed the establishment may be.

❡ The modern world has not permeated all these establishments. Credit cards are not always accepted and sometimes the rooms and furniture can be basic. There are no 5-star, resort-style religious accommodations, and some convents and monasteries impose curfews— although usually they're generous, it's always best to check when you book.

❡ Sometimes there are added bonuses. Many ancient convents and monasteries are repositories for valuable artistic treasures, and some have given shelter to the works of artists and writers who are long gone from this world. A painting hanging in an Austrian monastery was recently identified as a genuine Rubens titled *Massacre of the Innocents*, worth over €76 million. *The Last Supper* by Franciabigio (1484–1525), painted in 1514, is in a convent in

Florence. In another, Fra Angelico's (1400–1455) ancient frescoes adorn the walls. The poet Dante Aligheri (1265–1321) wrote in the garden of a convent on the outskirts of Florence. More recently, renowned Czech artist Petr Brandl (1688–1739) painted and decorated the interior of the Brevnov Monastery church in Prague.

❡ I have enjoyed staying in many of the accommodations listed in this book and appreciate the helpful, informative feedback I have received from numerous others who likewise have stayed in convents and monasteries across Europe. The priests, monks, nuns and lay staff I have approached in regard to this guide have been helpful and encouraging and in the most cordial manner have either given me access to their establishments or enthusiastically offered photographs and information.

❡ However, while monks and nuns do live a life of prayer and devotion they are not always as easily identified as they may have been in the past. That gardener, tractor driver or good-looking young man showing you to your room might well be a monk; and the chatty, casually dressed waitress cheerfully serving you breakfast is most likely a nun.

TRISH CLARK March 2008

How to use this book

ACCOMMODATION ⸙ The book describes *two different categories of accommodation*; **Open Houses** and **Spiritual Retreats**. Lists of **Additional Accommodation** covering both categories are also included.

⸙ **Open Houses** include convents, monasteries and Christian hotels which are open to tourists and holidaymakers. Men, women, children, couples and individuals of any religious persuasion can use this accommodation (except where otherwise specified). Christian hotels are linked to Protestant churches and are run in an atmosphere of cordial hospitality and Christian spirit.

⸙ **Spiritual Retreats** are suitable only for those men and women who wish to embrace a spiritual dimension in the course of their holiday—a day of meditation, a period of quiet reflection, a religious retreat, or a pilgrimage.

⸙ **Additional Accommodation** includes suitable establishments for tourists or for those on a spiritual journey. Pilgrims are also welcome to stay in accommodation available to tourists.

⸙ When **requesting accommodation** it's easiest to use fax or email with a clear message written in English and where possible translated into the local language. Free language translation tools online can be used for this purpose.

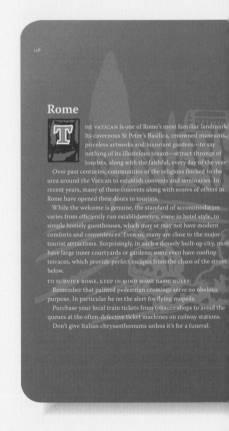

⸙ Simple **maps** (not to scale) show the location of the accommodation. Detailed maps are available from tourist offices or may be found on the Internet.

⸙ Some accommodation offers **accessibility** for the mobility disabled; this is indicated with an icon.

⸙ **Restrictions** may apply to certain accommodation such as female-only or male-only access; these are shown in each entry.

⸙ **Prices** shown are approximate, and are based on a twin share, per person per night basis for the low season. Prices for accommodation at Spiritual Retreats usually need to be negotiated on enquiry.

ITALY
Open Houses
Rome Aventino

01

Villa Rosa

The Villa Rosa Convent is situated in a quiet, exclusive suburb of well-kept villas, and a couple of embassies, away from crowds, traffic and the noise of the city. The convent is run by the International Order of Dominican Sisters and is around the corner from the 4th-century **church of Santa Prisca** and 0.5 kilometres from **Circus Maximus**, the stadium where the Romans staged their chariot races. The villa is on the **Aventine Hill**, one of the Seven Hills of Rome, with extensive views over the city. The single, double and triple guestrooms are spread over four floors and can be accessed by a lift. All guestrooms have private bathrooms. Breakfast is the only meal catered for. The sisters take holidays each August when the villa is closed down for the month. The convent has no car parking facilities and no credit cards are accepted. Many of the sisters are of Irish background and English is widely spoken here.

✉ Via delle Terme Deciane, 5
00153 Rome (RM)

from €45.00 pp, including breakfast

+39 (0) 6 57 17 091
+39 (0) 6 57 45 275

villarosa0006@libero.it

The nearest train station is Circo Massimo which is 600 metres from the convent.

Sunday Mass 0800 & 1900 (1900 in June) Church of Santa Prisca, Piazza Santa Prisca, 00153 Rome (RM)

Open to both men and women

PLACES OF INTEREST ❧ A section at the end of each geographical region provides information about the most popular pilgrimages in each area.

PILGRIMAGES ❧ A section at the end of each geographical region provides information about the most popular pilgrimages in each area.

PLACES OF INTEREST ❧ in the local area and surrounds are listed under each reviewed property, and include sightseeing and day trips.

FOOD AND DRINK ❧ comprises a small listing of popular and distinctive local restaurants and cafés.

✉ Address
Accommodation price
✆ Telephone
Fax
Email
Directions
Church services
Accessibility
€ Meal price range
  low price   €
  mid price   €€€
  high price   €€€€€

Open to both men and women
Open to women only
Open to men only
Open to groups only
Open to Priests only
T Tourist Accommodation
S Spiritual Retreat
ST Tourist Accommodation with Spiritual Retreat Option

Aus

YOU CAN'T ATTRACT THE MASSES WITH religion these days. In an era where the church is in such dire straits as it is here, opening up the cloisters also opens up a potential bridge to people and the possibility that they will once again seek dialogue with us.

FATHER DR MAXIMILIAN KRAUSGRUBER, O.CIST
ABBEY OF ZWETTL, AUSTRIA

tria

CZECH REPUBLIC

GERMANY

SWITZERLAND

ITALY

SLOVENIA

CROATIA

HUNGARY

BURGENLAND

VORARLBERG

TYROL

EAST TYROL

SALZBURG

UPPER AUSTRIA

LOWER AUSTRIA

VIENNA

STYRIA

CARINTHIA

Mehrerau
Hohenweiler
Bregenz
Götzis
St Gerold
Gaschurn

Reutte

Stams

Innsbruck
St Georgenberg-Fiecht
Maurach am Achensee

Bad Gastein

Ramingstein

Gosau

Salzburg
Michaelbeuern

Aspach
Feldkirchen an der Donau
Schlägl

Kremsmünster
Schlierbach

Albernsdorf
Linz

Tragwein
Bad Kreuzen

Seitenstetten

Geras
Zwettl
Altenburg

Göttweig
Heiligenkreuz
Lilienfeld

Mariazell

Maria Luggau

Wernberg
Feldkirchen
Gurk
St Lambrecht

St Paul im Lavanttal
St Georgen am Längsee

Seckau
Rein
Graz
Heiligenkreuz am Wassen
Fehring

Seebenstein
Oberpullendorf

Mönchhof
Eisenstadt

Vienna
Kleinzell
Heiligenkreuz

AUSTRIA

COUNTRY OF LAVISH NATURAL BEAUTY, Austria must truly be one of God's special places. Indeed, many of Austria's ancient abbeys, monasteries and convents are set against such stunning backdrops that it is difficult to deny a 'divine touch'. Most are situated in the north of the country, with others scattered along the banks of the **Danube** and in the country's alpine areas. A good number are to be found in Austria's spa regions and are run by nuns trained in health and beauty therapies who take a hands-on role in pampering their guests.

More than a place to sleep, Austria's monasteries are unique retreats from the hectic pace of everyday life. Once almost isolated from the outside world, it is now not uncommon for the country's religious orders to offer physical refuge along with the spiritual. Austere monks' cells have surrendered to more material comforts and these days Austrian monasteries usually have busy restaurants or cafés and a monastery shop attached to the premises, with the residents lending a helping hand as part of their ministry.

Austria's magnificent churches and abbeys are also the repositories of centuries of religious art, precious books and handwritten manuscripts once only available to the local parish but now openly shared with tourists and visitors.

Vienna

THEY SAY THAT MUSIC NOURISHES THE SOUL and what better place to stir the spirit than Vienna where the genius of **Strauss**, **Mozart** and **Beethoven** can be heard in venues all over the city—including Vienna's churches and abbeys. The ancient convents and monasteries of Vienna have long been centres of religion and enlightenment and a number of them take in overnight guests.

Many of Vienna's religious buildings can be found within the radius of the 4-kilometre **Ringstraße**, (*Ring Boulevard*) built by Emperor Franz Joseph in 1857 in preference to city walls. The **Capuchin Church** (the final resting place of Austrian royalty), **Schotten Abbey** (the home of Benedictine monks since 1155) and the lesser-known **Gothic Minorite Church** are icons of culture and Christianity; all lie within the ring road—considered the heart of historical and cultural Vienna. However, if it's Vienna's soul you are searching for, look no further than the medieval **Stephansdom**, the city's first cathedral, whose soaring steeples have towered over Vienna's old town for centuries.

For another kind of soul-stirring experience, head for the cosy, intimate atmosphere of a traditional Viennese *kaffeehaus* (coffee house).

Schotten Abbey

Established by Irish Benedictines in 1155, **Schotten Abbey** is situated in the historic centre of Vienna, near the Spanish Riding School and the Hofburg. Today the abbey is still home to Benedictine monks who run a prestigious high school for boys (Johann Strauss was once a pupil) and a busy bed and breakfast guesthouse which can sleep up to 30 people. Spacious single, double and triple guestrooms all have an en suite bathroom attached. Breakfast is the only meal served but the abbey is close to restaurants and coffee houses, shops and major tourist attractions. An underground (pay) parking station is nearby.

❡ The monks' valuable art collection is on display in the abbey museum and exhibits include paintings, tapestries and a **600-year-old Gothic 'winged' altar**, highly prized for a painting depicting the Holy Family's flight into Egypt, with 15th-century Vienna in the background. The abbey library's collection of 200,000 books and manuscripts dates back to the 16th century. The abbey church is often the venue for classical concerts.

❡ The monastery shop sells food, wine and souvenir items made by the monks and each December, a festive Christmas market is set up on the square outside the monastery.

✉ Freyung 6
A-1010 Vienna

🏨 from €45.00 pp

☎ +43 (0) 1 534 98
📠 +43 (0) 1 534 98 105

✉ gastmeister@
schottenstift.at

☞ The nearest train stations to the abbey are **Herrengasse** and **Schottentor**. Herrengasse is only a few blocks away. Schottentor is a little further but still within walking distance.

✝ **Sunday Mass**
1100 & 1900
Schotten Abbey
Freyung 6
A-1010 Vienna

Open to both men and women

Open Houses
Vienna

PLACES OF INTEREST ⟨ If you find yourself in **Vienna** on New Year's Eve, you can waltz the night away at the grandest ball in all Austria; the Imperial Ball (*Kaiserball*), held in the elegant **Hofburg Imperial Palace**, attracts over 3000 guests each year. Footmen in full dress uniform will attend to your every need and midnight is greeted by singers and dancers of the Vienna State Opera. If you left your dancing shoes at home, you can always catch the *Neujahrskonzert* (New Year's Concert) at the **Wiener Musikverein concert hall**.

⟨ If Strauss is not to your liking, each June the city presents the *Donauinselfest*, an open-air festival of rock and pop music which is held on Vienna's man-made **Danube Island**. And whenever they're in town, the **Vienna Boys' Choir** performs each Sunday (although *not* from late June through until early September) during the 0915 Mass in the **Burgkapelle**, the Gothic palace chapel of the Hofburg. Tickets (for seating) are available from the ticket office at the Burgkapelle which is open on Friday between 1100–1300 and 1500–1700. No tickets are required for standing room and this area is open from 0830 on the day of the Mass.

⟨ You could spend endless hours in Vienna's coffee shops, wine taverns and markets, but if you're in the mood for an excursion visit the 1400-roomed **Schloß Schönbrunn** on the city outskirts. Once the **Imperial Summer Palace** and the birthplace of Emperor Franz Joseph, it is now listed as a world heritage cultural site; the world's largest zoo forms part of the estate. The Schönbrunn Palace Theatre, the city's oldest, hosts a **Summer Music Festival** during July and August.

⟨ **Vienna Prater** is an enormous estate (once a royal hunting ground) in the centre of Vienna, where *heurigen*, cafés, a **giant ferris wheel** and all manner of entertainment attract visitors all year round. The ferris wheel achieved worldwide fame when it was featured in scenes of the movie *The Third Man* by English novelist **Graham Greene**. The original English version is screened at the **Burgkino Theatre** at Opernring 19 at least one evening per week.

❡ The **Vienna State Opera House** at Opernring 2 was founded during the reign of Emperor Franz Joseph and is the centre of Viennese cultural life; it has one of the largest stages in Europe. The opera season commences towards the end of October each year and concert tickets are much sought after. Guided tours of the Opera House with a visit backstage are conducted during the year.

❡ If you're in the mood for shopping the **Leoville Factory Outlet** in Leobersdorf is a mere 30-minute train trip south of Vienna and well worth it for the bargain priced **European labels**. Take the *Südbahn* (train) from Wien Meidling or Wien Südbahnhof to the Leobersdorf train station.

FOOD AND DRINK ✦ **Melker Stiftskeller** was once used to store wine from the vineyards of the **Benedictine Monastery of Melk**. The monks converted the cellars into a multi-roomed underground restaurant which they still own. Traditional Austrian cuisine is served and the wine list includes selections from the vineyards of the Melk monastery.

✉ Schottengasse 3

☎ +43 (0) 1 533 5530   €€

❡ The historical **Café Central** has been a favourite gathering place of artists and writers for over 100 years and is still a haven of old world charm. After he left school and before he was rejected by the **Vienna Academy of Fine Arts**, a young **Adolf Hitler** had some success selling his paintings to patrons of the café.

✉ Herrengasse

☎ +43 (0) 1 544 376 324   €€€€€

❡ Homesick Australians can catch up on the news and sport at **Crossfields Aussie Pub**, in central Vienna, and feast on kangaroo, crocodile or beef burgers. Cold Aussie beer is on tap.

✉ Maysedergasse 5

☎ +43 (0) 1 241 002 20   €€€

❡ However, those preferring a little more sophistication will feel quite at home in the gracious ambience of the **Café Mozart**, also of *The Third Man* fame and just a few steps away in Albertinaplatz. You could try the delicate **Mannerschnitten** (*Viennese hazelnut wafers*)—a perfect complement to a milky **Franziskaner coffee**, named after the colour of a Franciscan monk's habit. A **Kapuziner**, named after the colour of a Capuchin monk's habit, is a little stronger.

✉ Albertinaplatz

☎ +43 (0) 1 241 0000   €€€€

Burgenland

BURGENLAND LIES ON THE AUSTRIA–HUNGARY BORDER in the thermal spa region of Austria. Its staked claim to fame is as the Austrian province which receives the most sunshine—a happy coincidence because as much as a quarter of the province is made up of lakes and national parks. The area around **Lake Neusiedl** is especially popular with holidaymakers, and as a weekend getaway for tired and stressed city folk.

The region is a prolific producer of white wine. **Grapevines** flourish in the gentle climate and local vintners willingly share their passion—and maybe even a few drops—with visitors.

In need of some pampering? In the north of the province the **Cistercian Abbey of Marienkron** is one of a number of monastery / health resorts offering spas and saunas, facials, massages and a wide range of health treatments along with accommodation.

OPEN HOUSE

02

Marienkron Abbey and Hotel

The Sisters of the Cistercian Order founded this health and relaxation complex in the grounds of the **Marienkron Abbey Estate**. Previously the sisters' main source of income was from breeding chickens on the abbey's farm. This was tiring work and once too often a hardworking nun would fall asleep during prayer time. Justifiably unhappy with this state of affairs the Abbess proposed turning the farm into a health complex, and convinced the local bank manager to support the project. While the complex was constructed, the sisters learned healing therapies and studied hospitality and accounting. Under the control of the sisters, the business achieved great success; so much so that a hotel was later established to cope with the demand. The sisters are assisted by other health professionals who aim to provide a holistic regenerating cure for the body, soul and spirit based on the **Kneipp philosophy** of water, herbs, plants, movement and nutrition. The centre offers a range of activities for guests including Nordic walking, cycling, aerobics, yoga and swimming. Tours through the area's vineyards can be arranged.

❡ Accommodation is available in the abbey hotel which is owned and run by the nuns. The accommodation ranges from single and double guestrooms of various standards to 4-star suites. All rooms are en suite and equipped with television, radio, telephone, hairdryer and bathrobes. The hotel features a **gourmet restaurant**, a **café** and a **wine tavern**. Parking is available. Guests can participate in prayers with the sisters and attend daily Mass if they wish.

✉ Klostergasse 3
A-7123 Mönchhof

🛏 2-night all inclusive package from €200.00 pp (single room)

📞 +43 (0) 2173 8020 544
📠 +43 (0) 2173 8020 540

✉ reservierung@marienkron.at

☞ The nearest train station is **Mönchhof-Halbturn** which can be reached from Vienna's **Südbahnhof** station in an hour. Take a taxi from the station to Marienkron Abbey, a journey of 10 kilometres south. It is worthwhile checking with the sisters to see if a pick-up from the station can be arranged. Mönchhof is 70 kilometres south-east of Vienna.

✝ **Sunday Mass 0915 (may change)** Marienkron Abbey Church, Klostergasse 3 A-7123 Mönchhof

⚭ Open to both men and women

Open Houses
Burgenland Mönchhof

PLACES OF INTEREST ☙ **Mönchhof** is situated on the eastern side of **Lake Neusiedl**. A major attraction of the town is a permanent exhibition of a 20th-century village in the local **outdoor museum**. The museum 'village' consists of dwellings, a town square, a church, a pub and a scattering of shops, all stocked and furnished as they were in the early 1900s. These days a **farmers' market** is held in the Mönchhof town square each Friday.

❡ The picturesque holiday village of **Podersdorf** on the edge of **Lake Neusiedl**, has a number of rental outlets where visitors can hire boats and bicycles and explore the lake and its environs more thoroughly, or maybe learn how to stay upright on a sailboard at one of the windsurfing schools in the area. Podersdorf is 10 kilometres south-west of Mönchhof. Keen walkers could pick up a map from a local tourist office and follow one of the **themed walking trails** which weave through the province. Many make the trip to the little village of **Rust**, situated on the opposite side of the lake where, from April through to August, hundreds of **storks** take time out from delivering babies to build their nests on the roofs and in the chimney pots of the village houses.

❡ The walled, medieval, Hungarian town of **Győr**, 60 kilometres south-east of **Mönchhof**, has much to interest the tourist, including a string of protected buildings and ancient monuments. The oldest building is an **Episcopal Palace** which was established by St István (*Stephan*), the first King of Hungary (975–1038). The private chapel of today's **Bishop of Győr** is within the 17th-century cathedral which stands opposite the palace. The UNESCO-listed **Benedictine Archabbey in Pannonhalma** in Hungary is situated 18 kilometres south of Győr and has been home to the order since the year 996. The monks conduct guided tours of the historical buildings and the abbey winery. The **abbey shop** stocks wine, herbal teas and liqueurs produced by the monks.

✝ Sunday Mass 0900, 1000 & 1130

❧ Austria's first designer clothing factory outlet, **McArthur Glen**, at Parndorf, 20 kilometres north of Mönchhof, boasts over 120 shops selling Europe's top designer brands. The centre is located just off the A4 motorway which links Vienna to Budapest. Travel light or with an empty suitcase and fill it with McArthur Glen goodies. It is recommended that any serious shopping be attended to before setting out on the wine trails!

❧ A floating stage on **Lake Neusiedl** is the setting for an annual **Operetta Festival** which is held every summer near the town of **Mörbisch**.

❧ The village of **Stoob**, south of Mönchhof, has a thriving **pottery** industry and during summer local artists run courses for aspiring potters.

❧ Mönchhof is 20 kilometres from the border town of **Hegyeshalom**, in Hungary. **Budapest** is just 3 hours away by train. Both destinations can be undertaken as day trips.

FOOD AND DRINK ❦ The village of **Mönchhof** is surrounded by vineyards and wine estates with plenty of opportunities to taste the local **Riesling** and sample the *burgenlandische* hospitality. Wine taverns, vineyards and eating houses can be easily reached from the Marienkron complex which is less than 1 kilometre from the centre of town. Of course, the popular restaurant located in the abbey hotel is an excellent choice for a fine, well prepared meal.

✉ Marienkron Abbey Restaurant

☏ +43 (0) 2173 8020 544 €€

❧ The **House of Hafner** in Mönchhof produces the luscious sweet whites the area is known for, and also a unique **kosher wine** variety which is made under the strict supervision of a rabbi. More traditional wine is a speciality of the **Pillinger** family in Mönchhof who have a vineyard for a backyard and an informal outdoor eating area where **hearty snacks and wine** are served.

House of Hafner

✉ Halbturner Street 17

Pillinger

✉ Stiftsgasse 54 €

❧ *Many of Austria's restaurants and inns close down over the winter months and often for short periods during the summer. Please check before heading out.*

Lower Austria / Niederösterreich

AUSTRIA'S LARGEST PROVINCE INCLUDES the enclave of Vienna—and its famous woods! All year round there's always plenty going on. The province is laced with hiking trails and walking paths. There are themed routes such as the **wine trails**, the **cider road** and the **flower trail** to follow, and seemingly countless museums and castles and churches to visit.

Concerts, plays and musical programs are presented in the province's monasteries throughout the year. Indeed, given there are more monasteries in Lower Austria than in any other part of the country, there is an abundance of choices for either lazy holidaying, stimulating sightseeing or some serious soul cleansing.

Many monasteries in the province conduct educational courses for the general public on subjects as diverse as **art, music, cookery** and **Chinese medicine**. Monastery tours can be taken, souvenirs purchased and in many the produce from the monks' gardens and vineyards can be enjoyed.

03

Kurhotel Salzerbad

If seeking out a serene environment, travel to **Kleinzell**, 70 kilometres south of Vienna. The owners of this Christian hotel have created a comfortable, relaxed atmosphere and the service they offer makes each guest feel special. Although there are 130 comfortably furnished single and double guestrooms and suites, an **Austrian-style restaurant** and a well-stocked wine bar, the hotel still retains a warm, friendly ambience. Guestrooms are fitted with television, hairdryer and mini-bar.

❦ This health and leisure hotel has all the modern facilities of a 4-star spa property including a massage room, sauna and solarium and is within walking distance of the local **golf course**. Therapies offered include acupuncture, homeopathy and traditional Chinese medicine and water therapies based on the Kneipp hydrotherapy method. Activities available in the immediate area include hiking, cycling, tennis, mini golf and swimming in the hotel's **indoor pool**. Car parking is provided.

✉ Kleinzell 96
A-3171 Kleinzell bei Hainfeld

🏨 from €45.00 pp

☎ +43 (0) **2766 3710**
📠 +43 (0) **2766 3711 1**

✉ info@salzerbad.at

☞ Take the train to **Rainfeld-Kleinzell** station and then a taxi or bus to the hotel which is 6 kilometres away.

✝ **Sunday Mass**
0830
Parish Church of Kleinzell
A-3171 Kleinzell bei Hainfeld

⚤ Open to both men and women

Open Houses

Lower Austria / Niederösterreich Kleinzell

PLACES OF INTEREST ❧ **Kleinzell** is a tiny, postcard-pretty village situated in the foothills of the **Austrian Alps**. For the artist who wants to produce a painting as a keepsake, Kleinzell is the perfect model. Kleinzell's snowfields have kilometres of **cross-country ski runs** and two ski lifts. For those who have never ventured onto skis and have no intention of doing so, there are over 100 kilometres of marked **walking trails** in the area. If walking doesn't quite appeal, you can always take a sled, at least in the winter. **St Polten**, 35 kilometres north of Kleinzell, is the capital of Lower Austria. It is well known for its Baroque cathedral, a pedestrian-only town centre, and its reputation for fine galleries focusing on modern and contemporary art. The city is thought to be the oldest in Austria, having been established by Roman Emperor Hadrian in 121AD, then called Aelium Cetium.

❡ The **Mariazellerbahn**, a scenic passenger and tourist train, chugs up the mountains between St Polten and Mariazell in Styria, a one-way journey of 2.5 hours. Mariazell is 50 kilometres south of Kleinzell. The 12th-century **Mariazell Basilica** attracts pilgrims who come to pray before a miraculous lime wood statue of the Virgin Mary which was originally carved by Magnus, a Benedictine monk from the Abbey of St Lambrecht and placed in the branch of a tree where the basilica now stands. The statue can be seen in the **Chapel of Miracles**, within the Mariazell Basilica.

☩ Sunday Mass 0800, 1000, 1115 & 1830

❡ Over the past 9 centuries the Cistercian **Heiligenkreuz Abbey** has acquired a renowned collection of priceless medieval treasures including monuments, artworks and a 50,000-volume library. Tourists can visit the abbey and during some liturgical services join the monks in prayer. Guided tours of the abbey must be pre-booked with the monks; however, the monastery restaurant and shop is open to everyone. The complex is 15 kilometres west of Vienna. Mary Vetsera (1871–1889), mistress of Crown Prince Rudolf (1858–1889), the son of Emperor Franz Josef and Empress Elisabeth, who died in mysterious circumstances with her prince at **Schloss Mayerling** nearby, is buried in the **Heiligenkreuz Abbey** cemetery.

☩ Sunday Mass 0830, 0930, 1100 & 1845

❧ Not far away is one of the smallest and most unusual chapels in the country, the 200-year-old **Barbara Chapel**, situated far underground in an old mining shaft off the *Seegrotte* (Lake Grotto), Europe's largest underground lake, in **Hinterbrühl**, a small town 30 kilometres south-west of Vienna. The chapel holds only a small number of people, and every four years on the first Sunday in December, a Mass is celebrated for lost comrades in a larger area deeper in the mine. The Archbishop of Vienna celebrates the Mass accompanied by the Vienna Boys' Choir and a congregation of around 3000. The most recent Mass was held in 2007.

❧ Relax and roll the dice in the refined elegance of Baden Casino's gaming halls. The **Baden Casino** in the Kaiser-Franz-Ring is situated in the town of Baden, between Vienna and Kleinzell, and is one of the largest casinos in Austria and one of the oldest in Europe.

FOOD AND DRINK ❧ For one month each year, commencing in early September, the **Baden Grape Cure Festival** takes place in the town's main marketplace. Grapes that have not been used for winemaking are used in a 'cure' program to benefit health and increase energy. Those who take the cure consume grapes in specified amounts along with litres of grape juice. An integral part of the cure is a program of musical events, vineyard and cellar tours.

❧ Baden's Römertherme (*Roman baths*) is one of the largest spa centres in Europe. Although in a land-locked country, the Römertherme spa boasts a long, wide, white sandy beach along with thermal pools, saunas and steam baths and an array of beauty treatments are available. The centre's **Restaurant Quirinus** is open every day for coffee and snacks, a glass of wine or a full meal.

✉ Brusattiplatz 4

☎ +43 (0) 2252 450 30–402   €€→€€€€

❧ If strolling through the village of Kleinzell you can't miss the **Mohr café/restaurant** which bears a faint resemblance to an old-fashioned corner store. Drop in for a coffee and a bite to eat, sit under an umbrella and enjoy the casual, rustic environment and traditional home-style cooking.

☎ +43 (0) 2766 235   €

Open Houses

Lower Austria / Niederösterreich Zwettl

04

Abbey of Zwettl

If seeking out a peaceful hideaway, travel to Zwettl, 120 kilometres north-west of **Vienna**. The abbey was founded in 1138 and is one of many European monasteries in the hands of the Catholic Cistercian Order. Accommodation in the abbey guesthouse is in single, double, triple or quad rooms, or in a hostel section which is popular with young travellers. Some guestrooms have en suite facilities. The abbey tavern is well known for its hearty servings and is patronised by the villagers and tourists alike. Fish, especially carp from the monastery's lakes, often feature on the menu. The tavern sells local beer and wine which can also be purchased in the monks' gift shop.

❡ A permanent exhibition of art and history can be seen in the abbey's old underground wine cellars. The book collection on display in the **Zwettl Abbey library** includes 60,000 books and manuscripts, the oldest of which dates back to the 12th century. A 14th-century illustrated work titled *The Book of Zwettl* details the history of the monastery over the centuries. The abbey is often the venue for concerts and cultural events. A monastery **Organ Festival** is held in June and July each year; the program may include recitals by the abbey's own Zwettler Boys' Choir.

✉ Stift-Zwettl 1
A-3910 Zwettl

🛏 from €45.00 pp
(single room)

📞 +43 (0) 2822 2020 217
📠 +43 (0) 2822 2020 240

✉ gastpater@stift-zwettl.at

☞ Take the train to the **Zwettl** main station, followed by a taxi to the abbey which is on the eastern outskirts of the town, approximately 3 kilometres and just a few minutes' drive from the station.

✝ **Sunday Mass**
Summer: 0800, 0900, 1000 1100
Winter: 0800, 0900 & 1030
Abbey of Zwettl
Stift-Zwettl 1
A-3910 Zwettl

⛪ Open to both men and women

PLACES OF INTEREST ❧ Set in an idyllic landscape dotted with castles, abbeys and monasteries, the town and cultural centre of **Zwettl** is a good choice to start a walking or cycling holiday. Before you leave you could spoil yourself with a pair of Austrian leather walking shoes, handmade by **shoemaker Johann Rabl**, at Florianigasse 17.

❧ During September the **Festival of Craftsmen** takes place in the village, with music, street dancing and other outdoor entertainment together with market stalls selling locally made handcrafts and produce. Woodcarver Christian Chadek-Franzus hand-crafts unique wooden handbags, hairclips and even wooden ties and briefcases. His gallery is at Landstraße 61. Not far away the colourful creations of local artist Marina Anton are on display in the **Anton Gallery** at Landstraße 65.

❧ There is a horse riding centre in the grounds of the former **Castle of Rosenau**, 12 kilometres west of the abbey, where horse sleigh rides can be taken during the winter months. The castle is home to the **Museum of Freemasonry** which provides an insight into the sometimes mysterious world of the Freemasons.

❧ The formidable 12th-century **Castle Rappottenstein** in the town of Rappottenstein, south of Zwettl, is an imposing medieval fortress and one of the best preserved castles in the country. The castle is owned and occupied by an Austrian family who open the doors to the public during the summer when it is also the venue for cultural and musical events.

❧ The man-made **Lake Ottenstein**, 15 kilometres east of Zwettl, is a summer haven for water lovers. Landlubbers could perhaps take to the hiking and cycling paths through the wooded areas surrounding the lake or play a round at the Ottenstein Golf Club. The local castle, the 16th-century **Schloss Ottenstein**, is known for its *Päpstezimmer* (Pope's room) where the walls are lined with 241 portraits of every Pope between the reign of St Peter (32–37) and Blessed Innocent XI (1691–1700).

Open Houses

Lower Austria / Niederösterreich Zwettl

❦ The history and development of this part of the country is unfolded at the **local culture Museum** (*Dorfmuseum*) in Roiten, 16 kilometres south of Zwettl. The museum was designed by Austrian architect and painter **Friedensreich Hundertwasser** (1928–2000), who was born in Vienna. Visit *www. kunsthauswien.com*, the Kunsthauswien Museum website, for much more information about Hundertwasser; including the fact that 'according to his wishes he was…buried in harmony with nature on his land in New Zealand, in the *Garden of the Happy Deads*, under a tulip tree'.

FOOD AND DRINK ❦ After an energetic day of shopping or sightseeing, you could quench your thirst at the **Zwettler Brauhaus** with a glass or two of delicious, local Zwettler beer. Alternatively, the tavern and restaurant attached to the monastery are open most days 0800 to midnight.
☎ +43 (0) 2822 540 66   €€
❦ At the **Sonnetor shop** at Sprögnitz 12 in Zwettl, tea lovers can choose from a selection of locally grown **organic fruit and herbal teas**, some with curious names like Gunpowder, Shalom and Santa's Secret.
✉ Sprögnitz 12

❦ For a bite to eat on the run, buy a sausage from one of the vendors' stalls set up in the Zwettl marketplace. Hot drinks are served at the **Café Fröschl** which also includes a handy bakery.
✉ Hamerlingstraße 11
☎ +43 (0) 2822 5242 9   €
❦ If visiting the Castle of Rosenau on a Sunday you could have lunch at the **Heuriger Meierhof** in the Rosenau village. Here wines from all over Austria can be sampled while you indulge in an 'all you can eat' smorgasbord of sausages, pork, dumplings and potato salad.
☎ +43 (0) 2822 5849 4   €€€
❦ The **Schloss Restaurant** in Castle Ottenstein specialises in robust, medieval style 'knights' meals'.
☎ +43 (0) 2826 8254   €€€

Salzburg

A CITY OF MUSIC AND CULTURE, Salzburg is considered by many as the centre of Austrian music. This is largely on account of it being the birthplace of **Mozart**, whose compositions of sacred music can be heard in churches and cathedrals all over this beautiful town. During the 17th century the city's Catholic and political hierarchy established magnificent churches and grand monasteries so Salzburg would rival the Vatican in Rome and spectacularly created the classical, stylish city, so admired today.

Centuries earlier, in 714AD, St Rupert (the first bishop of Salzburg) founded the great **Nonnberg Nunnery**, which has overlooked the city from its hillside perch for almost 1300 years. The nunnery, formally titled **St Ehrentraud Abbey**, after its first abbess, is the oldest women's monastery in Austria. Up until the mid-19th century only daughters of the aristocracy were allowed to enter the Nonnberg Convent. Today overnight guests join with the nuns in days of prayer and silence.

Salzburg has strong associations with the film *The Sound of Music*, several parts of the movie being set there. Nonnberg Abbey, where Fräulein Maria (played by Julie Andrews) trained as a nun and later married the handsome Captain von Trapp, can be reached on foot from central Salzburg's **Kapitelplatz Square**. Or take the funicular.

Hotel Helenenburg

The Hotel Helenenburg is a modern, well furnished, comfortable hotel run by the **Diakoniewerk Christian Evangelist Society**. Most of the guestrooms have en suites but some share bathrooms off the hallway. All rooms have a balcony with front-facing rooms looking over the **Gastein Valley**. All meals are available.

❧ Facilities include sauna, gym, spas, thermal baths and hot springs. Hiking weeks, health days and three-night 'taster' packages are part of the services offered. The hotel provides free maps and equipment such as Nordic walking sticks to walkers and hikers. Musical events, book readings and art exhibitions are often held here. The hotel has a lift and free parking is provided.

❧ **Empress Elisabeth**, accompanied by her daughter **Archduchess Valerie**, once booked the entire hotel for a few weeks of recuperative water therapy. Sisi was a passionate traveller, who was assassinated as she boarded a steamer for a trip across the lake whilst on holiday in Geneva in 1898. She was 60 years old. Hollywood actress Ava Gardner played the role of the Empress in the 1968 film *Mayerling*.

Kötschachtaler Straße 18
A-5640 Bad Gastein

from €40.00 pp, including breakfast

+43 (0) 6434 3727
+43 (0) 6434 3727 88

info@helenenburg.at

Take the train to **Bad Gastein station**. The hotel owners offer a (pre-arranged) pick-up service from the station.

Sunday Service
0930
Evangelist Christophorus Church
A-5640 Bad Gastein

Open to both men and women

PLACES OF INTEREST ❧ **Bad Gastein** is a popular, stylish spa town in an area known for its healing thermal springs and crisp mountain air. There is a large casino here but for those who prefer their sport out of doors there is a challenging 18-hole alpine golf course 2 kilometres from the town. Skiers and snowboarders can surf the snow to their hearts' content during the winter months. There are over 300 kilometres of trails and tracks for the use of walkers and bikers in summer. Alpine restaurants and mountain huts cater for the weary.

❡ Mozart's mother once holidayed in Bad Gastein and the local square is named in her son's honour. And while Mozart's music is played in taverns and restaurants all over the region, the sound of music in the **Mozartplatz** each evening is most likely disco coming from one of the nightclubs in the square. Bad Gastein's Casino is an informal venue for an evening of *après ski*. However, the town's nightclubs, bars and restaurants cater for all tastes.

❡ Day trips can be taken to **Vienna** or **Salzburg** from Bad Gastein or from **Bad Hofgastein**, a slightly smaller resort town 7 kilometres north. Both towns have good shopping facilities and the area has many cosy, traditional-style restaurants, cafés and taverns to choose from.

❡ The **Gasteiner Heilstollen**, a curative tunnel on the outskirts of Bad Gastein, is an old gold mine reputed to have therapeutic properties. Access to the tunnel is by train which takes approximately 10 minutes to reach the treatment area 1.8 kilometres inside the mountain. Skiers often have a session in the tunnel after a day on the pistes to relax and rejuvenate in the soothing warmth of the mountain. The **Gasteiner Museum** at Kaiser Franz Josef Straße 1 is dedicated to the history of the spas in the area and especially to the Gasteiner Heilstollen. Exhibits include objects of bathing history, baths, spa equipment and artworks.

❡ The saunas in the resorts of this area are often nude and some are mixed so it might be a good idea to make some enquiries before rushing in.

Open Houses

Salzburg Bad Gastein

❧ The **Hohe Tauern National Park** surrounds Bad Gastein. This enormous recreation area reaches into the provinces of **Salzburg**, **Carinthia** and **Tyrol**. Among the 90 kilometres of established winter walking paths are scenic glacier and waterfall trails. Most trails are signposted and maps are available from local tourist offices or from the National Park Authority headquarters in **Neukirchen am Großvenediger**. The park is traffic free but hikers can use a special **park 'taxi' service** (which can also transport mountain bikes) to reach or return from a particular area.

FOOD AND DRINK ❧ **Klammstein Castle** near Dorfgastein, 15 kilometres north of Bad Gastein, has a cheery restaurant where ghost tours and treasure hunts come with the ever popular 'knights' feast'.

☎ +43 (0) 6433 7603 €€€

❧ Bad Gastein has no shortage of eating establishments and wine bars. Choices range from classy, expensive, gourmet restaurants with breathtaking views to typical Austrian taverns serving Austrian specialities. You could try the schnitzel at the **K. u. K. Nostalgia** restaurant, in the Hotel Sponfeldner which overlooks the famous waterfall cascading through the centre of town. (K. u. K. are letters once used by Austrian royalty, meaning 'Imperial and Royal'.)

☎ +43 (0) 6434 300 90 €€€

❧ And while you will have to pay for the **sausages and pizza** at the restaurant in the local **Congress Centre**, the breathtaking view is free.

☎ +43 (0) 6434 2223 0 €€€

❧ Relax in **Bad Hofgastein's Schmaranz Brewery** where a tasty, organic '**white beer**' is brewed. The brewery's tavern and restaurant is open every day from 1500 and usually attracts an energetic *après ski* crowd.

☎ +43 (0) 6432 6719 40 €€€

Institute St Sebastian

The Institute St Sebastian is conveniently situated in the centre of 'old' Salzburg in a quiet area near many of the city's tourist attractions. It is possible to see much of Salzburg on foot from the hostel. In the past it has been a monastery and a hospital for the needy. Today it is run as a tourist hostel by the Catholic Church in partnership with the Austrian government.

❧ This spacious complex offers dormitory accommodation and guestrooms for up to four people. Some guestrooms have an en suite and share bathrooms are on each floor. The hostel is equipped with telephone, television and an Internet connection. There is a self-service kitchen, laundry, lift, sun terrace and guest lounges. The institute has a 'no lock out, no curfew' policy and is open all year. Senior visitors and children are welcome as there is no age limit imposed.

❧ Mozart's wife Constanze (1763–1842) and his father Leopold (1719–1787) are buried in the **St Sebastian cemetery** in the grounds of the church in Linzer Gasse which is attached to the institute.

✉ Linzer Gasse 41
A-5020 Salzburg

🛏 from €30.00 pp

☎ +43 (0) 662 8713 86
📠 +43 (0) 662 8713 8685

✎ office@
st-sebastian-salzburg.at

☞ The institute is approximately 1 kilometre south of **Salzburg's Hauptbahnhof** train station.

✝ **Sunday Mass**
0900
Church of St Sebastian,
Linzer Gasse 41
A-5020 Salzburg

✝ **0830, 1000, 1130**
Salzburg Cathedral
Domplatz
A-5020 Salzburg

⚥ Open to both men and women

Open Houses
Salzburg

PLACES OF INTEREST ❦ The churches and squares of **Salzburg's Old Town** are dramatically overlooked by the 1000-year-old **Hohensalzburg Fortress** which was originally built as a safety house for the town's clergy. The Old Town of Salzburg was recently granted world heritage status by UNESCO.

❧ Salzburg's medieval Abbey of St Peter was established for monks of the Benedictine Order by St Rupert in 696. Along with the **Franciscan Church** (*Franziskanerkirche*) the abbey is one of the oldest buildings in the town. A 13-year-old Mozart wrote the *Dominicus Mass* for his friend the Abbot Hagenauer; and years later presented his composition *Mass in C Minor* in the abbey church with wife Constanze the lead vocalist. The composer's sister Maria Anna Berchtold zu Sonnenburg (1751–1829) is buried in the abbey cemetery.

❧ Visitors to the town in July and August will be able to join the locals in celebrating the life of Mozart during the annual **Salzburg Festival**, which is heavily reliant on Mozart's works. The annual **Mozart Week** is held near the composer's birthday on 27 January and provides another opportunity to hear his music.

❧ The city's summer palace at **Hellbrunn** in south Salzburg was built on the whimsy of Markus Sittikus, the **Archbishop of Salzburg**, who presided over matters religious in the town from 1612 to 1619. A mechanical theatre illustrates life in a traditional Austrian village and the pavilion used in the movie *The Sound of Music* is in the grounds. A word of warning: if visiting the palace, don't sit down without thoroughly inspecting the seat. The Archbishop had quite a sense of humour and there are numerous **hidden trick fountains** which are known to soak the unsuspecting, sometimes to their embarrassment.

The **Silent Night Memorial Chapel** in Stille Nacht Platz, Oberndorf, 19 kilometres north of Salzburg is the church where the Christmas Carol *Silent Night* was sung for the first time on Christmas Eve, 1818. Every Christmas Eve at 1700 a memorial Silent Night church service is held in front of the tiny chapel to mark the occasion.

In the centre of **Obertrum**, 16 kilometres north of Salzburg, the **Josef Sigl Brauerei** has been brewing the most popular beverage in town, Trumer Pils, for over 400 years. On special occasions the town fountain flows with Trumer instead of water.

Christmas markets take place throughout Salzburg during December, the most spectacular being held in the Salzburg cathedral square.

FOOD AND DRINK Try a refreshing stein of beer in Salzburg's **Augustiner Monastery Brewery**. Now half-owned by the **Benedictines of Michaelbeuern**, this lively beer hall was until recently run by Augustinian monks who brewed the beer and waited on the tables. The complex is part of the old Augustine monastery in the **Mülln district**, just outside the town centre. The vast indoor beer halls and outdoor beer gardens can hold over 2500 people.

+43 (0) 662 4312 46 €

More genteel visitors can partake of coffee and *Mozartkugel* (a delicious chocolate ball layered with pistachio, marzipan, nougat and chocolate created in honour of the composer) at the **Café Fürst** in the Alter Markt.

+43 (0) 662 8437 590 €€€

Stiftskeller St Peter in St Peter's Monastery in Salzburg is the oldest restaurant in Austria, having been established by Benedictine monks in 803. A roaming musician entertains guests with the music of Mozart in the evenings.

+43 (0) 662 8412 680 €→€€€€€

Josef Holzermayr Confectionary Shop in Salzburg's Alter Markt delivers *Mozartkugel* (low-fat variety available) anywhere in the world. Among the assortment of sweets and chocolates are edible Christmas tree decorations.

Styria / Steiermark

 TYRIA ENJOYS A REPUTATION FOR BEING THE CULINARY heart of Austria. But **Graz**, once the medieval capital of the province, is probably best known these days as the birthplace of Arnold Schwarzenegger (b 1947). The region is also home to some of the oldest monasteries in Austria. In the north of the province, the Styrian town of **Mariazell**, a place of pilgrimage since the 14th century, marks the end of an ancient monastery-lined pilgrimage trail which runs all the way from **Vienna**, some 160 kilometres away. Known as the **Via Sacra**, pilgrims still use this route today as they have done since its inception in 1632.

Styria has a chequered religious history. When the Austrian government launched an attack on religious houses during the 18th century, scores of convents and monasteries in Styria were wiped out, abandoned by their religious owners. Nonetheless, the great **Benedictine abbeys of Rein** and **St Lambrecht** and the **Franciscan Monastery** in **Graz** survived. The abbeys date back to the 11th and 13th centuries and remain treasure troves of art and antiquity for overnight guests and day-trippers alike.

OPEN HOUSE

07

Abbey of St Lambrecht

This 11th-century Benedictine abbey is in an enviable position, surrounded by national park and encircled by the mountains of **Grebenzen**. The tiny town of St Lambrecht is ideally placed for an active break—snow sports in winter and mountain climbing, fishing or hiking in summer.

¶ Accommodation is provided in the abbey in dormitories (mainly for young people) or in simple rooms in the abbey's guesthouse. All guestrooms share a bathroom on the same floor. Throughout the year the abbey hosts numerous concerts, exhibitions and cultural events, many of which draw large numbers of tourists to the area.

¶ The monks maintain a collection of 15th- and 16th-century sculptures and paintings. A stuffed bird museum and a museum depicting the history of the surrounding rural area were both established by monk collectors during their time at the abbey. All are open to the public.

¶ The monastery shop retails wine from the monks' vineyards as well as liqueurs made from herbs and plants grown in the monastery garden. The shop stocks the St Lambrecht's recipe book, a practical souvenir as you'll be able to treat the family to some traditional Austrian fare when you get home.

Haupstraße 1
A-8813 St Lambrecht

price to be negotiated

+43 (0) **3585 2305 22**
+43 (0) **3585 2305 20**

gastmeister@stift-stlambrecht.at

Take the train to **Mariahof-St Lambrecht**.
The abbey is 8 kilometres from the train station.

Sunday Mass
0800 & 1015
St Peter's Church
Abbey of St Lambrecht
A-8813 St Lambrecht

Open to both men and women

Open Houses
Styria / Steiermark St Lambrecht

PLACES OF INTEREST The village of **St Lambrecht** is situated 40 kilometres south-west of **Judenburg** in the centre of the Grebenzen nature reserve, a hikers' and skiers' paradise. For some downhill thrills try the St Lambrecht summer toboggan run. Take the ski lift up the **Grebenzen Mountain** behind the monastery and ride a toboggan almost 2 kilometres back down.

¶ If you are visiting Styria during mid-June to the end of July you will be in time for the **Styriarte Festival of Music**. The festival features artists and ensembles performing classical pieces from the Middle Ages to the 19th century in castles, abbeys and historical settings. **Graz**, Styria's cultural capital, hosts performances in the 17th-century **Eggenberg Palace** which has 24 state rooms and a window for each week of the year. The palace is on the world heritage list. Graz is 120 kilometres east of St Lambrecht.

¶ The **Piber Stud Farm** (*Lipizzanergestüt*) where the famous Lipizzaner horses of the Spanish Riding School in Vienna are bred is in the town of **Piber** between Graz and St Lambrecht. Occasionally the owners host concerts featuring the horses performing with musical groups such as the **Vienna Boys' Choir**. Guided tours of the farm and visits to the stables are conducted throughout the year and a program of concerts, training and rehearsals is organised for the public.

¶ The south of the province, known as the *Weinstraße* or **Wine Road**, is dominated by large vineyards. If wine tasting is not your cup of tea, there are several themed driving routes, along flower or apple trails. The culture trail links museums, galleries, historic villages and ancient churches. Maps are available from local tourist offices. St Lambrecht is on the wood route, a themed trail leading through Styria's densely forested regions. Keen cyclists could follow the route of the **Tour de Mur** cycling race which follows the **River Mur** from **Muhr** in Salzburg to **Bad Radkersburg** in Styria. The scenic 340-kilometre long, 5-night route through vineyards, villages and national parks can also be done in shorter stages. The actual **race** itself is held in May each year and attracts thousands of participants riding anything non-motorised with wheels.

¶ For more leisurely sightseeing, book a ticket on the UNESCO-listed **Semmering Railway**. On the mountainous sector between **Mürzzuschlag** in Styria and **Gloggnitz** in Lower Austria passengers share the sky-high view with the local buzzards.

❧ Kids will love the **Vivarium Water Park** in **Mariahof** where an Amazon-like rainforest is inhabited by monkeys, alligators and live piranhas. However, the park's freshwater swimming pools are guaranteed carnivore-free.

FOOD AND DRINK ❧ **St Lambrecht** is a tiny village with a couple of good cafés. The **Pristovnik** serves pasta and pizza, while the **Café Hinterhofer** is a good choice for the ever-popular *kaffee und kuchen* (coffee and cake). Full meals with wine are also available. Both cafés have garden areas but more formal dining facilities can be found in the guesthouses and inns in the town.

Pristovnik

☎ +43 (0) 3585 2436   €

Café Hinterhofer

☎ +43 (0) 3585 2131   €

❧ **Styria's** famous culinary specialities can be sampled at any of the region's **farmers' markets**. Produce markets take place in the Lendplatz and on the Kaiser-Joseph-Platz in Graz every day except Sunday. Markets in **Murau**, 12 kilometres north-west of St Lambrecht, and in **Neumarkt**, 10 kilometres east, are held every Friday morning in the town squares.

❧ Liquid refreshment in the form of **Gösser Beer** (Austria's finest beer, according to locals) can be enjoyed in any of the taverns and beer gardens in the town. The locally produced variety is the most popular brand in Styria. It was **Benedictine nuns** of the local convent, **Stift-Göss**, who first established a brewery in **Leoben** in 1020 and brewed the beer themselves, considering the product 'liquid bread' which they are said to have distributed freely. The nuns have long gone but a brewery is still active. The remains of the ancient convent and the nuns' now restored church are local tourist attractions. The brewery tavern serves full meals.

Gösser Brauerei

☎ +43 (0) 3842 2853 0   €€→€€€

Upper Austria / Oberösterreich

PPER AUSTRIA IS CLAIMED BY MANY TO BE THE country's most scenic province—and the village of **Hallstatt,** on the shores of **Hallstätter** (*Lake Hallstatt*) is often said to be the most beautiful lakeside village in the world. No surprise then that the monasteries and convents of the region are found in stunningly picturesque settings.

The province boasts first-class skiing facilities, with kilometres of cross-country ski trails and walking and cycling paths. The multiple-use trails meander across the hills and meadows and around the lakes of the **Salzammergut** region leading to spectacular views. The area is ideal for swimming during the summer months.

A vibrant cultural scene exists in the province with opera festivals, concerts and musical events staged in towns and villages all year round.

Shimmering lakes, crisp, invigorating mountain air and the healing qualities of the mineral-rich thermal springs throughout the region have led to the development of numerous spa and health resorts. Utilising the natural waters on monastery estates, many of these are run by nuns who offer programs designed to revitalise the body as well as the soul.

08

Guesthouse Weikersdorf

Situated in a rural setting on the outskirts of the
village of **Alberndorf** approximately 30 kilometres
south of the Czech border, the guesthouse is run by the
Diakoniewerk Christian Evangelist Society. It has 40
single, double and triple guestrooms. Most guestrooms
share a bathroom but 9 rooms have en suites. The dining
room is large enough to seat all the guests, should they
decide to eat at the same time. All meals and in-between
snacks are available. A small chapel for the use of guests
is inside the building.

❧ The guesthouse can be used by extended family
groups, social groups and for business getaways.
The house has modern conference facilities with
provision for up to 80 people. Although small numbers
of people are catered for, group bookings are preferred.
Car parking is available.

❧ The complex is situated in a picturesque area with
opportunities for walking, hiking and horse riding
in summer and cross-country skiing in winter.
A 4-kilometre **Biblical Hiking Trail** first established
in 1828 commences at the Alberndorf parish church
on a return route through the nearby forest and
past numerous religious artworks, monuments and
prayer stations.

✉ Weikersdorf 7
A-4211 Alberndorf in
der Riedmark

🏨 from €25.00 pp

☎ +43 (0) 7235 7102
📠 +43 (0) 7235 7102 20

✍ weikersdorf@
diakoniewerk.at

☞ Take the train to **Linz**
and a bus or taxi to
Alberndorf which is
20 kilometres north
of Linz, the capital of
Upper Austria.

✝ **Sunday Service**
0930
Evangelist Church of
Gallneukirchen,
Hauptstraße 1
A-4210 Gallneukirchen
bei Linz

⚭ Open to both men and
women

Open Houses
Upper Austria / Oberösterreich
Alberndorf in der Riedmark

PLACES OF INTEREST ❧ Visitors can take advantage of the local walking and cycling trails or visit the 12th-century ruins of **Schloß-Riedegg** at **Gallneukirchen**. The castle is the home of an **African Museum** which displays a collection of traditional African artwork and artefacts. Adjoining the castle ruins is a monastery run by the order of **Mariannhill Missionaries** who care for the castle site and the museum and run a busy youth hostel.

❦ **Lasberg**, a pretty village in the richly landscaped **Mühlviertel** region, is 17 kilometres north-east of **Alberndorf**. This scenic area can be explored on any of the numerous walking trails, most of which are serviced by **alpine inns** where walkers can take refuge and refuel on generous servings of Austrian country-style food while taking in the views. On the way to **Lasberg** you could stop at the village of **Kefermarkt** to see an exquisite 15th-century hand-carved wooden altar in the village church. During the **snow season** the Mühlviertel is a winter paradise for cross-country skiing and snowboarding. The themed driving routes lead to museums, weaving mills, vineyards, castles and mountain villages. Maps are available from local tourist offices.

❦ A self-guided **Old Town Walk** leads to places of interest in the Linz old town including **Linz Castle**, the old cathedral, churches and the city hall. **Adolf Hitler** lived at Humboldtstraße 31 during his teenage years. Maps of various walking tours are available at the local tourist office.

❦ The Gothic **Church of St Nicholas** in the attractive little village of **Rožmberk nad Vltavou**, across the Czech–Austrian border, is 45 kilometres from Alberndorf. It dates from the 15th century. Interior frescoes include a 17th-century depiction of the death of the Virgin Mary and one of Christ on the Cross from the same period. The restored, 13th-century **Rožmberk nad Vltavou Castle** is the centrepiece of the village which overlooks the Vltava River. The castle is open for most of spring and summer. Once the home of the aristocratic Rosenberg family, it is quite grand with frescoes, panelled ceilings, historic works of art and even a drawbridge. Keep an eye out for the 'White Lady', the resident **castle ghost**.

FOOD AND DRINK ✆ Linz is renowned for its great choice of restaurants serving not only good solid Austrian fare but also meals from the cuisines of Africa, China, Italy and Mexico. And a stein of Austrian beer is never too far away.

❡ The **Wienerwald fast food restaurant chain** has two outlets in Linz. Something of an upmarket McDonald's, Wienerwald restaurants offer eat-in, take-away and home delivery services. Soup, burgers, grills, schnitzels, salads and dessert are the basis of the menu and these simple, well-priced restaurants can be found throughout the country.

✉ Promenade 22

✆ +43 (0) 50 1516 401   €

✉ Freinbergstraße 18

✆ +43 (0) 50 1516 402   €

❡ The Linz tourist office in the **Hauptplatz** has maps and details of tourist walks around the historic 'old town' which provide many opportunities to stop off for some refreshment. The **Klosterhof Restaurant and beer garden** is in the grounds of a former monastery in Landstraße, in the centre of town. An evening meal here will often include a recital by a leading musician or a classical band.

✉ Landstraße

✆ +43 (0) 732 7733 73   €€€

❡ The town's best-known *kaffeehaus*, the **Café Brandl**, is around the corner from the Klosterhof. Delicious jam-filled **Linzer Torte**, the city's favourite cake, made from a recipe over 300 years old, can be indulged in here, or in numerous other cafés throughout the town.

✉ Bismarckstraße

✆ +43 (0) 732 7736 350   €€

Kneipp Health & Spa Centre

This monastery / spa centre is owned and operated by the sisters of Marienschwestern vom Karmel. It is a most idyllic location for the Kneipp cure of recovery, restoration and relaxation which is practised by the sisters who work alongside health professionals. **Father Sebastian Kneipp** (1824–1897), a German priest and holistic healer, pioneered the method which is widely used throughout Austria.

❡ Most of the comfortable, spotlessly clean single, double and family rooms are en suite and the centre's chefs place particular emphasis on healthy eating using home-grown herbs and vegetables. The sisters mix freely with the guests and engage in outdoor activities such as walking excursions, hiking and exercise classes. Laughter and easy conversation create an atmosphere of pleasant companionship. The centre has a chapel, gymnasium, sauna, treatment rooms, a guests' library, shop and café. There is a lift, conference facilities and a parking area.

✉ Marienschwestern von Karmel
Kneippstraße 1
A-5252 Aspach

🛏 from €54.00 pp, including breakfast

☎ +43 (0) **7755 7051**
📠 +43 (0) **7755 7051** 35

✉ *kurhaus.aspach@ marienschwestern.at*

☞ Take the train to **Ried im Innkreis**, 16 kilometres east of Aspach from where a bus or taxi can be taken to the centre. Pre-arranged transfers can be organised. Aspach is 260 kilometres west of Vienna.

✝ **Sunday Mass**
0900
Aspach Parish Church
Marktplatz 1
A-5252 Aspach

⚤ Open to both men and women

PLACES OF INTEREST ❦ The **village of Aspach** has a population of around 2000 people. It is situated on the edge of the **Kobernaußerwald Forest** which is crossed by over 60 kilometres of walking and cycling trails. For those interested in taking a trail ride horse stables are located on the outskirts of Aspach. The **Aspach summer concert season** gets under way each summer when concerts and other musical events are held in venues around the village, including the Kneipp Centre. Paintings, sculptures and artwork are on display (and for sale) at the Aspach studio of local artist Wolfgang Maxlmoser at Pfarrgrund 3.

❦ An impressive 55,000-volume library, medieval ceiling frescoes and the vast collection of religious art belonging to the **Augustinian Canons** of the **Monastery of Reichersberg am Inn**, 18 kilometres north of Aspach, can be viewed by the public during a guided tour. In 2002 a painting on loan to the monastery for some 30 years was revealed as a **genuine Rubens**. The owner, an elderly lady, was left the painting but was not fond of the violent scene it depicted and so allowed the monastery to display it until she learnt its value. Titled *Massacre of the Innocents* the painting was auctioned by Sotheby's London and sold for more than €76 million.

✝ Sunday Mass 0930

❦ Enjoy a cruise on **Lake Traunsee** where dozens of boats and the paddle steamer *Gisela*, once a favourite of the Austrian royal family, make regular trips all year round. The boats are heated in winter. Departures are from **Gmunden** and **Ebensee**. Gmunden is 60 kilometres south of Aspach.

Open Houses
Upper Austria / Oberösterreich Aspach

❡ The **Gmundner Ceramic Factory** at Keramikstraße 24 in Gmunden is the largest ceramic factory in Austria. Guided tours take place Monday to Friday. The factory shop sells a vast range of ceramic souvenirs, vases and dishes of all shapes and sizes. The factory has a small take-away food area where simple meals are available.

❡ Take a factory tour and watch the glass-makers at work at the **Riedel Glass Factory** in the village of **Schneegattern**, 25 kilometres south of Aspach. Riedel glasses are said to enhance the aroma and taste of the wine, and there is a unique shape for each grape variety.

❡ The skilful, experienced sportsmen of the **Roman Moser Fishing School** at Kuferzeile 23 in Gmunden conduct fly fishing lessons for rainbow trout during April and May each year. Fishing season in Upper Austria begins in April until some time in October.

FOOD AND DRINK ❧ **Upper Austria** is famous for its beer and dumplings. Regular dumpling weeks are held when all sorts of the doughy delicacies can be ordered: potato, bread, meat, cabbage, even leftovers. **Cabbage dumplings** were a favourite of Emperor Franz Josef as was boiled beef (*tafelspitz*), a robust meat and vegetable dish which can be served as two or three courses.

❡ The **Reichersberg am Inn Monastery Bräustüberl** (*beer hall*) and restaurant has a reputation for serving good food at moderate prices. The outdoor area is particularly inviting. On a warm summer day wooden tables are set out under shady trees, attracting a regular clientele of well fed locals and day visitors.

☎ +43 (0)7758 2324   €€

❡ Take a scenic walk to the **Restaurant Orther Stub'n** in **Gmunden's castle**, **Schloss Orth**, which is reached via a long pedestrian bridge extending over **Lake Traunsee**. The menu covers everything from coffee or a light snack to a three course candle-lit dinner.

☎ +43 (0)7612 6249 9   €€€

Kneipp Health and Spa Centre

This is another friendly yet professional spa centre owned and operated by the sisters of Marienschwestern vom Karmel. The sisters live a life of prayer combined with their work in the health centre and in the outside community. The complex is on the outskirts of the 500-year-old village of **Bad Kreuzen** and overlooks the forests of the **Wolfsschlucht Gorge**, a mecca for ramblers and hiking enthusiasts.

❡ The sisters have a commitment to providing a restful ambience for those seeking to regain physical, spiritual and mental energies. The single, double and multiple guestrooms are comfortable and well appointed and most have en suites.

❡ As in all Marienschwestern centres, fresh, healthy food plays a vital role and the restaurant menu embraces healthy, guilt-free gourmet cuisine. A sister will often lead guests on an excursion into the countryside to gather herbs for the kitchen. The centre is fully equipped with saunas, a gymnasium, an indoor swimming pool, massage areas and mineral spa baths. There is a communal lounge room, library, television room, shop and chapel.

✉ Marienschwestern vom Karmel
A-4362 Bad Kreuzen
106

🛏 from €47.00 pp, including breakfast

☎ +43 (0) 7266 6281
📠 +43 (0) 7266 6281 50

✉ kurhaus.badkreuzen@
marienschwestern.at

☞ Take the train to **Grein** and the bus to **Bad Kreuzen**. Grein is only 7 kilometres south of Bad Kreuzen. A taxi is the other alternative.

✝ **Sunday Mass**
0730 & 0900
Catholic Church of Bad Kreuzen
A-4362 Bad Kreuzen

⚥ Open to both men and women

Open Houses

Upper Austria / Oberösterreich Bad Kreuzen

PLACES OF INTEREST ❧ The old market town of **Bad Kreuzen** is located halfway between Vienna and Salzburg in the Mühlviertel farming region. The local **Burg Kreuzen Castle** was built around 900AD and has become a vantage point for the views down the **Danube Valley**. Part of the castle operates as a **youth hostel**. There is an on-site café.

❧ Walking and hiking are enjoyable pastimes for visitors and locals alike. The **Wolfsschlucht Gorge** is close to the resort and some of the trails through the area lead up to the Burg Kreuzen Castle. Maps are available from the tourist office in the main street of Bad Kreuzen.

❧ The **Castle of Greinburg** overshadows the town of **Grein**, just a few kilometres south of Bad Kreuzen, a town known for its hospitality and restaurants. The 15th-century castle, once owned for a short time by Queen Victoria of the United Kingdom, is worth the short (but strenuous) hike up the hill. The castle is the cultural centre of the town and hosts concerts, operas, balls and artistic events. Or just enjoy some wicked indulgence at one of the traditional inns or restaurants on the banks of the **Danube** below.

❧ **Christkindl Pilgrimage Church** in the enclave of **Christkindl** is a place of pilgrimage to a tiny wax statue of Christ which stands upon the main altar. This miraculous statue is said to have cured a local man of epilepsy in the early 18th century and has attracted pilgrims ever since. A **children's Mass** is celebrated in the church at 1400 each Christmas Eve followed later by Midnight Mass. Christkindl is 60 kilometres south of **Bad Kreuzen**.

✝ Sunday Mass 0800 & 0930,
    except 0900 only *during September & October*

❧ **Christkindl Post Office** in the tiny village of Christkindl is open for 6 weeks each year from the second-last week in November, when **Christmas mail** from all over the world arrives to be posted again, this time bearing the Christkindl Post Office stamp. Walk the scenic route along the medieval streets of **Steyr** to Christkindl, a distance of 2.5 kilometres. Over the Christmas season an old-time bus departs from the town square in Steyr for the short journey. In the spirit of Christmas the **Museum of Christmas-Tree Decorations** in Steyr's Michaelerplatz displays thousands of **antique Christmas decorations** and Christmas trees, figurines, toys, and dolls houses.

❧ If driving back to Vienna you could take the scenic **Romantic Road** which leads through the wine country and past a handful of monasteries including **Melk**, **Göttweig** and **Klosterneuburg**.

FOOD AND DRINK ❧ A **roving restaurant tour** (combined with a guided walking tour of the town, led by a night-watchman in traditional dress) departs from the **Steyr Town Hall** each Thursday between April and September at 2100. The tour commences with a welcoming glass of champagne before setting out for the local parish church to climb to the top of the church steeple. Climbers are rewarded with picture-postcard views of the charming, 'quaint' old town of Steyr. During the walk appetisers, an entrée, a main course and dessert are each served in a different restaurant—a great way to sample regional Austrian cuisine. The local tourist office can provide details.   €€€

❧ The monasteries in the area cater for hungry tourists and the great abbeys of **Melk** and **Göttweig** offer a range of informal choices for indoor and outdoor eating and drinking. Don't leave without inspecting the wine cellars of both monasteries where estate bottled collections and boutique labels are for sale and despatched around the world.

Melk

☎ +43 (0) 2752 5255 5   €€

Göttweig

☎ +43 (0) 2732 8558 1225   €€

❧ First-class inns and restaurants can easily be stumbled upon in and around the pretty cobblestone town of **Grein** and some have lovely aspects over the River Danube.

Kneipp Health & Spa Centre

This monastery / spa centre is located near the **River Danube** in an area of health resorts and mineral springs. The Marienschwestern sisters have created an informal, easy-going atmosphere which encourages guests to relax and feel comfortable. The guestrooms are cosy and well furnished and are available in single, double or family configurations. All have en suites. Children are welcome and are encouraged to participate in many of the therapies.

❡ A high level of personal service is offered in a warm and companionable manner and as in all Marienschwestern centres particular attention is directed to providing healthy, carefully prepared food. Wine is served with meals.

❡ The nuns and staff at the resort take the same holistic approach to improving health and well-being as is found in the sister centres in **Upper Austria**. Guests are pampered with massages, body wraps, a cellulite cure and indulgent warm water treatments, and can also use the local golf course and tennis courts. Stables and horse riding facilities can be found in the area. The centre has a beauty and cosmetic section for facials and skin treatments. The centre was completely renovated in 2007 and guests can now avail themselves of cooking lessons conducted by the centre's chefs.

OPEN HOUSE

✉ Marienschwestern von Karmel Bad Mühllacken 55 A-4101 Feldkirchen an der Donau

🛏 from €54.00 pp, including breakfast

📞 +43 (0) **7233 7215**
📠 +43 (0) **7233 7215 414**

✎ kurhaus. badmuehllacken@ marienschwestern.at

☞ Take the train to **Linz** and then a bus or taxi to the centre. You could contact the centre to see if a pick-up can be arranged. **Feldkirchen an der Donau** is 20 kilometres west of Linz.

✝ **Sunday Mass**
0800
Marienschwestern Chapel
Bad Mühllacken 55
A-4101 Feldkirchen an der Donau

👥 Open to both men and women

PLACES OF INTEREST ❦ The **Kneipp Health and Spa Centre** in Feldkirchen is situated in the **Pesenbachtal** nature reserve, a popular walking and hiking area. The gently hilly landscapes of the region make it an ideal walking area and there are a number of trails to choose from. The picturesque 9-kilometre **Kerzenstein Walking Trail** leads from **Bad Mühllacken** near **Feldkirchen** to the town of **Gerling**. Stop off for coffee and cake and enjoy some postcard views from one of the traditional inns along the way.

❦ The 12th-century Augustinian **Monastery of St Florian** is 10 kilometres south-east of Feldkirchen. The monastery is well known for its three organs, including the Bruckner organ, named after composer Anton Bruckner, a former organist at St Florian's. The organs are often used to accompany the internationally renowned **St Florian's Boys' Choir**. Between May and mid-October on every day except Tuesday and Saturday a 20-minute recital is performed on the **Bruckner organ** at 1430 (small charge).

† Sunday Mass 0700, 0830, 1000 & 1900

❦ The **Bruckner Festival** of classical (and in recent times electronic) music is held in the **Linz Brucknerhaus concert hall** and other historical venues, including the local abbeys, every September–October in honour of Austrian composer Anton Bruckner (1824–1896). The festival attracts musicians and performers from all corners of the globe.

❦ The high-tech **Ars Electronica Centre** in Linz and its **Museum of the Future**, is a must-see for *Dr Who* fans of all ages.

Open Houses
Upper Austria / Oberösterreich Feldkirchen an der Donau

❧ The **Pöstlingbergbahn** is one of the world's steepest tram lines and runs from **Urfahr** station in Linz to the top of the **Pöstlingberg** (*mountain*) almost 3 kilometres away. The views over Linz and the rich, ornate interior of the little church sitting on the top of the mountain, enhance the experience. The **Linz Zoo** at Windflachweg 1 in Linz is situated halfway up the Pöstlingberg. The **scenic tram** makes a stop at the zoo.

❧ The **cruise boat** *MFS Kaiserin Elisabeth* operates return day trips (some train travel involved) out of Linz and on to **Grein** and **Spitz** through the world heritage-listed **Wachau Valley** where vineyards and peaceful cobblestone villages, medieval castles and monasteries are strewn along the **Danube**.

FOOD AND DRINK ❧ The town of **Feldkirchen an der Donau** has a number of good, reasonably priced cafés and restaurants-cum-guesthouses. The **Café Rechberger** is one of the closest to the **Kneipp Centre** and others can be found in the marketplace.

✉ Pesenbachtal 6
☏ +43 (0) 7233 6559   €

❧ Take home some Yuletide knick-knacks from the **Christmas market** held in **Feldkirchen** each December.

❧ The Premonstratensian fathers of the **Monastery of Schlägl**, 40 kilometres north of Feldkirchen, support themselves by working in the 800 hectares of monastery-owned forest as well as undertaking brewing and culinary pursuits. Relax under an umbrella in the monastery's outdoor restaurant, or eat inside and sample the produce from the monastery's market garden. Guests can choose from eight varieties of **Schlägl beer**, brewed on-site by the monks.

☏ +43 (0) 7281 8801 280   €€
☩ Sunday Mass 0830 & 1000

❧ No-one will go hungry at **St Florian Monastery** either. Listed on the menu is **Monastery Soup**, a hearty, creamy, thick vegetable soup with chunks of bread added at the last minute. Guaranteed to provide healthy sustenance, for monks and magnates alike.

☏ +43 (0) 7224 8902 70   €€

Open Houses

Upper Austria / Oberösterreich Gosau

12

Haus der Begegnung

The Haus der Begegnung Christian Hotel is situated on 1 hectare of land at the base of the **Dachstein Mountains** and has views over the **Gosau Valley**. It is a large complex of houses and apartments suitable for groups, families and solo travellers. Accommodation is provided in a **3-star guesthouse** where the double guestrooms and family rooms each have an en suite bathroom, a safe and a hairdryer. Separate apartments and houses on the property are ideal for family groups. The apartments are self-contained and suitable for up to four persons. Apartments with front-facing rooms have valley views.

❧ Snacks and meals are available in the dining room where large helpings of dumplings and strudel are the norm, as is an expanding waistline. The option of full board is available. There is a games room, children's playground, sauna and parking area. The local ski bus stops outside the hotel which is well positioned for mountain climbing and hiking, and in winter, cross-country skiing.

✉ Haus 438
A-4824 Gosau

🛏 from €37.00 pp,
including breakfast

📞 +43 (0) 6136 8242
📠 +43 (0) 6136 82424

✉ hausderbegegnung@
eunet.at

🚂 Take the train to
Steeg-Gosau station
which is 10 kilometres
from the village of
Gosau. Take a taxi to
the guesthouse.

✝ **Sunday Service
0900 (may change)**
Evangelical Church
A-4824 Gosau

⚥ Open to both men and
women

Open Houses

Upper Austria / Oberösterreich Gosau

PLACES OF INTEREST ❧ The **Gosau tourist train** runs on tractor power. It is known as the 'slow' train because it ever so leisurely winds and climbs through the picturesque countryside of the **Salzkammergut** region. A local guide is usually on board to entertain with folk music.

❧ If it's more glorious scenery you're after head for the tranquil, picture-perfect village of **Hallstatt**, 14 kilometres east of **Gosau**, which looks even more beautiful from a cruise boat out on the lake. The village of **Bad Ischl**, north of Hallstatt, was once the preferred summer holiday destination of Austrian emperors. Their holiday house is now open for inspection.

❧ The town of **Bad Goisern**, 15 kilometres from Gosau, is famous for its Goiserers, the comfortable and expertly crafted handmade mountain boots. These make a practical and lasting keepsake to take home. You could break them in around **Lake Gosau**, 12 kilometres out of the town and in a picturesque walking and hiking area. The lake is almost entirely surrounded by mountains. A local bus (Postbus) departs from Gosau and makes a number of stops near the lake. Well-established walking paths branch off from the lake and most lead to breathtaking views. All the trails are well marked. **Salzburg** is an hour's drive from Gosau. The villages of **Bad Ischl**, **Obertraun** and **Hallstatt** can also be easily reached from Gosau by local bus.

❡ The world's oldest salt mines and **subterranean salt lake** lie in an elevated valley 850 metres above **Hallstatt**. Children enjoy the guided tours of the mine, especially the cable car ride to the top and sliding down the old miners' shoots inside to reach the lake. The lake is artificially lit and various exhibits provide visitors with an insight into the life of a salt miner. Some tours include a visit to the '**man preserved in salt**', a prehistoric miner whose body was discovered in 1734.

❡ **Christmas markets** are held each December in **Gosau** and **Hallstatt** when the shops in the towns are open until late (usually until 2100) and the sights and sounds and festive atmosphere add to the excitement of the Christmas season.

FOOD AND DRINK Should you find yourself in **Bad Ischl**, you could have a bite to eat at one of the **Zauner cake shops and cafés** on the Pfarrgasse, the main shopping street, or on the Esplanade. Even if you're watching the figure, allow yourself the deliciously naughty purchase of a slice of their heavenly home-made chocolate cake. It is said to lose its calories upon being cut. During their sojurns in Bad Ischl, Franz Josef and Sisi ordered the Imperial pastries from the Zauner Café.

📞 +43 (0) 6132 2331 013   €€€€

❡ If checking out a pair of Goiserers, take a walk around the charming town of **Bad Goisern**. On the central Marktstraße you will find the inviting **Café Maislinger** where fresh bread and **exquisite pastries** are baked on the premises. The café is often the venue for local musical events.

📞 +43 (0) 6135 2056 2   €€€

❡ The family-run **Restaurant Gosauerhof**, part of the Hotel Gosauerhof, serves homely Austrian dishes in a cosy atmosphere.

📞 +43 (0) 6136 8229   €€

❡ The elegant restaurant of the **Hotel Koller**, situated on the outskirts of Gosau and reminiscent of a stately hunting lodge, enjoys an enviable reputation for serving fine Austrian cuisine.

📞 +43 (0) 6136 8841   €€€€€

Vorarlberg

T HE TINY, ALPINE PROVINCE OF VORARLBERG, the most isolated of Austria's provinces, borders **Switzerland**, **Liechtenstein** and **Germany**. The ultra smart ski resorts of the **Arlberg**, offering impeccable pistes and extensive ski runs, are a match for many in France and Switzerland and are a magnet to a rich and glamorous clientele, particularly the villages of **Lech** and **Zürs**.

In summer, motorcyclists are attracted to the quiet scenic roads of the **Silvretta Mountains**, the **Arlberg** and the **Montafon** whilst hikers and mountain bikers can choose from a multitude of bike and walking trails of varying stages of difficulty.

The pristine alpine landscape of Vorarlberg is the perfect stage for outdoor summer music festivals. Each July and August there is a month-long **summer opera festival** on the world's largest floating stage on the shores of **Lake Constance**.

Much of this area is dairy country, and the province is renowned for its cheese. Monks in the province still practise animal husbandry and grow vegetables, allowing the monasteries to be relatively self-sufficient. However, compared to the other Austrian provinces, religious houses in Vorarlberg are rather few and far between.

Hotel Saladina

The 3-star Christian Hotel Saladina is a traditional
Austrian hotel situated in the centre of the alpine village
of **Gaschurn** in the **Montafon Valley**, the heart of the
Austrian Alps. The hotel has a comfortable, homely
atmosphere and its 19 guestrooms are all complete
with balconies and en suites. Furnished in traditional,
rustic Montafon-style, the guestrooms are equipped
with a television, telephone, mini-bar, CD player and a
hairdryer. Half or full board is available.

¶ The Saladina's epicurean restaurant flows on to an
outdoor terrace for eating under the stars when the
weather permits. Fondue is a house speciality. The hotel
is ideally positioned for winter sports activities in the
Silvretta Nova alpine region. Facilities include heated
outdoor pool, sauna, solarium, a conference centre,
parking and wheelchair access.

✉ Gaschurn 200
A-6793 Gaschurn

🏨 from €65.00 pp,
including half-board

📞 +43 (0) 5558 8204 0
📠 +43 (0) 5558 8204 21

✎ service@saladina.com

☞ Take the train to
**Bludenz Express
train station**. From
here take the bus or a
taxi to **Gaschurn**, 26
kilometres south.

♱ **Sunday Mass
1000**
Church of St Michael
Kirchplatz
A-6793 Gaschurn

⚒ Discuss your needs in
advance of arriving,
ideally when booking.

⚥ Open to both men and
women

Open Houses
Vorarlberg Gaschurn

PLACES OF INTEREST ❦ The village of
Gaschurn and its sister village **Partenen**
sit side by side in the mountains of
the **Montafon**, among a landscape of
lakes, waterfalls, mineral springs and
mountain trails. **Galtur** is the highest
ski village in the area (situated at 1585
metres above sea level) and is the setting
for the gruesome short story *An Alpine
Idyll* written by Ernest Hemingway
(1899–1961) whilst in Galtur on a skiing
holiday. The highest ski lift in the area is
2864 metres above sea level. The region
has over 200 kilometres of downhill ski
runs, cross-country ski tracks and signposted winter footpaths.

❦ In summer, the locals head to the
Mountain Beach Park for a revitalising
dip in a combination of man-made
swimming pools and natural lakes.
Sports addicts may prefer **Gaschurn's
outdoor aerobics centre** and the '**4000
Steps to Heaven**', an outdoor staircase
which has an incline of 86 degrees. The
current record for climbing these stairs
is around 21 minutes. For reasons of
safety the steps can only be accessed
during the warmer months.

❦ The annual **Schubertiade Festival**
held all summer long, often in
the pretty, ornamental village of
Schwarzenberg, celebrates the life and
musical achievements of Franz Schubert
(1797–1828). The chocolate-box alpine
background only adds to the enjoyment
of this maestro's music. Concerts are
also performed in the Renaissance
Palace of Hohenems, 20 kilometres
south-west of Schwarzenberg.

❧ The toboggan run in **Gaschurn** has been designed especially for learners and is just 500 metres long. For real thrills the run at **St Gallenkirch**, 5 kilometres north of Gaschurn, is over 5 kilometres in length; it is floodlit, with a lift for the return journey.

❧ The traditional ceremony of **Funkensonntag** (*Fiery Sunday*) takes place on the first Sunday in Lent in Gaschurn and other Austrian ski towns. The occasion marks the end of winter with a huge bonfire, fireworks and much feasting and frivolity.

FOOD AND DRINK ❧ The **Restaurant Fässle Nova** in Gaschurn's Sporthotel is an epicurean restaurant which is mentioned in France's leading food guide, **Gault-Millau**. Less finicky bon-vivants are catered for in more traditional-style cafés within the complex and live music in the evenings ensures a buzzy *aprés ski* scene. Not to be outdone the **Post-Hotel Rössle**, in the same street, attracts serious food connoisseurs to its elegant, candle-lit dining room and a cool, stylish crowd to its trendy café and bars.

Restaurant Fässle Nova

☎ +43 (0) 5558 8888 €€€€€

Post-Hotel Rössle

☎ +43 (0) 5558 8333 0 €€€€€

❧ **Schattenburg Castle** in the town of **Feldkirch** near the Swiss border is one of the province's best preserved. Its fortress-like appearance perfectly sets the mood for the display of antique armoury and weapons inside. The castle's aptly named restaurant, **Knights**, claims to serve the **biggest Wiener schnitzels in Austria**—guaranteed to be at least 30 cm in length.

☎ +43 (0) 5522 7244 4 €€€

❧ **Small Christmas markets** are held in most villages in the Gaschurn area for those brave enough to defy the elements but rest assured, consoling mugs of hot, spicy, mulled wine are always on hand.

14

Probstei St Gerold

The ancient Benedictine monastery of St Gerold has been offering hospitality for almost 1000 years. The monastery is situated on a slope of the **Große Walsertal Mountain** in a rural alpine landscape away from the tourist areas.

❦ Today, only a lone monk lives here, ably assisted by a band of hardworking locals. The house is almost self-sufficient and the monastery's 50-bed guesthouse is equipped with modern conveniences. The 27 single or multiple guestrooms are all en suite with a television. Families are welcome.

❦ Meals are taken in the former **monastic refectory** where dishes include those prepared from old monastic recipes. Fruit and vegetables grown in the monastery's market garden are used where possible.

❦ An indoor swimming pool and sauna, a children's playground and horse stables form part of the monastery complex. Riding lessons and trail rides can be arranged.

❦ *Some years ago we wanted to stay in a monastery for just one night. The whole family fell in love with the place; we felt at home and enjoyed our stay so much that we try to go back whenever we can.*
WERNER KONRAD BLENK AND THE BLENK FAMILY—
CHRISTIANE, JOSEFINE, MORITZ AND TILMAN
FORMERLY OF VORARLBERG AND NOW OF THE
HUNTER VALLEY, AUSTRALIA

✉ A-6721 St Gerold

🛏 from €47.00 pp,
including breakfast

☎ +43 (0) 5550 2121
📠 +43 (0) 5550 2121 19

✉ propstei@
propstei-stgerold.at

☞ Take the train to
Bludenz or **Feldkirch**
and then the local
bus or a taxi to the
monastery, which is
15 kilometres north
of Bludenz and 20
kilometres east of
Feldkirch.

✝ **Sunday Mass**
0900
Church of St Gerold
A-6721 St Gerold

♿ Discuss your needs in
advance of arriving,
ideally when booking.

⚥ Open to both men and
women

PLACES OF INTEREST ❧ There are over 400 kilometres of walking paths and all-season hiking trails around **Bludenz**. If you dare, take the chairlift up to the **Hirschberg and Bizau ski resort**, 40 kilometres north of St Gerold; get back down in double-quick time on the all-season sled run. The track is almost 2 kilometres long and has 80 turns. Such a high speed trip is bound to get the blood pumping, although it is not recommended for the nervous or those with weak hearts.

❦ Ride the cable car at **Bregenz**, 50 kilometres north of St Gerold, from the base station near the harbour to the peak of the **Pfänder Mountain**. Enjoy the panoramas over **Lake Constance, Germany, Austria** and **Switzerland** on the way. Once at the top you could visit the **alpine wildlife park** and watch a 'birds of prey' exhibition or wander amongst the native goats and deer. Or relax and have a drink and a bite to eat on the verandah of the **Berghaus Pfänder restaurant** and enjoy the view.

❦ The **Capuchin Monastery** at Bahnhofstraße 4 in Feldkirch was established in 1605 and is still a full working monastery to this day. The Patron Saint of Vorarlberg, **St Fidelis of Sigmaringen**, was once a Capuchin friar attached to the Feldkirch monastery. Fidelis was martyred in 1622; his relics lie inside the monastery church.

✝ Sunday Mass 0900

❦ The **Liechtenstein border** is just 20 kilometres west of St Gerold; the town of **Vaduz**, the capital of the tiny principality of **Liechtenstein**, is a further 15 kilometres. **Germany** and **Switzerland** can be easily accessed from St Gerold and Feldkirch.

❦ Vaduz is noted for its unusual museums including a **Postage Stamp Museum**, a **Calculator** and **Typewriter Museum** and, more typical of the area, a **Ski Museum**.

❦ The oldest craft workshop and pottery factory in Liechtenstein, Schädler Ceramics, is at Churer Straße 3 in **Nendeln**, 6 kilometres north of Vaduz. The ceramics centre is open to visitors Monday to Friday between 0800 and 1700.

Open Houses

Vorarlberg St Gerold

FOOD AND DRINK ✦ The centre of the quiet, attractive town of Feldkirch is a medieval cobblestone 'old town' where the **market square** is usually bustling with buskers and street performers. Each Tuesday, Thursday and Saturday the local farmers sell their produce here. Bread, sausages, cheese and fruit can always be purchased. For something a little more formal the **Restaurant Johanniterhof** serves cheap, tasty meals and the Rauch Café is good for a coffee and a snack. Both are in the marketplace.

Restaurant Johanniterhof

☎ +43 (0) 5522 8299 01   €€

Rauch Café

☎ +43 (0) 5522 7635 5   €

❡ The **Bludenz tourist office** in Werdenbergerstraße can provide maps of local hiking paths, some leading from one farm to another. As well as being a great way to see the beautiful countryside the farmers sell their produce direct to the passing public and many farmhouses have cafés and restaurants attached.

❡ Meanwhile, chocolate heaven is not far away. Take a factory tour of the **Suchard chocolate factory** near the Bludenz train station where the famous *Milka* brand is made.

✉ Fohrenburgstr 4

☎ +43 (0) 5552 6093 04

❡ Chocoholics flock to one of Austria's largest **chocolate festivals** held in Bludenz each July. Just enjoy, and diet when you get home.

Marienschwestern Centre

This centre is situated in a scenic, rural area on the northern outskirts of Vienna, 10 kilometres from the city centre. It is run by the Catholic Marienschwestern sisters and operates primarily as a spiritual meeting centre. Groups and families are particularly welcome; however, tourists on holiday can stay at the centre if rooms are available.

❡ The double guestrooms are modern and most have en suite facilities. Those without an en suite have a toilet and wash basin provided. Apart from conference rooms and meeting facilities there is a comfortable lounge area and dining room. A small shop sells religious objects and souvenirs and there is plenty of spacious, green surrounds for walking or cycling. The house is open all year round and guests are welcome to participate in liturgical services with the sisters. Buses travel from **Kahlenberg** into Vienna on a regular basis from a bus stop located near the convent. A tiny pilgrimage church and Marian shrine in the convent grounds draws pilgrims from all over Europe. The Blessed Sacrament is exposed in the church each day between 1430 and 1530.

❡ The wine area of **Grinzing** and the **Augustinian Monastery of Klosterneuburg** can be easily reached from here.

✉ Schönstatt am Kahlenberg
A-1190 Vienna

💶 from €35.00 pp, including breakfast

☎ +43 (0) **1 320 1307**
📠 +43 (0) **1 320 1307 302**

✎ contact@ schoenstattzentrum-wien.at

☞ Take bus number 38A from **Heiligenstadt** train station to the **Kahlenberg**.

✝ **Sunday Mass**
1000
Kahlenberg Pilgrimage Church
Schönstatt am Kahlenberg
A-1190 Vienna

⚭ Open to both men and women

Spiritual Retreats
Vienna

PLACES OF INTEREST ❧ The **Kahlenberg** (*mountain*) on the fringe of the city is a popular weekend escape for many Viennese. On the edge of the **Vienna Woods**, the area is ideal for walking and hiking. Signposted trails lead through beech and pine woods and on to Grinzing, Vienna's wine-growing district. A spectacular view of Vienna can be enjoyed from the lookout at the top of the Kahlenberg. If you fancy a drink or a bite to eat while taking in the view, the **Café Sobieski**, a popular local eatery and wine bar, is easily accessible from the lookout. The café is named after the Polish King Sobieski who, with his troops, famously repelled a Turkish invasion of Vienna from the Kahlenberg in 1683.

❧ Composer Ludwig Van Beethoven was once a resident of the Döbling area at the foot of the Kahlenberg. A **Beethoven Memorial** in the form of a museum is at Döblinger Hauptstraße 92 in the house where the composer once lived (1803).

❧ Learn to dance to Beethoven's music or waltz to Strauss' 'Blue Danube' at one of Vienna's Dancing Schools. The **Elmayer Dancing School** is in the Palais Pallavicini near the Spanish Riding School, **Professor Wagner's School** is at Fleischmarkt 3–5 and the **Watzek School** is at Salzgries 12, all in the centre of Vienna. If you prefer to learn how to whip up an authentic strudel or a plate of dumplings, Viennese chef Bernhard Baumgartner runs an **Austrian Cooking School** which caters for tourists. Bernhard can be contacted at *bernhard@austriancookingschool.com*

❧ If you have some time to spare or feel the need for some quiet relaxation simply sit at the bus stop outside the famous **Vienna State Opera House**, opposite the **Hotel Bristol**, and watch the always elegantly attired Viennese come and go. This is also the point from which many tour buses depart.

❧ The interior of the **Universitätkirche** (*University or Jesuit Church*) at Dr Ignaz-Seipel-Platz 1, is elaborately decorated with an extravagant use of marble, ceiling frescoes and wall murals. The church ceiling was painted by Jesuit brother and artist Andrea Pozzo (1642–1709) and his illusory *trompe l'oeil* dome is considered a masterpiece.

✝ Sunday Mass 1030 & 1215

¶ Vienna has many quaint, traditional shops. The embroidery shop, **Ludwig Nowotny** at Freisingergasse 4, specialises in petit-point from centuries old, original patterns. **Mörtz** the shoemaker at Windmühlgasse 9, hand-crafts made-to-measure walking and mountain boots. For a touch of elegance, lace handkerchiefs can be bought where Empress Marie Therese (1717–1780) purchased hers at **Zur Schwäbischen Jungfrau**, at Graben 26. The shops are all within short walking distance of each other with the exception of Mörtz which is located in a street off the **Mariahilferstraße**.

FOOD AND DRINK ¶ **Demel**, the 200-year-old Imperial court confectioners, is where Empress Elisabeth (1837–1898), known as **Sisi**, once purchased her candied violets. Cakes, traditional Viennese pastries and chocolates are also sold. Visitors to Demel can relax in the polished refinement of the upstairs 'salons' and enjoy the decadent creations of the bakery below.

✉ Kohlmarkt 14

✆ +43 (0) 1 535 1717 0   €€€€€

¶ If the Empress was here today she would most certainly request her groceries from (Julius) **Meinl am Graben** the city's most upmarket food emporium. Classic Austrian cuisine and the best of Austrian wine are on the menu at the **Meinl am Graben restaurant** which is known as one of Vienna's best eating places. If the budget doesn't extend to fine dining there are always the street corner sausage (*würste*) stands.

✉ Kohlmarkt

✆ +43 (0) 1 532 3334 ext 6000   €€€€€

¶ Closer to the Marienschwestern Centre, in the village of **Nussdorf**, the **Café Bamkraxler** is an informal local eating place serving Salzburg Augustiner Bräu (*beer*) brewed in the Mulln Brewery in Salzburg, which is partly owned by Benedictine monks.

✉ Kahlenberger Straße

✆ +43 (0) 1 318 8800   €€

¶ The village and vineyards of **Grinzing** hosts numerous *heurigen* (wine taverns) which serve home-grown wine with home-cooked Austrian cuisine, all in a casual village atmosphere. A marked walking trail leads from Grinzing up to the **Kahlenberg** Mountain. At a leisurely pace the walk should not take more than 75 minutes.

Spiritual Retreats
Vienna

Missionary Sisters of Canisius

The convent is run by the **Canisius Sisters** and is situated in a leafy corner on the edge of the Vienna Woods on the western outskirts of Vienna between the centre of the city and the town of **Mauerbach**. The large, double-storey manor that houses the convent is dominated by the addition of a striking modern-day chapel with high ceilings and colourful, iridescent stained-glass windows.

¶ The convent is open to women only and the sisters welcome individuals or small groups to join them for prayer, meditation and spiritual guidance. Facilities are simple and as the guest area of the convent is quite small the sisters can only accommodate a limited number of guests at any one time. The convent has spacious gardens but limited car parking.

✉ Kreuzwiesengasse 9
A-1170 Vienna

💰 price to be negotiated

📞 +43 (0) 1 486 2550
📠 +43 (0) 1 486 2550 90

✉ carmen.huetter@aon.at

☞ The nearest train station is **Gersthof** which is 3 kilometres from the convent. Take a taxi from here.

✝ **Sunday Mass**
0900
Chapel of the
Missionary Sisters of
Canisius
Kreuzwiesengasse 9
A-1170 Vienna

👤 Open to women only

PLACES OF INTEREST ✏ The convent is situated in a woody area of parks and gardens. Opposite the convent, the English-style gardens of the **Potzleinsdorfer Schloss Park** are in glorious full bloom each April.

¶ Many Viennese spend their idle hours on **Danube Island**, a 21-kilometre long artificial strip in the River Danube and located in the 22nd District. Visitors can catch some sun on kilometres of sandy beach, hire a boat or a bicycle, walk, swim, or just relax and sip something cold at one of the umpteen cafés and bars. Take the U1 line to **Donauinsel**.

¶ From Gertshof train station it is a 45-minute ride into Stephansplatz station and a short walk to **The Royal Apartments** of Empress Elisabeth (Sisi) and her husband Emperor Franz Joseph (1830–1916) which are on display at the Hofburg, the former Imperial Palace. One of the unusual exhibits is Sisi's gymnasium equipment. She was a fitness fanatic a century before it became trendy! The world-famous **Spanish Riding School** forms part of the complex. Sisi's favourite furniture is on display at the **Imperial Furniture Collection** at Andreasgasse 7.

¶ Franz Josef and Sisi were married in the **Augustinian Church** in Josefpltz near the Hofburg in 1754. Each Sunday at 1100 (during the summer months) a theatrical High Mass is celebrated in the church accompanied by the music of the **Augustinerkirche Orchestra**.

¶ To the left of the 17th-century Baroque **Capuchin Church** at Tegetthoffstraße 2 in a quiet corner of the Neuer Markt is the unimposing entrance to the **Imperial Crypt** (*Kaisergruft*) where Emperor Franz Joseph and Empress Elisabeth are buried along with 144 other royals. The royal hearts are kept separately in the Augustinian Church and the royal intestines in the catacombs of **St Stephen's Cathedral**.

✉ Capuchin Church

✝ Sunday Mass 1000, 1130 & 1600

Spiritual Retreats
Vienna

❡ Austrian artist Gustav Klimt's romantic interpretation *The Kiss* hangs in the Austrian Gallery in the upper Belvedere Palace in Vienna's south and the artistic works of Austrian Expressionist painter Egon Schiele (1890–1918) can be seen at the **Leopold Museum** in Museumsplatz. Egon Schiele was a past student of the Augustinian Canons of Klosterneuburg.

❡ Shops and department stores of the **Mariahilfer Straße** are open every day except Sunday. Sale times are late January and late June / July. Vienna is considered a safe city for women travelling alone. However, those inclined could use Vienna's **'ladies only' taxi service**.

☎ +43 (0) 60 160

FOOD AND DRINK ❦ Feast on fine Viennese fare at the **Luise's Wilhelm Busch traditional restaurant** or enjoy a mug of refreshing Zwettler beer at the Busch heuriger. The restaurant is situated behind the **Church of St Anna**, approximately 1 kilometre from the convent.

✉ Dornbachstraße 114

☎ +43 (0) 1 489 7091   €€€

❡ **Café Sacher Wien** in the Hotel Sacher, is the home of the famous Sacher-Torte, which is still made to the original recipe.

✉ Philharmonikerstraße 4

☎ +43 (0) 1 514 560   €€€€€

❡ **Griechenbeisl Inn** was first established in 1447 and is the city's oldest restaurant. Over the years renowned artists, writers, musicians and composers have eaten here; many of the walls are covered in memorabilia.

✉ Fleishmarkt 11

☎ +43 (0) 1 533 1977   €€€€

❡ Once owned by monks and used as a storage area for wine, the **Augustinerkeller** is situated in the Hofburg Palace complex and is now a popular wine bar and restaurant, serving schnitzel and strudel and other local specialities. A roving accordion player provides entertainment in the evening when the atmosphere is always lively.

✉ Augustinerstraße 1

☎ +43 (0) 1 533 1026   €€€

❡ The imposing, 12th-century **Augustinian Monastery of Klosterneuburg** is situated in the Vienna Woods, 12 kilometres north of Vienna. The monks conduct guided tours of the abbey which include the multi-layered underground wine cellars. Cellar tours conclude with a tasting of Klosterneuburg's wine (small charge).

⛪ Sunday Mass 0700, 0800, 0930, 1100 & 1800

17

Abbey of Altenburg

The Benedictine monks of the Abbey of Altenburg
offer accommodation to males only, along with an
invitation to participate in the spiritual activities of the
community. Overnight guests generally lend a welcome
hand with the daily chores, by way of contributing to
the upkeep of this busy abbey. The monastery is almost
self-sufficient as the monks work in the vineyards, the
market garden and in the abbey's manicured formal
gardens using agricultural methods developed by their
predecessors.

❡ The abbey has a fascinating history and, by virtue of
its past, is perfect for those seeking spiritual renewal.
It was founded in 1144 but over the centuries fell into
ruin. A new abbey was constructed above these ruins.
During excavations in the latter part of the 20th century
the ruins were unearthed and restoration of much of
the original abbey was carried out. These days the new
abbey stands above the original one.

❡ The restoration work has been meticulous and even
the stained-glass windows of the original abbey have
been reinstated. Today both the medieval abbey and its
more modern relative are open for the public to enjoy.
As the abbeys have at various times been occupied by
monks from the 12th century onwards, they truly are
living history. Altenburg is 85 kilometres north-west
of Vienna.

✉ Abbot Placidus Much-
Straße 1
A-3591 Altenburg

🏨 from €45.00 pp

☎ +43 (0) 2982 3451
📠 +43 (0) 2982 3451 13

✉ info@stift-altenburg.at

🚉 Take the train to **Horn**
then transfer to a bus
to **Altenburg**. The
bus continues on to
Zwettl, 38 kilometres
west of **Altenburg**.

✝ **Sunday Mass
0700 & 1000**
Abbey of Altenburg
Abbot Placidus Much-
Straße 1
A-3591 Altenburg

⚥ Open to men only

Spiritual Retreats

Lower Austria / Niederösterreich Altenburg

PLACES OF INTEREST ❧ **Altenburg Abbey** is rich with artistic treasures. The Austrian painter **Paul Troger** (1698–1762) created the frescoes in the abbey church and in the abbey's celebrated Baroque library. Paul Troger also designed the eerily beautiful crypt under the library, in the style of grotesque Baroque.

❧ True to its name, the garden of the 12th-century **Castle of Rosenburg**, 4 kilometres south of Altenburg is, for much of the year, a sea of classical, multi-hued roses. However, the medieval spirit lives on at Rosenburg and the castle's original tournament courtyard, which dates back to the Norman and Viking times, is used for falconry displays, sometimes with a fanfare and starring knights on horseback in true medieval style.

❧ The renaissance **Castle of Greillenstein** is 6 kilometres west of Altenburg. The castle's owners run popular night-time candlelight 'spirit' tours of the castle and the grounds where encounters with ghosts have been reported. Tours begin with a hearty meal accompanied by local Austrian wine to make the sightings a little easier.

❧ Austria's oldest town, **Krems**, is over 1000 years old. In a prominent wine-growing area, the town is 40 kilometres south of Altenburg and is surrounded by vineyards. Krems is a university and festival town which participates in the country's annual **Donaufestival** (*Danube Festival*) held each April. The locals provide a ready-made audience for the performances of modern music and dance.

❧ The **Church of Maria Dreieichen** has been a place of pilgrimage since 1656 when a local man, Matthias Weinberger, placed a wax statue of the Madonna in the fork of an oak tree growing near the village. The statue was said to have miraculous properties and when it melted after a fire during the late 17th century a new image was created. The Church of Maria Dreieichen is still a place of pilgrimage today and the remains of the original oak tree can be seen behind the high altar. The church is 10 kilometres east of Altenburg and administered by the monks of Altenburg Abbey.

FOOD AND DRINK ❧ The casual, relaxed ambience of the **Altenburg Abbey restaurant and tavern**, as well as the generous platters, ensures a liberal sprinkling of neighbourhood clientele. The abbey café is open for snacks, light meals and hot drinks.

☏ +43 (0) 2982 3451 76　　❝

❧ Spitz, where waterside inns and informal cafés are scattered along the banks of the Danube and from where a car ferry regularly makes a return trip across the river, is south of Altenburg and only 18 kilometres from the restaurants and winery of the great Abbey of Melk. **The Abbey of Melk** has a number of indoor and outdoor eating options. The menu covers a varied range of snacks, drinks and full meals. Set menus can be arranged for group bookings.

☏ +43 (0) 2752 5255 5　　❝

❧ **Znojmo** in the Czech Republic is 50 kilometres north of Altenburg in the Czech wine region. The local Moravian vineyards can be visited by following a section of the 160-kilometre long **Wine Road** which commences in the town.

Spiritual Retreats
Lower Austria / Niederösterreich Geras

Hotel Alter Schüttkasten

The Premonstratensian abbey at Geras was founded by Count Ulrich of Pernegg in 1153. At the same time an associate monastery was established for the women of the order in a castle at **Pernegg**, 10 kilometres south. Premonstratensians follow the Rule of St Augustine and are also known as Norbertines.

❡ These days the abbey and the monastery are both well suited for those seeking spiritual renewal. Though nuns no longer live at Pernegg it is still owned by the order and is a centre of spiritual healing.

❡ Visitors have a choice of accommodation options. The Premonstratensians operate a hotel at Geras, the **Hotel Alter Schüttkasten**, which has 40 double and single rooms. A separate building located near the monastery's art and craft studio accommodates guests taking one of the live-in craft or academic courses offered by the monks each year. There is also a guesthouse at the monastery in Pernegg. All guestrooms in the overall complex have en suite bathrooms. Meals are served in the restaurant of the Hotel Schüttkasten or in the dining room of the monastery at Pernegg. Seasonal specialities are always on the menu, including freshly caught fish from the abbey's lakes. A **beer garden** is open during the warmer months.

✉ Abbey of Geras
Vorstadt 11
A-2093 Geras

🛏 from €43.00 pp, breakfast included

☎ +43 (0) **2912 332**
📠 +43 (0) **2912 332 33**

✐ info@schuettkasten.com

🚆 Take the train to **Hötzelsdorf-Geras** station which is 6 kilometres south of the abbey and 4 kilometres from **Pernegg**. A pick-up is generally necessary as taxis are not always available.

✝ **Sunday Mass**
0900, 1030 & 1900
Abbey of Geras
Vorstadt 11
A-2093 Geras

⚥ Open to both men and women

PLACES OF INTEREST ❧ **The Abbey of Geras** is situated in the hilly Waldviertal region, near the Czech border amid 134 hectares of pine tree forest. Former Geras monk Father Hermann-Josef Weidinger (1918–2004) achieved fame in Austria as a leading herbalist, often using the herbs of the abbey garden 'pharmacy'. An advocate of elderberry, he once said it was his favourite herb because 'it is good for the soul'. Today, a walk through the garden is an engrossing sensory experience at the end of which the monks' herbal products, including a variety of health promoting herbal teas, can be purchased. In later years Father Weidinger consulted at the Paracelsus House Nature Cure Centre in Karlstein, 25 kilometres west of the Abbey of Geras.

❡ The **Reblaus Express Scenic Railway** runs between Retz and the walled town of Drosendorf on the Czech border, stopping at 10 stations en route, a one-way journey of 40 kilometres. The train rolls through farmland and forests winding around vineyards and past farmhouses and slowing at scenic viewpoints for photo opportunities. On the first Sunday of each month passengers can continue on to Vranov, in the Czech Republic, 30 kilometres from Drosendorf Station. The border crossing is 9 kilometres north of Geras.

❡ The 11th-century **Raabs Castle** in Raabs an der Thaya, 17 kilometres west of Geras, is the area's regional centre of music and culture. During the Raabs Cultural Summer Festival a program of concerts, plays and art exhibitions is staged within the walls of the medieval castle. **International Master Classes** for students of the violin, cello and chamber music are conducted by some of Austria's most experienced musicians. Students live in at the castle. Some of the oldest ruins in Austria, those of the **Castle Kollmitz** at Kollmitzdörfl, are nearby.

Spiritual Retreats
Lower Austria / Niederösterreich Geras

❦ **The Market Square** in Retz is one of the most beautiful in Austria. The yellow, church-like building at one end of the square is the Town Hall (*Rathaus*); inside is a striking Gothic chapel which is sometimes used for wedding ceremonies. The fortress-like **Hardegg Castle**, in the smallest town in Austria (15 kilometres north of Retz), is also used for weddings.

❦ The **Haugschlag** and **Waldviertel** Championship Golf Courses are north-west of Geras near the Czech border and are said to be among the best courses in Austria. From some holes stray golf balls could quite easily be lost in the Czech Republic. The 27-hole Mnich and the 9-hole Nová Bystřice golf courses form part of the **Monachus Golf Resort** and lie on the Czech side of the border. These courses are accessible from Haugschlag via an exclusive border crossing established especially for golfers and golf carts. The border crossing is open between 0600 and 2200 each day. The clubs are unique in that golfers are allowed to bring their dogs along.

FOOD AND DRINK ❦ The wine town of **Retz** is situated 24 kilometres east of Geras. The town's market square is the rooftop of Austria's largest wine cellar, a network of underground caves dating back to the 13th century. The caves were once used to store the area's wine stocks.

❦ **Retz Wine Tasting Trail** leads from the town past dozens of local vineyards. Maps are available from the local tourist office.

❦ The Old Town dates back to the 12th century and, as well as being ideal for a stroll round some historical sites, there are a number of good restaurants and pizzerias in the vicinity. An authentic Austrian café or pastry shop is never too far away and the **Cyril Blei bakery** in the main square is often packed with passers-by who find the melt-in-the-mouth delicacies too good to resist.

☏ +43 (0) 2942 2807 8   €

❦ Those with a sweet tooth will feel right at home at the **Wickliky Café**, where *Guglhupf* (pronounced *Googlehoopf*—a traditional Austrian coffee cake), fruity strudel and cream filled pastries are baked every day.

✉ Znaimerstraße 2

☏ +43 (0) 2942 2348   €

Spiritual Retreats
Lower Austria / Niederösterreich Lilienfeld

Abbey of Lilienfeld

The abbey is situated in the village of Lilienfeld in the foothills of the Alps and welcomes both men and women for overnight stays for short periods of time. It is especially popular with younger people due to its close vicinity to some of the best skiing areas in Austria. Visitors can overnight in the abbey guesthouse and experience the peaceful atmosphere so essential to spiritual renewal. Guestrooms are available on an ensuite or share bathroom basis. Guests of the abbey are welcome to join in the monks' daily schedule of prayer and Mass but there is no obligation to do so. Breakfast is the only meal served.

❧ Founded in 1202, this Cistercian abbey is one of the largest medieval monasteries in Austria. It is on the **Vienna–Mariazell pilgrimage route** south of St Polton and houses a relic said to be from the original Cross.

❧ Each July the monks run a series of summer schools which attract international teaching specialists. Students travel from around the globe to study music and art under these leading tutors. During this time concerts and religious services in the abbey are accompanied by the music of the students. Musical and cultural events take place at the abbey all year round. An **Advent market** is held at the abbey on the first weekend in December.

✉ Klosterrotte 1
A-3180 Lilienfeld

🏨 from €45.00 pp

☎ +43 (0) 2762 5242 037
📠 +43 (0) 2762 5242 037

✉ p.pius@aon.at

☞ Take the train to
Lilienfeld which is
less than 1 kilometre
from the abbey and 83
kilometres south-west
of **Vienna**.

✝ **Sunday Mass**
0900 & 1000
Abbey of Lilienfeld
Klosterrotte 1
A-3180 Lilienfeld

⚭ Open to both men and
women

Spiritual Retreats

Lower Austria / Niederösterreich Lilienfeld

PLACES OF INTEREST ❦ The foothills around Lilienfeld are snow-covered each winter and skiing is a popular activity. There are two chairlifts leading from the village to the slopes of **Muckenkogel**, above. The slopes are suitable for both beginners and experts alike. For a more exhilarating, rollercoaster ride, venture onto the '**Eibl Jet**' in Türnitz, 15 kilometres south. This all-season, 1-kilometre long sled track has a vertical drop of 110 metres—guaranteed to make even the bravest hold their breath and offer up a silent prayer.

❡ In summer the ski trails convert to well-marked and generally easy walking trails. Austrian Mathias Zdarsky is said to have been the world's first ski instructor. He honed his skills on the hills around Lilienfeld and the town's **Zdarsky Ski Museum** is named in his honour.

❡ Classical music enthusiasts should enjoy the concerts which are held throughout the year in the **Abbey of Melk**, 40 kilometres north of Lilienfeld. Music from the 17th and 18th century is often featured, with occasional guest appearances from international ensembles and soloists. The formidable, 11th-century stronghold is one of Austria's most significant abbeys and dominates the tiny town from its hilltop position. Unfortunately the abbey is not open to overnight guests, but visitors can inspect the treasures in the abbey museum and the extravagantly decorated abbey church. While there, be sure to wander along the **Kaisergang** (*Emperor's Gallery*), a long corridor lined with portraits of Austria's monarchs, into the abbey's opulent library and a collection of over 85,000 books.

✝ Sunday Mass 0930

From Melk a cruise boat departs for the lovely old town of Krems, sailing down the **River Wachau** through world heritage-listed scenery. The cruise takes about 1 ¾ hours. From Vienna an all-inclusive ticket can be purchased at the **Westbahnhof** train station which includes entrance to the abbey, the cruise to Krems and the return train.

Ybbsitz, 70 kilometres west of Lilienfeld, is a stop on the **Iron Trail** driving route. It is known for its forges and blacksmithing. The **blacksmiths' Christmas market** is held in the town during the third week of December with local blacksmiths demonstrating their art. Metalwork classes can be arranged at the Forging Centre in the town.

The stately **Herzogenburg Monastery** was established during the Middle Ages and the present building originates in the 13th century. The Augustinian canons who live here conduct tours of the monastery from April to October. The monastery's library of rare books and manuscripts and the monks' collection of Gothic art are included in the tour. Herzogenburg is near St Polten and 40 kilometres north of Lilienfeld.

✝ Sunday Mass 0800, 0930 & 1830

An **Advent market** is held at the abbey in Lilienfeld on the first weekend in December.

FOOD AND DRINK If passing by the Abbey of Lilienfeld, you will see a shop near the entrance to the estate where wines from the monks' Pfaffstätten vineyards, east of Lilienfeld, can be purchased. The abbey has no dining facilities for day or overnight visitors but cafés and eating places can be found in the village. The monks at the **Abbey of Herzogenburg** also sell their wine in the same way.

The town of **Herzogenburg** is well serviced by restaurants and taverns, and the wine villages of **Nussdorf**, **Traismauer** and **Inzersdorf** also cater for the hungry and thirsty.

A corner of the ancient **Carthusian monastery** in Gaming, west of Lilienfeld, is now the Restaurant Kartausenkeller where authentic Austrian fare is served in the refectory once used by the monks. Much of the monastery has been restored and sections are open to the public.

📞 +43 (0)7485 972 48 €€€

The **Abbey of Melk** has a double-level, 600-seat restaurant offering an a la carte menu and a wine list which includes a selection from the abbey winery. A separate garden café serves coffee, cake and snacks.

✉ Stiftsrestaurant Melk

📞 +43 (0)2752 525 55 €€

Abbey of Mariastern

The Abbey of Mariastern is situated near the base of the **Pfänder Mountains**, 15 kilometres north of **Bregenz** and just a short walk from the German border. The heart of this 16th-century monastery is a strikingly simple two-level stone church. The main monastery building was once a former castle.

❦ Mariastern is a busy working monastery run by a zealous community of **Cistercian nuns**. The sisters manage an eclectic program of prayer evenings, religious discussions and days of meditation as well as welcoming guests and running a busy guesthouse. The monastery has two apartments for the use of overnight visitors and eight single and five tastefully furnished double guestrooms, mostly en suite. The sisters lead a structured life of prayer, work and worship. Guests are invited to join them in liturgical services.

❦ The sisters use their work time to make candles, religious cards and other hand-crafted goods which are sold in the abbey shop along with wine, books and souvenirs.

✉ Gwiggen 1
A-6914 Hohenweiler

🛏 from €33.00 pp,
including breakfast

✆ +43 (0) 5573 8223 4
✆ +43 (0) 5573 8223 46

✉ schwestern@
mariastern-gwiggen.at

☞ Take the train to
Bregenz station.
From here take
the bus on Line 19
to **Hohenweiler /
Gwiggen** and get off
at the abbey, which
is 10 kilometres from
Bregenz.

✝ **Sunday Mass**
0815
Abbey of Mariastern
A-6914 Hohenweiler

♀ Women only

PLACES OF INTEREST ❧ **Heli-skiing** on the slopes of **Lech** is a must for thrill seekers. For something requiring less staying power, take the local shuttle bus and have a look around the other resort villages on the Arlberg. The bus links Lech and Zürs with St Anton, St Jakob, St Christophe and Stuben. St Anton is the largest ski resort; Lech and Zürs are the most expensive.

❧ A few kilometres from Hohenweiler are departure points for **cruise boat tours** of **Lake Constance**. The boats pull in to many of the Austrian, German and Swiss towns situated on the lake. The stunningly handsome German town of **Lindau** is on an island in Lake Constance and can be accessed by bridge. Lindau is 11 kilometres south-west of Hohenweiler.

❧ The Swiss–Austrian border post of Diepoldsau near Hohenems is 35 kilometres south of Hohenweiler. A further 25 kilometres west is the Swiss town of **Appenzell**, an oasis of peace. Its residents are happily at odds with each other on religious issues, the town being divided into two separate and autonomous religious halves of 'Protestant' and 'Catholic', each operating independently of the other.

Spiritual Retreats
Vorarlberg Hohenweiler

❧ The **Island of Mainau** in Lake Constance, Germany is referred to locally as the 'flower island'. Garden lovers should enjoy the island landscape of rose gardens, parks, butterfly house and arboretums. The monastic **Island of Reichenau**, also in Lake Constance, is world heritage-listed for the **Benedictine Abbey of Reichenau** which was founded by St Pirmin in 726. Today, this peaceful isle is mostly farmland, as it was centuries ago when vast fields of crops were sown for the abbey. The water pitcher, said to have been used by Christ to turn water into wine at the Wedding Feast of Cana, is stored in the abbey church.

❧ On the shores of Lake Constance, the unique **Zeppelin Museum** can be found in a disused railway station in **Friedrichshafen**. The museum is dedicated to the history of the airship and displays a partial reconstruction of the doomed *Hindenburg*, which burst into flames whilst landing in New Jersey in 1937. The town is 25 kilometres west of Bregenz.

FOOD AND DRINK ✦ Eat your way along the **Bregenzerwald cheese trail** which links tiny villages, traditional inns and family-owned dairies. Farmhouse cheesemakers produce unique varieties of cheese all along the trail. Look out for *Käsknopfle*, a cheese dumpling, and *Kässpätzle*, a delicious regional cheese and noodle speciality.

❧ The **Cistercian Monastery of Mehrerau** is in an idyllic location on the shores of **Lake Constance**. The monks work in the gardens and vineyards cultivating produce for the monastery restaurant and wine cellar. The monastery is a peaceful and picturesque haven for a relaxed lunch in the garden of the **Klosterkellar wine tavern**.

☎ +43 (0) 5574 8677 0   €€

✝ Sunday Mass 0730, 0900 & 1045

Vienna

❧ The **Via Francigena** (*Highway to Heaven*) is an ancient pilgrimage route from Canterbury in England to the burial place of St Peter in the Vatican, Rome; a journey of around 1900 kilometres. Pilgrims who wish to join the trail from Austria could follow the route of the **Way of St James** which commences at the Hainburger Gate in the town of **Hainburg an der Donau**, 50 kilometres east of Vienna, and follow the trail to **Melk**, **Linz**, **Salzburg** and through **Vorarlberg**, finally linking with the **Via Francigena** at **Lausanne** in Switzerland. From Lausanne, pilgrims can continue on through France and Spain to the Shrine of **St James de Compostela** in Galicia or head along the Via Francigena to **Aosta**, **Pavia**, **Lucca**, **Siena** and finally **Rome**. The trail to Rome is approximately 1000 kilometres from Lausanne.

❧ **Via Slavica Pilgrimage**, a lesser known route, follows an ancient trail from **Vienna** to the **Vatican** in Rome, with a choice of travelling through **Ljubljana** in Slovenia, or along the **Via Sacra** in Austria to **Mariazell** and through **Arnoldstein** in Carinthia, **Tarviso** and **Udine** in Italy, to the ancient Roman city of **Aquileia** and on to **Assisi** and **Rome** (over 1200 kilometres).

❧ The **Via Sacra** is an ancient pilgrims' route leading from Vienna through Lower Austria to **Mariazell** in Styria and on to a miraculous 12th-century statue of the Madonna in the **Mariazell Basilica**. The trail leads past a chain of religious shrines, pilgrimage churches and through abbey towns (approximately 140 kilometres).

❧ The **Vienna to Mariazell Pilgrimage Trail** commences at **St Stephan's Cathedral** in Vienna and weaves through **Heiligenkreuz**, **Mayerling**, **Kaumberg**, **Kieneck** and **St Ägyd** and on to **Mariazell**. The trail joins the **Via Sacra** at **Heiligenkreuz** and leaves it at **Kaumberg**, 20 kilometres south-west.

❧ An impressive **Ash Wednesday Procession** in **St Stephen's Cathedral** is led by the Archbishop of Vienna. The traditional ceremony is attended by large numbers of devout locals. Each week-day and on Sunday at 1700 a public prayer service with the exposition of the Blessed Sacrament is held in **St Stephan's Cathedral** (*Stephansdom*) in Vienna. The ceremony takes place in front of a 15th-century Neustädter altar which is to the left of the cathedral's main altar. The cathedral is open each morning at 0600 and the doors are closed after evening blessing at 2145.

✝ Sunday Mass 0730, 0900, 1015, 1115, 1200, 1730, 1800, 1900 & 2100

Vienna

❧ **The Schatzkammer** (*Imperial Treasury*) in Vienna's **Hofburg** is a reservoir of royal and religious heirlooms including the Imperial Crown, a piece of the lance believed to have pierced the side of the crucified Christ and a nail said to be from the Holy Cross.

❧ In a tradition dating back 350 years, a popular **Easter, Lenten market fair** is held in the square outside the **Kalvarienberg** (*Calvary*) **Church** in Hernals in Vienna's 17th district. During the 17th century a **Way of The Cross** (sections of which still remain) led to the Kalvarienberg Church. These days the Way of the Cross is in an enclosed area near the church and is open to pilgrims every day between Ash Wednesday and Easter Monday. The Kalvarienberg Church opens daily from 0700 until 2100.

† Sunday Mass 0745, 0900 & 1900

Burgenland

❧ A pilgrimage route from **Burgenland** to the **Mariazell Shrine** in **Styria** commences from **Eisenstadt**. Known as the **Mariazell Trail** the route leads through the castle town of **Forchtenstein**, through **Würflach**, **Puchberg am Schneeber**, **Schwarzau im Gebirge** in Lower Austria and on to **Mariazell** (approximately 130 kilometres).

❧ From Eisenstadt's **Mount Calvary Church** (*Kalvarienbergkirche*), also known as Haydn's Church because composer Joseph Haydn is buried here, pilgrims can follow an unusual Kalvarienberg (*Way of The Cross*) in and around the church and past numerous prayer stations and religious monuments. The panoramic views from some stations are a bonus.

Carinthia

❧ The town of **Frauenkirchen**, 6 kilometres south of **Mönchhof** (see Open Houses accommodation) has been a place of pilgrimage since 1335. The original pilgrimage church was destroyed by the Turks in 1683 and a new church was built in its place. **The Basilica Maria auf der Heide** (*St Mary's on the Heath*) houses a 12th-century statue of the Virgin Mary from the original church known as the **Shrine of Frauenkirchen**. Pilgrims can walk an unusual (and short) **Kalvarienberg** which has been erected in a rising, circular fashion near the basilica.

✉ Basilica of Frauenkirchen

✝ Sunday Mass 0900 & 1000

❧ The town of **St Margarethen**, on the western side of **Lake Neusiedl**, south of Vienna, stages a passion play every 5 years. The play is held in a cavernous old former Roman quarry with performances taking place over a 3-month period. The next passion play is scheduled for June, 2011.

❧ The province of Carinthia adjoins Salzburg and Styria and is the home of **The Vierberge-Wallfahrt**, an ancient, 40-kilometre pilgrimage trail which winds over the mountains of **Magdalensberg**, **Ulrichsberg**, **Veitsberg** and **Lorenziberg**. The annual pilgrimage takes place on the second Friday after Easter and begins with a Mass celebrated at midnight on the Magdalensberg Mountain. The trail is dotted with shrines and monuments, and during the pilgrimage a Mass is celebrated on each mountain. The tradition is to complete the pilgrimage within 24 hours.

❧ The **Domitian Pilgrimage Trail** commences at the **Church of Christ the Saviour** at **Millstatt** south-west of **St Lambrecht**. The church is the burial place of St Domitian, a Slovenian saint who designed the trial. Pilgrims follow a return route past churches, shrines and monuments and through **Obermillstatt**, **Lammersdorf**, **Sappl**, **Matzelsdorf** and **Pesenthein**. The trail takes an average 7–8 hours to complete.

❧ Pope John Paul II visited the **Basilica of Maria Luggau**, in the south of the province, in 1986 to pray before a 16th-century painting of the Blessed Virgin, said to have miraculous properties. The basilica is under the care of the Catholic Servite Order and the friars live in a monastery attached to the church.

Lower Austria

❧ An ancient pilgrims' trail leads from **Schwarzenbach** in Lower Austria past a tiny, wooden pilgrimage church and on to **Annaberg** in the Lilienfeld district, a distance of just over 20 kilometres. The legend is that Jesus, Mary and Joseph used this trail when fleeing Egypt. Some say that a footprint set in stone belongs to Mary. To-wards the end of the trail pilgrims follow a Way of the Cross with 14 separate prayer stations leading up to the parish church.

✝ Sunday Mass 1000

❧ One of Austria's most popular pilgrimage destinations is the Gothic **Pieta of Our Lady** on the Maria Taferl hill near the town of **Pöchlam**. The pilgrimage site is linked to a series of reportedly miraculous healings.

✉ Basilica of Maria Taferl

✝ Sunday Mass

　Summer: 0700, 0830, 1000, 1100 & 1900

　Winter: 0700, 0830 & 1000

❧ The pilgrimage church of **Maria Dreieichen** (*Mother of Sorrows*) has been a place of pilgrimage since 1656 when a local man, Matthias Weinberger, placed a wax statue of the Madonna in the fork of an oak tree growing near the village. The statue was believed to have miraculous properties and a church was built to house it. When the statue melted after a fire in 1856 a new statue was crafted. The church is still a place of pilgrimage today and the remains of the original oak tree can be seen behind the high altar.

❧ The **Lower Austria pilgrimage trail** to the Mariazell shrine in Styria commences in the town of Nebelstein near the Czech border and passes through **Zwettl**, **Göttweig**, **St Polten** and **Türnitz**. At Türnitz pilgrims can join the **Via Sacra** pilgrimage trail and continue on to Mariazell.

❧ The **Kirchschlag passion play** is performed every 5 years (indoors in a building near the parish church) in the town of **Kirschschlag**, 100 kilometres south of Vienna. The next performance is in 2010.

❧ The **Dorfstetten passion play** takes place every 6 years, as has been the case since 1990. Dorfstetten is 20 kilometres east of Bad Kreuzen.

Salzburg

❧ **The Basilica of Maria Plain** is the pilgrim church of Salzburg. The basilica is embedded into the hills on the outskirts of Salzburg and overlooks the city from a spectacular vantage point. The original church was established in 1652 to house what is thought to be a miraculous image of the Blessed Virgin, which stands to-day at the front of the main altar. As with many hilltop churches in Austria, a **Kalvarienberg**, 14 prayer stations replicating Christ's journey to Calvary, has been established.

✝ Sunday Mass 0800, 0900, 1000, 1115

❧ The **Via Nova pilgrimage trail** has been established over an ancient pilgrims' route, commencing in **Metten** in Germany and linking the Austria / German border town of **Passau** to **Michaelbeuern, Seeham, Obertrum, St Gilgen** and **St Wolfgang im Salzkammergut** (300 kilometres). The trail leads to pilgrim churches, shrines and places of religious interest (300 kilometres).

Styria

❧ The shrine of **Mariazell** is the most important in Austria and pilgrimage routes to the **Mariazell Basilica** can be followed from every province in the country. The shrine is dedicated to a miracle which occurred here in 1157 after a monk from the Monastery of St Lambrecht placed a wooden statue of the Madonna in the fork of a Linden tree growing near the town. Over the centuries the statue was believed to have miraculous properties. Amazingly, the original statue still stands in the basilica which has been built to protect it.

❧ The **Styrian Mariazell Pilgrimage Trail** commences at the Austrian town of **Eibiswald** near the Slovenian border and leads through **Stainz, Graz, Schanzsattel, Mürzsteg** and on to the **Mariazell Basilica**.

❧ The **Hemma Trail** is an Austrian pilgrimage route leading to **Gurk** and to the shrine of (Countess) St Hemma (970–1054) who is buried in the Gurk Cathedral. The trail can be followed in shorter sections and commences from a number of towns including **Admont** (from the pilgrimage church of Frauenberg), **Mariahof, St Lambrecht, Karnburg, Ossiach** and **Millstatt**.

Styria

❦ The world's largest pilgrimage cross (40m high) was constructed in 2004 near the peak of the **Veitscher Ölberg** mountain close to the Styrian town of **Veitsch**. With stunning views and dedicated to world peace, the meshed wooden cross can be climbed from the inside where a section of the crossbar has been set aside for peaceful meditation. Entry is between 1000–1900 daily, for a small fee. Veitsch is 50 kilometres south of Mariazell.

❦ The pilgrimage church of **Frauenberg** is protected by the Benedictine monks of Admont Abbey. The church, atop a hill 6 kilometres west of Admont, is dedicated to Mary the Mother of God. A **Way of The Cross** surrounds the church.

  ✝ Sunday Mass 0900 & 1030

❦ A fabled monument known locally as **Der Teufelstein** or *Devil's Rock* stands on a rise on the outskirts of the town of Fischbach, north of Graz. The legend is that one Christmas night Lucifer decided to build a stairway to Heaven, using the rock. Once a site of pagan worship, the rock is now thought to be some sort of ancient cosmic symbol. The area around the rock is now a place for peaceful contemplation.

❦ A passion play is presented every 6 years in the town of **Feldkirchen an der Donau**, near **Graz**. The next performance will take place in 2013.

Tyrol

❦ The Benedictine **St Georgenberg-Fiecht Abbey** in the town of **Fiecht** is the starting point of pilgrimages to the site of the abbey's pilgrim church which stands on the wooded slopes of Mt St Georgenberg. Inside the church is a 15th-century Gothic Pieta and a reliquary of the Holy Blood said to date from 1310AD. It is said that during a celebration of Mass held in the church all those centuries ago the wine turned into blood. During the summer, pilgrimages to the shrine are often held in the evening.

  ✉ Pilgrim church

  ✝ Sunday Mass 0900, 1100 & 1500

❦ The pilgrimage chapel of **Mariastein**, between **Salzburg** and **Innsbruck**, is within the tower of a castle perched on top of a rocky escarpment. It is a 150-step climb to the top of the castle tower where a small chapel safeguards a miraculous statue of the Madonna and the Baby Jesus.

❦ The **Thiersee passion play** is staged every 6 years with the next performance due in 2011. Since 1979 in the Tyrolean town of **Erl**, a passion play has been presented every 6 years between May and October.

Upper Austria

❧ A pilgrim trail for cyclists has been established in Upper Austria and is known as the **Donau-Alpen-Adria Pilgrims' Trail**. The trail commences at the **Monastery of Mariahilf** near Passau on the Austrian/German border and continues on to Altenmarkt and the pilgrimage **Church of Maria Gail** in Austria. Continuing down through the north of Italy the trail leads to the Sanctuary of the Virgin Mary in Barbana, Veneto, an age-old place of pilgrimage (500 kilometres).

❧ Another **Mariahilf pilgrimage church** is situated in picturesque **Halstatt**, south-east of Salzburg, and has been attracting pilgrims since the 12th century. Overlooking the rooftops of the tiny village, with unparalleled views over **Lake Halstattersee**, the church is a haven of peace and tranquillity. Within the church is the Chapel of St Michael where an historic 'bonehouse' contains the skulls of many past residents of the village.

❧ Each year a colourful and theatrical **Corpus Christi procession** is held on **Lake Halstattersee**. Visitors can purchase a ticket for a seat on any of the colourful, decorated flotillas participating in the ceremony, which commences with the celebration of Mass in the **Mariahilf pilgrimage church**. The feast of Corpus Christi is the Thursday following the second Sunday after Pentecost. The procession is usually held on the Sunday following the Thursday feast day.

❧ The town of **Mettmach** hosts a passion play every 6 years with the last play presented in 2007.

❧ Some make a pilgrimage to the **Pfarrkirche** (*parish church*) in Mondsee on the outskirts of **Salzburg**, where the real-life Baron Georg Von Trapp married Fraulien Maria Augusta Kutschera on 26 November, 1927 and was launched into a lifetime of celebrity through the timeless film *The Sound of Music*. In 1939 Georg and Maria and family moved to Stowe in the mountains of Vermont, USA where they established an Austrian-style ski lodge and resort. Georg and Maria have passed on and the much heralded **Trapp Family Lodge** is now run by the youngest child Johannes. During World War I the Von Trapp family lived for a time at the **Abbey of Klosterneuberg**, near Vienna.

**Additional
Accommodation**

Vienna   Burgenland   Carinthia

MÖDLING

Ⓢ Bildungshaus
St Gabriel

✉ Gabrielerstraße 171
A-2340 Mödling

📞 +43 (0) 2236 8032 28
📠 +43 (0) 2236 8032 04

✉ ebh.stgabriel@steyler.at

⚭ Open to both men and women

VIENNA

Ⓢ House of Don Bosco
St Veit-Gasse 25
A-1130 Vienna

📞 +43 (0) 1 8783 9
📠 +43 (0) 1 8783 9414

✉ dbh@donbosco.at

⚭ Only groups of young people
may stay here

Ⓢ Kardinal König Haus

✉ Kardinal-König-Platz 3
A-1130 Vienna

📞 +43 (0) 1 8047 5934 69
📠 +43 (0) 1 8049 743

✉ kursanmeldung@
kardinal-koenig-haus.at

⚭ Open to both men and women

Ⓢ Schwestern vom
Göttlichen Erlöser

✉ Kaiserstraße 25–27
A-1070 Vienna

📞 +43 (0) 1 5236 444
📠 +43 (0) 1 5236 4448 33
*(Mark for the attention of
Sister Judith)*

✉ sr.judith@gmx.at

⚭ Women only

EISENSTADT

Ⓢ Haus der Begegnung

✉ Kalvarienbergplatz 11
A-7000 Eisenstadt

📞 +43 (0) 2682 6329 0
📠 +43 (0) 2682 63290 90

✉ bildungshaus@hdb-eisenstadt.at

⚭ Only groups may stay here

OBERPULLENDORF

Ⓢ St Stephen's House

✉ Schloßplatz 4
A-7350 Oberpullendorf

📞 +43 (0) 2612 4259 10
📞 +43 (0) 2612 4348 7
📠 +43 (0) 2612 4259 112

✉ bildungshaus@haus-st-stephan.at

⚭ Only groups may stay here

FELDKIRCHEN

Ⓣ Gästehaus Philippus

✉ Martin Luther Straße, 13
A-9560 Feldkirchen

📞 +43 (0) 4276 2201

✉ info@gastsein.at

⚭ Open to both men and women

GURK

Ⓢ St Hemma's
Guesthouse

✉ Domplatz 11
A-9342 Gurk

📞 +43 (0) 4266 8236 14
📠 +43 (0) 4266 8236 16

⚭ Open to both men and women

MARIA LUGGAU

Ⓢ Servitenkloster Maria
Luggau

✉ 9655 Maria Luggau

📞 +43 (0) 4716 601
📠 +43 (0) 4716 6011 7

✉ kloster.luggau@aon.at

⚭ Open to both men and women

Lower Austria

Salzburg

ST GEORGEN AM LÄNGSEE

Ⓢ Monastery of St Georgen am Längsee

✉ Schlossallee, 6
A-9313 St Georgen am
Längsee

☎ +43 (0) 4213 2046
📠 +43 (0) 4213 2046 46

✉ office@stift-stgeorgen.at

🕮 Open to both men and women

ST PAUL IM LAVANTTAL

Ⓢ Monastery of St Paul im Lavanttal

✉ Haupstraße, 1
A-9470 St Paul im Lavanttal

☎ +43 (0) 57 2019 22
📠 +43 (0) 57 2019 23

✉ stiftspfarre@stift-stpaul.at

🕮 Open to both men and women

WERNBERG

Ⓢ Kloster Wernberg

✉ Klosterweg, 2
A-9241 Wernberg

☎ +43 (0) 4252 2216
📠 +43 (0) 4252 2216 119

✉ pension@klosterwernberg.at

🕮 Open to both men and women

GÖTTWEIG

Ⓢ Abbey of Göttweig

✉ A-3511 Furth/Göttweig

☎ +43 (0) 2732 8558 1332
📠 +43 (0) 2732 8558 1244

✉ urlaub@stiftgoettweig.at

🕮 Open to both men and women

HEILIGENKREUZ

Ⓣ Abbey of Heiligenkreuz

✉ A-2532 Heiligenkreuz 1

☎ +43 (0) 2258 8703 101
📠 +43 (0) 2225 8703 114

✉ gastmeister@stift-heiligenkreuz.at

🕮 Open to both men and women

SEEBENSTEIN

Ⓢ Guesthouse Herminenhaus

✉ Schulschwestern Sisters
Schloßweg 5
A-2824 Seebenstein

☎ +43 (0) 2627 4720 7
📠 +43 (0) 2627 4720 719

✉ pension-herminenhaus@aon.at

🕮 Open to both men and women

SEITENSTETTEN

Ⓢ Abbey of Seitenstetten

✉ Am Klosterberg 1
A-3353 Seitenstetten

☎ +43 (0) 7477 4230 0
📠 +43 (0) 7477 4230 0025 0

✉ gastpater@stift-seitenstetten.at

🕮 Open to both men and women

MICHAELBEUERN

Ⓢ Abbey of Michaelbeuern

✉ Michaelbeuern 1
A-5152 Salzburg

☎ +43 (0) 6274 8116 304
📠 +43 (0) 6274 8116 3094

✉ bildungshaus@
abtei-michaelbeuern.at

🕮 Open to both men and women

RAMINGSTEIN

Ⓣ Burg Finstergrün

✉ Wald 65
A-5591 Ramingstein

☎ +43 (0) 6475 228
📠 +43 (0) 6475 228 4

✉ info@burg-finstergruen.at

🕮 Open to both men and women

SALZBURG

Ⓢ Abbey of Nonnberg

✉ Nonnberggasse 2
A-5020 Salzburg

☎ +43 (0) 662 84160 7
📠 +43 (0) 662 84980 0

✉ mp.nonnberg@aon.at

👤 Women only

Ⓢ Archabbey of St Peter

✉ Sankt Peter Bezirk
A-5010 Salzburg

☎ +43 (0) 662 84457 621
📠 +43 (0) 662 84457 680

✉ pater_karl@gmx.at

🕮 Open to both men and women

**Additional
Accommodation**

Styria

🕯 FEHRING

Ⓢ Abbey of St Gabriel

✉ Pertlstein 50
A-8350 Fehring

☎ +43 (0) 3155 2671 13
📠 +43 (0) 3155 2671 4

✉ hildegard.altmann.abtei@
utanet.at

🛏 Open to both men and women

🕯 HEILIGENKREUZ AM
WASSEN

Ⓢ Haus der Stille

✉ Rosental 50
A-8081 Heiligenkreuz am
Wassen

☎ +43 (0) 3135 8262 5
📠 +43 (0) 3135 8262 56

✉ info@haus-der-stille.at

🛏 Groups only

🕯 MARIAZELL

Ⓢ Salvatorian Guesthouse

✉ Abbot Severingasse 7
A-8630 Mariazell

☎ +43 (0) 3882 2216
📠 +43 (0) 3882 2216 11

✉ salvatorheim@mariazell.at

🛏 Open to both men and women

🕯 REIN

Ⓢ Abbey of Rein

✉ A-8103 Rein

☎ +43 (0) 3124 5162 123
📠 +43 (0) 3124 5162 134

✉ august.janisch@stift-rein.at

🛏 Men only

🕯 SECKAU

Ⓣ Hotel Hofwirt

✉ Zellenplatz 3
A-8732 Seckau

☎ +43 (0) 3514 5422 2
📠 +43 (0) 3514 5422 3

✉ hotel@hofwirt.at

🛏 Open to both men and women

Tyrol

🕯 INNSBRUCK

Ⓣ Widum Köfels
(country holiday house
for groups and families)

✉ c/– Redemptorist College
Maximilianstraße, 8
A-6020 Innsbruck

☎ +43 (0) 512 5953 2109
📠 +43 (0) 512 5953 2299

✉ gespraechsoase@cssr.at

🛏 Open to both men and women

🕯 MAURACH AM
ACHENSEE

Ⓢ Barmherzige Sisters

✉ Eben, 5
A-6212 Maurach am Achensee

☎ +43 (0) 5243 5948
📠 +43 (0) 5243 5948 4

✉ notburgaheim.eben@
barmherzige-schwestern.at

🛏 Open to both men and women

🕯 REUTTE

Ⓢ Franziskaner Kloster
Reutte

✉ Obermarkt 8
A-6600 Reutte

☎ +43 (0) 5672 6259 0
📠 +43 (0) 5672 6259 022

✉ pfarre.reutte@tirol.com

🛏 Men only

Upper Austria

Vorarlberg

⚜ STAMS

🅂🅃 Stift Stams

✉ A-6422 Stams

☎ +43 (0) 5263 6242 0
📠 +43 (0) 5263 5218

✉ gastpater@stiftstams.at

👥 Open to both men and women

⚜ ST GEORGENBERG / FIECHT

🅂 Abbey of St Georgenberg / Fiecht

✉ A-6134 Abtei Fiecht

☎ +43 (0) 5242 6327 645
📠 +43 (0) 676 3405 510

✉ raphael@st-georgenberg.at

👥 Open to both men and women

⚜ KREMSMÜNSTER

🅂 Abbey of Kremsmünster

✉ Burgfried 1
A-4550 Kremsmünster

☎ +43 (0) 7583 5275 0
📠 +43 (0) 7583 5275 18

✉ stift@kremsmuenster.at

👥 Open to both men and women

⚜ SCHLIERBACH

🅂 Bildungszentrum Stift Schlierbach

✉ Klosterstraße 1
A-4553 Schlierbach

☎ +43 (0) 7582 8301 3155
📠 +43 (0) 7582 81805 3

✉ bildungszentrum@stift-schlierbach.at

👥 Open to both men and women

⚜ SCHLÄGL

🅃 Abbey of Schlägl

✉ Schlägl 1
A-4160 Schlägl

☎ +43 (0) 7281 8801 400
📠 +43 (0) 7281 8801 227
✉ konvent@stift-schlaegl.at

👥 Open to both men and women

⚜ TRAGWEIN

🅂 Bildungshaus Greisinghof

✉ Mistelberg 20
A-4284 Tragwein

☎ +43 (0) 7263 8601 1
📠 +43 (0) 7263 8601 1

✉ bildungshaus@greisinghof.at

👥 Groups only

⚜ GÖTZIS

🅂 St Arbogast Hostel

✉ Montfortstraße 88
A-6840 Götzis

☎ +43 (0) 5523 6250 10
📠 +43 (0) 5523 6250 132

✉ arbogast@kath-kirche-vorarlberg.at

👥 Groups of young people only

⚜ MEHRERAU

🅃 Bernardi College

✉ Mehrerauerstraße 68
A-6903 Bregenz

☎ +43 (0) 5574 7143 869
📠 +43 (0) 5574 7143 869

✉ beherbergung@mehrerau.at

👥 Accommodation available only during summer school holidays (mid-July to late-August)

Czec
Rep

ALTHOUGH WE READ THAT WINE is not at all proper for monks, yet, because monks in our times cannot be persuaded of this, let us agree to this, at least, that we do not drink to satiety, but sparingly; because 'wine maketh even wise men fall off'. (Sir 19:2)

THE HOLY RULE OF ST BENEDICT
TRANSLATED BY REVEREND
BONIFACE VERHEYEN, OSB
ST BENEDICT'S ABBEY, ATCHISON,
KANSAS, US

CZECH REPUBLIC

OFTEN CALLED THE 'CROSSROADS OF EUROPE', the Czech Republic has, in recent years, become an increasingly popular destination for tourists and travellers of all ages and religious persuasions. The country's rich cultural heritage has proven to be a draw card for many. Seasons of concert and theatre, as well as literature festivals and major exhibitions make for a lively arts calendar. And there's entertainment for adults and children alike in the productions of the renowned Czech puppet theatres which have a long tradition of staging everything from opera to fairytales.

If you're restless for the open road, follow the scenic motoring routes. For an active holiday head for the walking trails or ski slopes, dependent on the season of your visit. Or take the time to explore the spa towns, castles and chateaux in a leisurely manner.

Like other European countries with a Christian heritage, beautiful old monasteries and convents abound. Many of those once confiscated by former regimes have now been returned to their original 'owners'—the religious orders. Sadly, a number of these historic buildings have suffered from years of neglect. However, many of the nuns and monks who now live in them have embarked on restoration and maintenance projects, raising funds by several means, including the taking-in of paying guests.

Prague

RAGUE COULD WELL BE CALLED the 'city of bells and spires', with some of the oldest belonging to the Church of Loreto. Its 27-bell carillon is timed to automatically play the hymn of praise, *We Greet Thee a Thousand Times*, every hour on the hour, each day of the year.

On the opposite side of Prague's **Vltava River**, King Wenceslas, Patron Saint of the Czech Republic, rides boldly down the square named in his honour. For decades **Wenceslas Square** was the site of demonstrations and rallies of dissent and is still the focal point of rallies and protests 20 years after the end of Communist rule.

The culture vulture can be well satiated during a visit to Prague. World class opera, ballet and classical music are performed at the **Prague State Opera** and the **National Theatre**. Mozart, literary legend Franz Kafka, Communism and puppetry are all commemorated in various museums. Galleries display works by Rubens and Titian along with renowned Czech artists and sculptors.

In spite of the former Communist regime, churches, monasteries and hundreds of religious shrines have survived to become some of Prague's prime tourist attractions. The Gothic **Cathedral of St Vitas** remains the seat of the city's Archbishop and Prague's religious epicentre. Religious freedom is now everybody's right in the Republic and visitors are free to attend the church services of numerous Christian denominations.

Open Houses
Prague

Casa Edith Stein

Originally a 15th-century farmhouse, this hotel is now part of the Convent of St Theresa, owned by the Carmelite Order of nuns. It is situated in the **Smíchov** area of Prague at the end of a quiet dead end street in a peaceful residential area not far from the city centre.

❦ Accommodation at the hotel consists of single, double and triple guestrooms and two apartments for small groups or families of four or five. Rooms are spacious and comfortable in a quaint old-fashioned way. All the guestrooms have a private bathroom as well as a telephone, satellite television, mini-bar and safe. There is a small chapel for the use of guests.

❦ The hotel restaurant is open for all meals and specialises in modern Italian cuisine. Children are made welcome. The English-speaking staff on reception can arrange theatre tickets, day trips and sightseeing excursions. There is secure car parking available in the courtyard. The hotel is open all year. Credit cards are accepted.

✉ U Perníkářky 2A/111
cz-150 00 Prague 5

🛏 from €45.00 pp

☎ +420 **257 220 501**
📠 +420 **257 220 497**

✉ *casaedithstein@volny.cz*

🚌 Bus numbers 149, 191 and 217 and tram numbers 4, 7, 9 and 10 stop near the hotel which is 4.5 kilometres from **Charles Bridge** and a 15-minute bus ride. From the airport the hotel is a 10-kilometre taxi ride.

✝ **Sunday Mass**
0830, 0930 & 1100
St Vitas Cathedral
Prague Castle Complex
Hradčany
Prague 1

⚭ Open to both men and women

Open Houses
Prague

PLACES OF INTEREST ✆ See Prague from a fresh perspective on a leisurely steamboat cruise on the **Vltava River**. Afterwards you could amble around this medieval city, relax in an outdoor café on the Old Town square and absorb the atmosphere of ancient Prague.

❡ Prague is also a great place to start a motoring holiday. The most popular scenic route is the 1000-kilometre **Castle Road**, which starts in **Prague** and ends in **Manheim**, Germany, passing around 70 castles along the way.

❡ If you prefer to walk, the **Czech Greenways**, a 400-kilometre hiking trail, links **Vienna** and **Prague**, leading through rural **Southern Bohemia** and **Moravia**. There's no rule that says you have to walk the whole length.

❡ The **Church of Our Lady Victorious**, at Karmelitská 9 in **Mala Strana** (*Little Quarter*) is the domicile of the miraculous wax statue of the Infant Jesus of Prague, Patron of children, schools, travellers and families. The statue's costumes are changed regularly by Carmelite nuns who live in the monastery next door. The **Museum of the Infant Jesus** of Prague is in the church complex and displays many of the outfits worn by the statue. Small souvenirs can be purchased from the church shop.

  ✟ Sunday Mass *Czech* 1000, *English* 1200,
      French 1700, *Italian* 1800

❡ The **Bertramka Mozart Museum**, at Mozartova 169 in the **Smíchov** district is a 2-kilometre downhill walk from the **Casa Edith Stein**. The museum is in the terraced stone villa where **Mozart** once lived and composed and hosts a program of concerts throughout the year. Along with an exhibition of the composer's tools of trade, displays include a lock of Mozart's hair. It is a short walk from the museum to **Petrin Hill Park**.

❡ To reach the Petrin Hill from **Charles Bridge** take the **funicular** from **Újezd Street**. The last stop will let you out near the mini Eiffel Tower (lookout tower) where you can take in a wide panorama of the city below.

❡ Tennis fans could visit the town of **Revnice**, 25 kilometres south of Prague, the birthplace of Czech tennis legend Martina Navratilova, who began her career at the Revnice Tennis Club. The medieval **Karlštejn Castle**, which towers above the town of **Karlštejn** near Revnice was the family home of King Charles IV (1316–1378) and can be visited on a day trip from Prague.

❡ The Czech Republic is known for its high quality Bohemian crystal. The famous names, Moser, Rott, Erpet, Slovimex, Bohemia and Celetná, can be found in the **Staré Město** (*Old Town*) and all carry a wide range of jewellery, figurines, candlesticks and light fittings.

It is difficult not to stumble across one of their outlets which are scattered throughout the city. The Czech 'blue onion' design porcelain is sold at **Dům porcelánu** at Jugoslavska 16 in the Nové Město (*New Town*). Crystal chess sets can usually be found at **Preciosa Glass** at Jindřišká 19, also in the New Town.

❧ The **John Lennon Memorial Peace Wall** in Velkoprevorske Náměstí in **Malá Strana** (*Little Quarter*) is an unofficial tourist site, which since the death of this singer, composer and member of the UK band the Beatles, has become an icon for free speech. Young people still visit the wall, near **Charles Bridge** on the castle side, to write messages, which these days are usually political or environmental.

❧ Smíchov residents do their shopping at the **Novy Smíchov** Shopping Centre at Plzeňská 8 at the **Andel Metro station** which has over 150 speciality shops and department stores and is the largest shopping centre in Prague.

FOOD AND DRINK ❧ The **Vecchio Borgo Italian Ristorante** is located in the Casa Edith Stein and caters to guests of the hotel and a loyal, local clientele. The family-friendly restaurant serves home-cooked Italian food (no pizza) at value for money prices. During the summer tables are set up on the terrace.

☎ +420 257 220 499 €€

❧ One of the most romantic restaurants in the city, the **Kampa Park Restaurant** in Mala Strana, is superbly positioned on the shores of the **Vltava**. Dine inside or on the verandah overlooking **Charles Bridge**. During the day flotillas of well-fed swans gracefully glide up and down the river, and in the evening, the lights of the city make an equally beautiful sight.

✉ Na Kampě 8в

☎ +420 257 532 685 €€€€€

❧ There is no better way to sample Czech beer than to take a tour of the **U Flekù Brewery** in Prague's **Nové Město**. The beer hall owned by the brewery can cater for over 1000 guests at a time. The pub's restaurants serve beer-flavoured cheese on just about everything, which really is something different to challenge the palate.

✉ Kremencova 11

☎ +420 224 934 019 €€€

❧ In 1880 Emperor Franz Joseph of Austria visited the **Staropramen Brewery**, a local Smíchov brewhouse, and pronounced the product 'excellent'. Today the brewery still invites guests to take a guided tour, which concludes according to tradition with a glass of Staropramen.

✉ Nadrazni 84

☎ +420 257 191 402 (296)

Church Pension Husův Dům

Situated in the centre of Prague this modern hostel is comfortable, well run and inexpensive. From the Church Pension it is only a 10-minute walk to Wenceslas Square and 2 kilometres to the main railway station.

❡ Run by the **Evangelical Church of Czech Brethren** the hostel has double, triple and quad rooms, some equipped with a wash basin. A few of the guestrooms have en suite bathrooms. There are showers and toilets on each of the five floors which are serviced by a small kitchen, a shared lounge for the general use of guests and a lift. Breakfast is the only meal available, but shops, cafés and bars are within easy walking distance of the hostel.

❡ Guests may check-in at any time but the office is only open between 0800 and 1630 each day. Please advise the staff beforehand if checking-in outside these hours so appropriate arrangements can be made.

❡ Staff can arrange sightseeing tours, restaurant bookings and walking tours. They can also reserve tickets for guests to attend concerts at the **Church of St Martin** in the Wall at Martinská 8, near the hostel.

✉ Jan Hus House
Jungmannova 9/22
cz-110 00 Prague 1

🏨 from €30.00 pp,
including breakfast

☎ +420 **296 245 432**
☎ +420 **603 554 785**
✆ +420 **224 999 238**

✉ *churchpension@srcce.cz*

☞ The hostel is situated 3 kilometres from Prague's main train station **Hlavní nádraží**. Trams number 9, 3, 14 and 24 stop near the hostel.

✝ **Sunday Service**
1100
Evangelical Lutheran Church of St Michael
V Jirchárích 14/152
cz-110 00 Prague 1

✝ **1100**
Anglican Church of Prague
U Klimenta
Klimentská 1
cz-110 00 Prague 1

⚥ Open to both men and women

PLACES OF INTEREST ❧ Laugh and be amazed at a **Czech Black Light Theatre performance** where the actors use darkness, the latest pyrotechnics and a good dose of music, magic and fantasy.

❡ Where else could you find cackling witches, Russian dolls and fairytale marionettes that jolt into life at a handclap but at Prague's popular and centrally located **Haveleská Market** (*Havelský trh*) in Havelský Street between the Old Town Square and Wenceslas Square. Each November, twinkling lights and, with luck, glistening white snow, transforms Havelský Street into a festive **Christmas market** where stallholders do a roaring trade in wooden toys, Christmas baubles, spicy sausages and mugs of hot, heartwarming 'grog', made with rum and lemon juice.

❡ Classical concerts are held regularly in the architecturally stunning **Chapel of Mirrors** in the historic **Klementinum** (*Clementinum*) cultural complex, near Charles Bridge, where 18th-century frescoes, elaborate ceiling mirrors, and embellished wood carvings provide a serious distraction to the activities on stage. The **Czech National Library** (and its 6 million volumes) is planning to move from the Klementinum to a controversial, futuristic new home in **Letna**, which is across the Čechův most (bridge) on the castle side of the city. The future building was the winner of a worldwide architectural design competition. Vast underground storage areas can hold millions of books, any of which can be extracted by a robot on request.

❡ The fascinating 15th-century astronomical clock on the **Old Town Hall** in Prague is one of the oldest clocks in Europe, and it is still in working order. Every hour onlookers gather to watch a mechanical display of the 12 apostles, Christ, a skeleton and a crowing cockerel. Test your heart rate by climbing the steps at the rear to view the fascinating machinations.

Open Houses
Prague

❡ Some of Prague's most important buildings include the **Convent of Saint Agnes of Bohemia** at U Milosrdnych 17, Staré Město. The convent was founded by St Agnes in the early 13th century, but these days is the home of the **Czech National Gallery** and a permanent exhibition of Czech painting and sculpture from the 19th century. If you are looking for a replacement **Stradivarius** you'll probably find one at the **Hrons Violin Shop** at Michalská 3 in the Old Town, where master craftsmen painstakingly restore antique stringed instruments.

❡ Upmarket designer shops and boutiques line either side of the appropriately named **Parízská** (*Paris*) Street between Prague's Old Town Square and the Jewish Quarter. Nearby, **Na Prikope**, home to shopping centres and retail outlets, is said to be in the top 20 most expensive streets in the world. International department stores, fashion shops and fast food outlets are located on the avenues around **Wenceslas Square**. Prague's main **railway station**, **Hlavní nádraží**, is near the high end of the square. Although the station is accessible to pedestrians by a number of underground tunnels, it is advisable to walk to the station via the overland route.

FOOD AND DRINK ❦ If something celebratory is called for then the **Francouzská Restaurace** (*French Restaurant*) in the **Municipal House Concert Hall**, in Staré Město should fit the bill. This timeless, classical restaurant serves fine French cuisine where the menu complements the elegant surroundings.

☎ +420 **222 002 770**   €€€€€

❡ In Celetna, a street running off **Old Town Square**, the **Grand Café Orient** has re-opened after being shut for 80 years. On the first floor of the **House of the Black Madonna** the gracious Art-deco café has been painstakingly revived in the original 'Cubist' style of architecture. Apart from the name, the house has no particular religious significance.

☎ +420 **224 224 240**   €€€

❡ The attractive, inviting restaurants lining the **Old Town Square** have some of the best people watching seats in town. However, dining on Prague's premier real estate is often reflected in the price, the food and the service.

Hotel Adalbert

The Hotel Adalbert is situated in the spacious grounds of the **Břevnov Monastery** estate, 4 kilometres west of **Prague Castle**. Named after the saint who helped found the monastery in 993, St Adalbert (Vojtěch) was a former Bishop of Prague and now Patron Saint of Bohemia. St Adalbert is buried in a chapel in Prague's **St Vitus Cathedral**.

❡ The Adalbert is a quiet and comfortable 3-star hotel accommodating guests in large single and double rooms and suites, all of which have a private bathroom. Some guestrooms look over the monastery garden and all rooms have satellite television, telephone, a room safe and Internet access. Facilities include a restaurant and bar with an enthusiastic local following, 24-hour reception, a lift and room service. The courtyard restaurant is open for lunch and dinner and a paved outdoor area is used during the warmer months. The hotel has wheelchair access and on-site parking is available in the grounds of the monastery for a small daily charge. Credit cards are accepted.

❡ Monks from Břevnov were among the first producers of wine and beer in the Czech Republic and initially planted grapes and hops in the grounds of the monastery in the year 993.

✉ Břevnovský klášter
Markétská 1
CZ-169 00 Prague 6

🛏 from €65.00 pp,
including breakfast

☎ +420 **220 406 170**
📠 +420 **220 406 190**

📧 recepce@hoteladalbert.cz

☞ Take tram number 22, 15 or 25 from **Station Hradčanská** on metro line A and get off at **Station Břevnov klášter** which is near the hotel. The hotel is 5 kilometres from the city centre.

✝ **Sunday Mass**
0730, 0900 & 1600
Basilica of St Margaret
Břevnovský klášter
Markétská 1
cz-169 00 Prague 6

♿ Discuss your needs in advance of arriving, ideally when booking.

⚥ Open to both men and women

Open Houses
Prague

PLACES OF INTEREST ❦ The **Břevnov Monastery** is the oldest in Bohemia and celebrated its 1000-year anniversary in 1993. The monastery is still occupied by Benedictine monks and the nuns of the order live in a separate convent on the estate. The monastery is open to the public every day for tours of the grounds, the abbey church and sections of the interior.

❡ The **16th-century Hvězda Summer Lodge** in the **Royal Hunting Park** is one of the most unusual buildings in Prague. It was built as a summer palace for the use of titled huntsmen and designed by Archduke Ferdinand II of Tyrol (1529–1595) in the shape of a 6-pointed star. The park was the inspiration of Emperor Ferdinand I, the Archduke of Tyrol's father, who purchased the land from the monks of Břevnov.

❡ Take a trip out of town to the 14th-century fairytale **Konopiště Castle**, near Benešov, 50 kilometres south of Prague to see how the other half lived. This castle was the former home of Archduke Franz Ferdinand (1863–1914), heir to the Austro-Hungarian throne, whose assassination led to the start of World War I. The sprawling estate includes hundreds of hectares of parkland and a rambling, English-style rose garden. Now the realm of the resident ghost, the castle's opulent interior boasts collections of precious porcelain, ancient weapons, hunting trophies and artworks.

❡ Charles Bridge joins the area of **Staré Město** with **Nové Město** and is a popular place for buskers and for Czech artists to sell their works. The 650-year-old bridge was built by King Charles IV and is lined with the statues of 30 saints. Tourists often have to queue to touch the bearded, **cross bearing statue of St John of Nepomuk** which is said to guarantee a return visit to the city. The statue marks the spot where St John was thrown from the bridge to his death in 1393.

❧ The **Loreto Church and the Holy House** at Loretánské náměstí 7, near **Prague Castle** is a place of pilgrimage to the **Santa Casa** (*Holy House*), a replica of the house said to have been occupied by the Virgin Mary and the Holy Family in Jerusalem. A diamond monstrance embedded with over 6000 diamonds as well as other precious religious artefacts are stored in the upstairs Treasury which is also open to the public. The complex is under the care of Capuchin fathers who live in a monastery nearby. Mass is celebrated in the **Church of the Nativity of Our Lord** (part of the complex) each Sunday at 1800 and on Saturday in the Santa Casa at 1930.

❧ One of Prague's foremost marionette theatres, the **Divadlo Spejbla a Hurvínka** (*Theatre of Spejbl and Hurvínek*) in **Dejvice** has been entertaining children and adults for almost 90 years with the father and son pair Speibl and Hurvínek, granny and dog Zeryk. Each performance takes around 75 minutes. A café is available for refreshments and a shop sells take-home marionettes and other souvenirs.

FOOD AND DRINK ❧ Hungry guests or day visitors to **Břevnov Monastery** may dine at the **Klášterní šenk restaurant**, adjacent to the **Hotel Adalbert**. Sizeable helpings of ducking, dumplings and goose are served around a roaring open fire with hefty mugs of Klaster beer. Local specialities include *Bramborak*, a Bohemian potato pancake filled with meat and veggies, and *Halusky*, which is fried potato gnocci with smoked meat or sheep's cheese. In summer tables are set up outside the restaurant. A half litre of monastery beer costs around €1.00, which is cheaper than a cappuccino.

☏ +420 **220 406 294**   €€

❧ Opposite the tram station **Drinopol**, near **Brevnov monastery**, the **Restaurantu U Bílého Lva** was once part of the monastery estate. Today this busy rustic waterhole caters for contemporary pilgrims with inexpensive Czech bar food, beer and a friendly pub atmosphere.

✉ Bělohorská 79

☏ +420 **233 355 909**   €

❧ An advantage of staying in the **Brevnov** area is that you will be close to the **U Marčanů restaurant** and wine bar, where the price of an evening meal includes a traditional folklore presentation of Czech music and dance.

✉ Veleslavinska 14

☏ +420 **235 360 623**   €€€

Hotel Jenerálka

The Hotel Jenerálka is situated within the walls of an historical 18th-century castle. Its guestrooms have been awarded 3 stars by the Czech Tourist Authority. The accommodation includes single, twin and triple rooms and 1- and 2-bedroom apartments. Rooms are available for disabled visitors.

¶ Most of the guestrooms have en suite bathrooms. Studio rooms and apartments have a bathroom and a kitchenette with refrigerator. All guestrooms have television. The hotel offers 24-hour reception, a guest lounge, a restaurant for breakfast and lunch, a lift, laundry, computer room and on-site parking. A gift shop sells postcards and souvenirs cheaper than shops in the centre of town. The hotel is run along 'eco' friendly lines and has recently introduced a program to increase the number of butterflies around the property.

¶ The Hotel Jenerálka is run by the **International Baptist Theological Seminary** in Prague. Located in the residential quarter of Dejvice, the hotel is approximately 20 minutes from the centre of Prague by bus. **Dejvice** is a quiet, well-to-do neighbourhood of embassies, parks and exclusive mansions.

¶ A taxi service centre is near the hotel and staff at reception can telephone for a cab if need be. If you choose to call a cab personally, you may prefer to use an English-speaking operator—the number to call for this service is 14014.

✉ Nad Habrovkou 3
cz-164 06 Prague 6

🏨 from €40.00 pp for a single room

☎ +420 **420 296 392 111**
📠 +420 **420 296 392 313**

✉ info@hotel-jeneralka.cz

☞ Take the metro to **Dejvická**. From **Dejvická Metro** Station take bus number 161, 254 or 312 to the **Jenerálka** or take a taxi. Metro and bus tickets are interchangeable. The hotel is approximately 10 kilometres from the centre of Prague.

⛪ **Sunday Service 1045**
International Baptist Theological Seminary, Nad Habrovkou 3, cz-164 00 Prague 6

♿ Discuss your needs in advance of arriving, ideally when booking.

⚥ Open to both men and women

PLACES OF INTEREST ❧ **Prague Castle** is one of the largest, ancient (9th century) castles in the world, covering an area of more than 7 hectares. It has been the home of heads of state, royalty and the Prague Bishop. Today it is the seat of the Czech President. It houses major works of art and regularly becomes the setting for performances of Shakespearean works. Within the castle grounds is the majestic Gothic **Cathedral of St Vitas**, protector of the Czech Crown Jewels and the burial place of prince and saint, Wenceslas. For the best view in town climb the 287 spiral steps to the top of the cathedral tower.

❡ Prague looked very different in the 1800s and on display at the **Prague City Museum** at Na porící 52, in the **Nové Mĕsto** is a 20-square metre wooden model of the town as it was during the early 19th century.

❡ For one-stop puppet and marionette shopping visit the puppet makers **Obchod Loutkamy** at Revolucní 14 near the **Metro station námestí Republiki**. The shop carries a wide range and the meticulous attention to detail is evident in each perfect piece. For something along cheaper lines pop into any of the puppet and hand-craft shops in almost every side street in the city and compare prices. Or try the markets. **The House of Sparkys** at Havířská 2, in **Staré Mĕsto** is the largest toy shop in the country and something of a children's nirvana. **The Puppet Museum** at Karlova 12, near Charles Bridge is a highlight for young and old. On show is a collection of intricately carved, historical and contemporary puppets hand-crafted by Czech woodcarvers.

❡ In 1989, the Premonstratensian monks of **Strahov Monastery** near Prague Castle re-opened the **monastic brewery** after it had been closed down during Communist rule. The tiny brewery is at Strahovske nadvori 301, in the grounds of the monastery. St Norbert beer is brewed on site and wine, also branded St Norbert, is served in the monastery restaurant and grown by the monks in their vineyards in Moravia. The monastery beer is not sold outside the monastery premises.

Open Houses
Prague

❦ **Prague Zoo** is situated on the Vltava River in the Letna district and suffered a heartbreaking loss of animals in floods which overwhelmed the city in 2002. However, the zoo is now operating as normal once again. Pack a picnic and relax in the zoo's peaceful surroundings or feed the kangaroos at 1215 on any day. The **Botanical Gardens of Prague** are close to the Prague Zoo and visitors can enjoy a relaxing stroll through the themed areas including a Japanese Cherry Grove and a Mediterranean Garden.

❦ **Troja Château**, at Trojského zámku 1, in the Letna district, was established in 1679 as the residence of a local aristocratic family. Designed in the style of a spacious Roman villa, the lavish interior now houses a vast collection of artworks and a wine museum which serves as a showcase for Czech wine growers. Czech wine varieties can be sampled here.

FOOD AND DRINK ❦ Guests of the Jeneralka won't have to travel into the city for entertainment and could take in a show at the **Dejvické Divadlo Theatre**, where a talented cast perform everything from Shakespeare to Hollywood classics. The theatre has a small café / restaurant.

✉ Zelená 1084/15A

☎ +420 233 339 108   €

❦ The restaurant of the **Hotel Jeneralka** is not open for dinner in the evening. However, a traditional Czech tavern is located at the gates of the hotel and a roast suckling pig is often on the barbeque.   €

❦ The Budweiser Brewery-owned **Budvarka pub and restaurant** in Dejvice serve their own brew and is part of the Budweiser chain. The wooded interior, local clientele and large platters make for an authentic Czech pub atmosphere.

✉ Wuchterlova 336/22

☎ +420 222 960 820   €€

❦ For something different try the Pizzeria /**Ristorante Canzone** in Dejvice which has a lengthy menu based on Italian and Croatian cuisine and is reasonably priced.

✉ Eliášova 7/331

☎ +420 224 325 226   €€

Bohemia

ISTORY BUFFS WILL BE FASCINATED by the medieval towns, Romanesque castles, churches, ruins and monasteries of this culturally significant region.

For the lovers of the outdoors, there are plenty of walking trails and cycling paths. Along the German border in the **Krušné hory** (*Ore Mountains*) and in the **Giant Mountains** (*Krkonoše*), a part of the Czech/Poland border, the trails become snow slopes and ski runs in winter with a host of rustic mountain lodges and ski resorts, where there is sure to be a mug of Bohemian beer waiting at the end of an exhilarating day on the pistes.

During the 14th century over 100 convents and monasteries were established in Bohemia, with the Catholic Church being a prominent landholder. However, many church buildings were wiped out during a succession of wars and revolts, and religious orders remained suppressed until the fall of Communism in 1989. Today the Jesuits, Cistercians, Benedictines and Premonstratensians are again active in Bohemia, occupying monasteries which are slowly returning to their former splendour.

Tourist offices can provide details of various trails that crisscross the region, including a motoring route which takes in Bohemia's significant religious sites.

05

Teplá Monastery

This 12th-century monastery is situated by a small lake outside the town of **Teplá**, 39 kilometres south of the spa town of **Karlovy Vary** (*Carlsbad*) and about 50 kilometres east of the German border. The monastery is in an area of much interest to the tourist with a good number usually intent on indulging in some water therapy at the spa towns Karlovy Vary and **Mariánské Lázně**.

❧ The monastery was formerly a large, busy community of monks of the Premonstratensian Order, but today just a handful still reside here. A separate section of the monastery has been converted into a comfortable, 60-room 3-star hotel which is open all year. Accommodation ranges from single and double guestrooms to comfortable, well-appointed apartments. All guestrooms have private bathrooms, telephones and televisions; some have views over the still substantial monastery estate. Conference and seminar facilities are on-site. Parking is available and credit cards are accepted.

❧ The hotel's refurbished 100-seat restaurant serves typical Czech cuisine including stag, wild pig and fish. There is a wine bar and the on-site beer hall serves a variety of Czech beer.

OPEN HOUSE

✉ Hotel Klášter TepláKlášter Teplá 10 cz-364 61 Teplá

🛏 from €55.00 pp, including breakfast

📞 +420 353 392 264
☎ +420 353 392 733
📠 +420 353 392 312

✉ recepce@ hotelklastertepla.cz

☞ Take the train or bus to **Teplá** (the bus is often quicker). **Tepla train station** is 2 kilometres from the monastery. The nearest bus stop is 100 metres from the hotel. **Prague** is 125 kilometres east of Teplá.

✝ **Sunday Mass 1000**
Monastery Church Klášter Teplá 10 cz-364 61 Teplá

⚭ Open to both men and women

PLACES OF INTEREST ⸿ Medieval artisans are responsible for the well preserved sculptures, frescoes and woodwork in the 12th-century Baroque **Church of the Annunciation**, attached to the Teplá Monastery. The shelves of the **Teplá Monastery Library** hold over 100,000 rare books, ancient documents and manuscripts dating back to 1197. All were untouched during the 40 years of Communist rule when the monks were expelled and the abbey was used as accommodation for Czech military forces.

⸿ A faint scent of sulphur hangs in the air in the gorgeous, picturesque spa town, **Karlovy Vary** (*Carlsbad*). The town's bathing and spa centres book out well ahead; however, if you haven't made a reservation, the centrally located **Castle Baths** (*Zámecké Lázně*) cater for walk-in clients as do the public springs and thermal pools—bring the swimming gear. It is almost mandatory to carry your own lázeňský pohárek (*spa drinking cup*) as you stroll along the promenades, past the Renaissance-style colonnades and 17th-century pavilions, sipping and stopping at will to refill from fountains or springs of varying temperature.

⸿ Popular cultural highlights of the town include an **International Film Festival** each July and a **Festival of Ancient Music** staged in August. A jewel of Baroque design, Karlovy's 18th-century **Church of St Mary Magdalene** is often the venue for classical concerts. Karlovy Vary is 40 kilometres north of Teplá.

⸿ Until recently, the small town of **Bečov nad Teplou**, 15 kilometres north of Teplá, was only known for the remarkable 15th-century frescoes on the walls of the Chapel of the **Visitation of the Virgin Mary** in the local Bečov Chateau. However, in 1985 a 13th-century bejewelled, gold and silver casket was discovered buried under the floor of the chapel. The reliquary, known as the **Shrine of St Maurus**, is priceless and is on display in the **Bečov Chateau**. St Maurus is believed to have died in the 6th century.

Open Houses
Bohemia Teplá

❧ Guided tours are conducted at the famous **Moser Glass and Crystal Factory** at Kapitána Jaroše (a small charge is made) and at the Becherovka Liquor Distillery and Museum at Tomáše Garrigue Masaryka 57, where this obscure but highly potent blend of herbs and alcohol is created.

❧ Thun porcelain is manufactured in the town and an annual Porcelain Festival takes place each September. The home of Czech Pilsner beer is in Plzeň (Pilsen), 50 kilometres south-east of Teplá, where the **Pilsner Urquell Brewery** conducts popular factory tours.

❧ Whilst in the Plzeň area you could visit one of the country's national monuments, the **Benedictine Kladruby Monastery**, founded by Prince Vladislav I in 1115AD and restored to its medieval grandeur by hundreds of Czech artisans during the 18th and 19th centuries.

FOOD AND DRINK ❦ **Spa Wafers**, a speciality of Mariánské Lázně, have been made by the Kolonáda Company for over 150 years. The wafers are thin enough not to undo any previous good work at the baths and are filled with delicious chocolate or nut paste. Purchase yours from either of the Kolonáda shops, at Hlavní 122 or Nehrova 29, both in Mariánské Lázně. The town is 18 kilometres west of Teplá.

❧ The **Restaurant Plzeňka** in Teplá is an authentic Czech eating house situated in a 16th-century coaching inn. The menu is Czech country-style and local beer and Moravian wine are served.

✉ Masarykovo nàmĕstí 142

☏ +420 353 394 213   €€

❧ For a change try the Guinness on tap at the **Irish pub** at Poštovní 96 in Mariánské Lázne or choose from over 60 brands of whisky at the Scottish pub in the **Hotel Edinburgh**.

❧ **Chodovar Brewery** in the town of Chodová Planá, 16 kilometres south of Teplá, has converted the basement of the brewery-owned Hotel U Sládka in Chodová Planá into a unique beer spa where visitors can take a soothing beer bath in the company's unique, freshly brewed 'bathing beer'. Finish with a hop massage, a beer shampoo and a glass of beer (for medicinal purposes only).

☏ +420 374 617 100

Moravia

 M ORAVIA IS THE CZECH REPUBLIC'S wine-growing region—so if you take your viniculture seriously you'll find following some of the walking trails through the Moravian vineyards very hard to resist. Some religious orders in Moravia continue to use traditional methods of vine growing and wine production, and still influence the region's wine culture. Many sell wine—and also offer hospitality—as a means of financially staying afloat.

The Znovín vineyard in the town of **Znojmo** has its headquarters in the former medieval **Premonstratensian Monastery of Louka** (*Loucký klášter*). Much of the Znovín wine is stored in vast, underground cellars, established by the Jesuits in the 18th century in the suburb of Přímětice. In the former Archbishop's Chateâu in **Kroměříž**, sacramental wine has been made for over 100 years. These historic cellars are now UNESCO-listed and open to the public.

These days many Moravian monasteries do 'double duty'. Apart from welcoming pilgrims and tourists for overnight stays, they lend themselves as inspiring, often grand venues for art exhibitions, musical performances and local cultural events.

Spiritual Retreats
Moravia Bystřice pod Hostýnem

Svatý Hostýn
(Holy Hostýn)

The spiritual refuge of Svatý Hostýn is situated 700 metres above sea level on the Hostýn Mountain. It attracts thousands of pilgrims each year to the Sanctuary of Our Lady, built in honour of the guardian of Moravia who is said to have protected the population against a Turkish invasion in 1241. Today the **Svatý Hostýn monastery** is run by Jesuit priests who minister to the multitude of day visitors and overnight guests. Accommodation at the monastery ranges from simple to superior guestrooms all with en suites. A large dining room caters for all meals which are available by prior arrangement.

❦ The **Basilica of the Assumption of Our Lady** was established in the 18th century and can hold 6000 worshippers at any one time. Almost 250 metres of wide stone staircase leads up to the entrance.

❦ Pilgrims can follow two '**Roads to Calvary**', the latest and most beautiful having been architecturally designed and established in 1912, and pray in the **Chapel of the Waters**, where the water is said to have miraculous properties. Austrian Emperor Franz Joseph I visited the sanctuary in 1897, the Czech President Vaclav Klaus in 2007. It remains the country's most visited place of pilgrimage.

✉ Svatý Hostýn 115
cz-768 61
Bystřice pod
Hostýnem

🏨 from €9.00 pp

☎ +420 **573 381 693**
📠 +420 **573 381 694**

✉ *matice@hostyn.cz*

☞ Take the train
to **Bystřice pod
Hostýnem**. A bus
runs from the town up
to the Svatý Hostýn
complex. If travelling
by car a permit may be
needed to motor up
the mountain. Contact
the monastery for
advice.

✝ **Sunday Mass
0700, 0900, 1015,
1130 & 1500**
Basilica of
The Assumption of
Our Lady
Svatý Hostýn 115
cz-768 61
Bystřice pod Hostýnem

👥 Open to both men and
women

PLACES OF INTEREST ❧ The small, quiet town of **Bystřice pod Hostýnem**, nestled at the foot of the Hostýn Mountain, is a common starting point for hiking and walking holidays. The town is surrounded by a beechwood forest which provides the wood for the local TON **furniture** factory to manufacture bentwood chairs and other 'bent' pieces of furniture. Every 2 years, fans of folk music gather in the town for the international folk music festival 'On Bystrice Square'.

❧ In the cold winter months, the **Hostyn Hills** attract downhill and cross-country skiers. One of the attractions is the 300-metre long run which is artificially lit for night skiing. When the snow finally melts mountain bikers, hikers and nature lovers take to the mountain's tracks and trails.

❧ Local artists and craftsmen display their works in a permanent exhibition at the **Chateâu of Bystřice pod Hostýnem** in the centre of the town. Concerts are held in the grounds of the chateau during the summer months. Discover more about the history of the area at the local folklore museum in the town of Rusava, 8 kilometres south of Bystřice pod Hostýnem. An outdoor museum with a display of traditional thatched cottages and various scenes depicting 18th-century village life can be explored in the village of Rymice, 11 kilometres from Bystřice pod Hostýnem.

❧ On the edge of the village of **Holešov**, 6 kilometres from Bystřice pod Hostýnem, stands the stately **Baroque Holešov Château**, where the manicured grounds and deer park are open to the public. If you are visiting Holešov in September you could compete in the annual **Watermelon Eating Championship**.

Spiritual Retreats
Moravia Bystřice pod Hostýnem

❧ Olomouc, once the capital of Moravia, is a town of onion-domed churches, ornate fountains and spacious cobblestone squares. **The Holy Trinity Column** on Olomouc's main town square was created by local sculptors and artists and took almost 40 years to complete. Work commenced in 1716 and the monument is now listed as a UNESCO landmark. A tiny chapel inside the monument is open on most mornings. Olomouc is 50 kilometres north-west of Bystřice pod Hostýnem.

❧ Castle Spilberk is in Brno, west of Bystřice pod Hostýnem and the region's capital. During the Nazi occupation, this 13th-century edifice was turned into an infamous prison where some 80,000 people were incarcerated.

❧ The Bata footwear company was first established in Zlin, 30 kilometres south of Bystřice pod Hostýnem and is reflected in the local **Shoe Museum** which has a collection of shoes, slippers and footwear from all over the world including a replica of a riding boot once worn by King Wenceslas.

❧ Souvenir hunters will be sure to find something to take home at **JK Truhlářství** at Ceskoslovenské brigády 131 in Bystrice pod Hostynem where a family of woodworkers use traditional methods to craft all kinds of small, wooden household objects and toys.

FOOD AND DRINK ❧ Don't be fooled if offered a **glass of Moravian** *burcak* (new wine) with its seemingly low 5 per cent alcohol content, because it continues to ferment after being swallowed.

❧ **Restaurant U Hanuša** in Bystřice pod Hostýnem is where the local sports fans go to drink beer and watch soccer on television. A restaurant and combined bar area make for a spirited, often noisy atmosphere. Soup, barbeque meats and salad make up the simple menu.

✉ Ceskoslovenské brigády 9

☎ +420 573 380 119   €

❧ Home-cooked Moravian specialities are always on the menu at the **Hospůdka U Krbu restaurant and bar** in Bystrice pod Hostynem.

✉ Přerovská 46

☎ +420 573 381 737   €

❧ Olomouc's much beloved cheese, the Olomoucké tvarůžky or **Olomouc curd cheese**, has been produced in the town since the 16th century and is so well thought of that the **Museum of Authentic Olomoucké Tvarůžky Cheese** has been dedicated to it. However, it is an acquired taste having only a 1 per cent fat content and a distinctive (rancid) odour.

Prague

❧ **The Loreto Pilgrimage Complex** is situated at Loretánské náměstí 7, near Prague Castle and attracts pilgrims to a 17th-century, faithfully copied replica of the **Santa Casa** (*Holy House*), said to be the home of the Holy Family in Nazareth. The pilgrimage complex is under the auspices of the Minor Capuchin Friars who live in a monastery nearby. It is believed the original Holy House is within the **Basilica di Santa Casa** in Loreto, in the province of Marche, Italy. Further information is provided in the Italian Pilgrimage section.

　† Saturday Mass Santa Casa 1930

　† Sunday Mass Loreto Church 1800

❧ In a glass reliquary inside the **Church of Our Lady Victorious** at Karmelitska 9, in Prague's Malá Strana, stands the miraculous wax statue of the immaculately dressed Infant Jesus of Prague. The church and the statue is a place of pilgrimage for those seeking the intercession or the blessing of the **Infant Jesus of Prague**. Over the centuries the statue has survived wars and desecration and came into the possession of the Carmelite Order in 1628. The statue's outfit is changed regularly by members of the Carmelite Sisters of the Child Jesus who live next door.

　† Sunday Mass *English* 1200, *Czech* 1000 & 1900, *French* 1700, *Italian* 1800

Bohemia

❧ **The Basilica of St Wenceslas** in Stará Boleslav is a major pilgrimage destination. It was at the entrance to this church (then called the Church of Sts Cosmos and Damian) that Prince Wenceslas I, Duke of Bohemia (907–c929) and later a Patron Saint of the Czech Republic, was murdered by or under his brother Boleslav's instructions. Deemed to have died a martyr's death, Wenceslas was proclaimed a saint and canonized some time during the 10th century. A 3-day long National St Wenceslas Pilgrimage takes place each September to mark the death of St Wenceslas on 28 September. Stará Boleslav is 25 kilometres north-east of Prague. Sunday Mass is celebrated in the town's Basilica of St Wenceslas at 0800. In ancient times a pilgrims' trail led from Prague to the pilgrimage site and was lined with dozens of chapels and monuments each spaced exactly the length of Prague's Charles Bridge. Most of the chapels have disappeared but some remains can still be found.

❧ The Jesuits came to **Římov** near České Budějovice in 1626 and were responsible for turning the town into a place of pilgrimage. The Římov Jesuits built an exact copy of the **Holy House of Loreto**, believed to be the home of the Holy Family in Nazareth. The fathers established a circuitous, 6-kilometre

Pilgrimages

Way of the Cross with 25 stations, each depicting a stage in Christ's journey to Calvary and spread throughout the scenic surrounds of the town.

❦ The pilgrimage **Church of the Visitation of Our Lady**, in Hejnice on the Czech, Polish and German borders, in the far north of the country, has been a place of pilgrimage since the 13th century to what is believed to be a miraculous statue of the Madonna and Child. The statue was placed on the site where the church now stands by a local craftsman, after the man's wife and child were cured of illness. The local **International Centre for Spiritual Rehabilitation** is run by monks of the Franciscan Order who conduct pilgrimages and other religious activities for visitors.

❦ The Catholic religious order the Redemptorists are custodians of the **Mountain of the Mother of God**, on the Polish border near the town of Králíky, which has been a place of pilgrimage for over 3 centuries. The object of pilgrims' venerations is an Image of the Blessed Virgin Mary claimed to have miraculous properties. A 'Holy Staircase' and a 1.5-kilometre, tree-lined, **Way of the Cross** lead from the town to the Redemptorist monastery and church.

† Sunday Mass 0830, 1000 & 1500

❦ A sandstone copy of the **Holy House of Loreto**, believed to be the house occupied by the Holy Family in Nazareth, stands in the grounds of a former **Capuchin Monastery** in Rumburk, 2 kilometres from the German border in far north Bohemia. Pilgrims worship before a statue of a 17th-century Black Madonna and Child which stands above the altar inside the Holy House and many follow a **Way of the Cross** which circles the building.

❦ **Svatá Hora** (*Holy Mountain*) and the **Basilica of the Assumption of Our Lady**, near the town of Příbram, 60 kilometres south-west of Prague is believed to have been a place of worship and pilgrimage since the 12th century. The complex consists of a centre basilica surrounded by four separate chapels dedicated to the Blessed Virgin. The Basilica of The Assumption of Our Lady was named in honour of a small, miraculous statue of the Holy Virgin which is kept inside. A 400-metre long **covered staircase** connects the lovely town of Příbram with the Svatá Hora complex.

† Sunday Mass 0600, 0730, 0900, 1100 & 1530

❧ The tiny village of **Velká Lhota** near the town of Telč, 160 kilometres south of Prague is of interest for the two Czech Evangelical churches, each in its own separate parish, which stand side by side in the little town. Both were established after a misunderstanding between the Lutherans and the Evangelists relating to a 'Patent of Tolerance', an 18th-century law permitting churches other than Catholic to be built. The area around the churches is known as the **Evangelistic Toleration Area**.

❧ The **Benedictine Abbey of St Wenceslas** in Klášterní Street in the town of Broumov near the Polish border is an offshoot of the Brevnov Benedictine Monastery in Prague and is recognised for the exact copy of the **Shroud of Turin** which is on view in the monks' refectory. Sunday Mass is celebrated in the abbey's **Church of Sts Peter and Paul** at 1030.

❧ The **Church of the Ascension of the Virgin Mary** in Přeštice is known to Czech pilgrims for a painting of the Blessed Virgin on the altar of the church, which is said to have miraculous properties. Přeštice is approximately 20 kilometres south of the town of Plzeň.

❧ The **Church of the Virgin Mary** in Klotovy, 80 kilometres south of Prague, can be reached via a **Way of the Cross** which leads pilgrims from the adjacent town of Tábor up to the pilgrimage church. The pealing of the church's impressive 10-bell carillon can sometimes be heard in the distance.

Moravia

❧ The **National Pilgrimage** takes place on 5 July each year to the **Basilica of Sts Cyril and Methodius** in Velehrad, 70 kilometres east of Brno in southern Moravia. The two brothers are responsible for the spread of Christianity throughout the country during the 9th century and share the title Patron Saints of Europe with St Benedict of Nursia and three women saints, Edith Stein, Bridget of Sweden and Catherine of Siena.

✝ Sunday Mass 0730, 1000 & 1500

❧ A miraculous sandstone statue of the Virgin Mary of Frỳdek stands on the 18th-century altar of the **Basilica of the Visitation of Our Lady** in Frỳdek-Místek on the far eastern side of the country near the Polish border. Our Lady of Frỳdek is associated with sight and hearing disorders.

❧ **The Basilica (Minor) of the Ascension of The Virgin Mary** in Bystřice pod Hostýnem is one of the most visited pilgrim destinations in the Czech Republic. Pilgrims come to pray before a miraculous statue of Our Lady of Holy Hostýn who is attributed with saving the people from the Tartars during a 12th-century invasion. The pilgrimage site is thought to have been visited by brothers and Saints, Cyril and Methodius, during the 9th century.

✝ Sunday Mass 0700, 0900, 1015, 1130 & 1500

❧ The magnificent Baroque pilgrimage **Church of the Birth of the Blessed Virgin** in Křtiny, 20 kilometres north of Brno, is known as the 'Pearl of Moravia'. The area has been associated with the Baptism of heathens by Sts Cyril and Methodius (Křtiny means *Christening*). Pilgrims pray before a 15th-century statue of the Blessed Virgin which is believed to have healing properties.

✝ Sunday Mass 0730, 0900 & 1030

❡ The Basilica Minor, the **Church of The Visitation of the Virgin Mary** on the Svatý Kopeček hill, overlooks the town of Samotišky near Olomouc and is part of a Premontratensian monastery. Svatý Kopeček was honoured with a visit by Pope John Paul II in 1995, who was joined by more than 100,000 pilgrims. Miracles are said to have occurred here and an interpretation of the **Holy Stairs** similar to those Jesus walked up to meet Pontius Pilate in Jerusalem, has been built within a chapel in the pilgrimage complex.

☦ Sunday Mass 0730, 0900, 1030 & 1500

❡ The iconic **Pilgrim Church of St John of Nepomuk** on the Zelena Hill near the town of Žd'ár nad Sázavou, north-west of Brno is a listed UNESCO world heritage site and considered a 'miracle' of architectural design. The church was designed by Czech-born architect Giovanni Santini (1677–1723) with encircling cloisters formed in the shape of a 5-pointed star, symbolising the wounds of the crucified Christ. St John Nepomuk is said to have been martyred in 1393 for refusing to reveal details of the Confession of the Catholic Queen of Bohemia. His body was thrown from Prague's Charles Bridge where 3 centuries later a statue was erected in his honour.

**Additional
Accommodation**

Prague

🏠 PRAGUE

🅣 Charles University Guest House and Apartments

✉ Protestant Theological Faculty
Černá 9
cz-115 55 Prague 1

📞+420 **221 988 214**
📠+420 **221 988 215**

✉ majordomus@etf.cuni.cz

🏤 Open to both men and women

🅣 Kostel U Jákobova Žebříku

✉ U Školské Zahrady 1
cz-182 00 Prague 8

📞+420 **284 680 145**
📠+420 **284 689 771**

✉ kosteljakob@mbox.vol.cz

🏤 Open to both men and women

🅣 Miss Sophie's Hostel

✉ Melounova 3
cz-120 00 Prague 2

📞+420 **296 303 530**

✉ reservation@miss-sophies.com

🏤 Open to both men and women

🅣 Sir Toby's Hostel

✉ Delnicka 24
cz-170 00 Prague 7

📞+420 **283 870 635**
📠+420 **283 870 636**

✉ info@sirtobys.com

🏤 Open to both men and women

Bohemia

🏠 DAČICE

🅢 Kostelní Vydří Carmelite Convent of Kostelní Vydří

✉ Kostelní Vydří, 58
cz-380 01 Dačice

📞+420 **384 420 119**

✉ kostelni.vydri@karmel.cz

⛪ Priests only may stay here

🏠 HEJNICE

🅢 International Centre for Spiritual Rehabilitation

✉ Klášterní 1
cz-463 62 Hejnice

📞+420 **482 360 211**
📠+420 **482 360 299**

✉ mcdo@mcdo.cz

🏤 Open to both men and women

🏠 JANSKÉ LÁZNĚ

🅣 Sola Fide

✉ Evangelisches Erholungssheim Johannisbad
cz-542 25 Janské Lázně
Bohemia

📞+420 **499 875 425**
📠+420 **499 875 425**

✉ solafide@mbox.vol.cz

🏤 Open to both men and women

🏠 KOLIN

🅢 Exerciční dům

✉ Kutnohorská 26
cz-280 02 Kolin Bohemia

📞+420 **321 721 959**
📠+420 **321 721 959**

✉ kolin@jesuit.cz

🏤 Open to both men and women

🏠 KRÁLÍKY

🅢 Poutní dům

✉ House of Pilgrimage
Králíky kláster
Dolní Hedeč 2
cz-561 69 Králíky

📞+420 **465 631 178**

✉ poutni.dum@kraliky-klaster.cz

🏤 Open to both men and women

🏠 PANSCHWITZ-KUCKAU
GERMANY

🅢 Kloster St Mariastern

✉ Cisinskistrasse 35
01920 Panschwitz-Kuckau
Germany

📞+49 (0) **35796 99445**
📠+49 (0) **35796 99433**

✉ gaestehaus@marienstern.de

🏤 Open to both men and women

Moravia

🏚 PŘÍBRAM

Ⓢ Svatá Hora
(Holy Mountain)

✉ Svatá Hora 591
   cz-261 80 Příbram

☎ +420 318 429 930
✆ +420 318 429 934

🖥 basilica@svata-hora.cz

🛏 Open to both men and women

🏚 TOUŽIM

Ⓢ Klášter Nový Dvůr

✉ Dobrá Voda 20
   cz-364 01 Toužim

☎ +420 353 300 500
✆ +420 353 300 521

🖥 bratr.hostitel@novydvur.cz

🛏 Open to both men and women

🏚 ŽELIV

ⓈⓉ Opatství Želiv

✉ Abbey of Želiv
   cz-394 44 Želiv

☎ +420 565 581 193
✆ +420 565 381 259

🖥 opatstvi.recepce@seznam.cz

🛏 Open to both men and women

🏚 BYSTŘICE POD HOSTÝNEM

Ⓣ Sola Gratia

✉ Lázně Vinohrádek 550
   cz-768 61 Bystřice pod
   Hostýnem

☎ +420 573 381 971
✆ +420 573 378 935

🖥 info@sola.cz

🛏 Open to both men and women

🏚 ČESKÝ TĚŠÍN

Ⓢ Exerciční dům

✉ Masarykovy sady 24
   cz-737 01 Český Těšín

☎ +420 558 761 423
✆ +420 558 761 420

🖥 c.tesin@jesuit.cz

🛏 Open to both men and women

🏚 VELEHRAD

Ⓢ Poutní a exercicní
dum Stojanov

✉ Pilgrimage House
   Salašská 62
   cz-687 06 Velehrad

☎ +420 572 571 531
✆ +420 572 571 420

🖥 velehrad@stojanov.cz

🛏 Open to both men and women

Ita

WHEN I EAT ALONE I FEEL LIKE A seminarian being punished. I tried it for one week and I was not comfortable. Then I searched through Sacred Scripture for something saying I had to eat alone. I found nothing, so I gave it up and it's much better now.

POPE JOHN XXIII

ITALY

A DOLCE VITA is Italy's gift to the world and the country's colourful, warm-hearted people passionately embrace their intoxicating lifestyle. Old and new unite in complete harmony, and the Italian family remains the very heart of society. But without doubt, Italy's spiritual heart is Vatican City in Rome, the headquarters of the Roman Catholic Church.

In a country of such profound artistic heritage, Italy's ancient monasteries and grand abbeys—seemingly timeless features of the Italian landscape—stand to this day as monuments to knowledge, religion and the genius of medieval architecture. Since the first convent-run B&B opened its doors to the public, thousands of religious houses have welcomed pilgrims and tourists, offering them friendliness, hospitality and inexpensive accommodation. Having run such operations for decades now, many Italian monks and nuns are well practised in the gentle art of hospitality.

Rome

HE VATICAN is one of Rome's most familiar landmarks. Its cavernous St Peter's Basilica, renowned museums, priceless artworks and luxuriant gardens—to say nothing of its illustrious tenant—attract throngs of tourists, along with the faithful, every day of the year.

Over past centuries, communities of the religious flocked to the area around the Vatican to establish convents and seminaries. In recent years, many of these convents along with scores of others in Rome have opened their doors to tourists.

While the welcome is genuine, the standard of accommodation varies from efficiently run establishments, some in hotel style, to simple homely guesthouses, which may or may not have modern comforts and conveniences. Even so, many are close to the major tourist attractions. Surprisingly, in such a densely built-up city, most have large inner courtyards or gardens; some even have rooftop terraces, which provide perfect escapes from the chaos of the streets below.

TO SURVIVE ROME, KEEP IN MIND SOME BASIC RULES:

Remember that painted pedestrian crossings serve no obvious purpose. In particular be on the alert for flying mopeds.

Purchase your local train tickets from tobacco shops to avoid the queues at the often-defective ticket machines on railway stations.

Don't give Italian chrysanthemums unless it's for a funeral.

01

Villa Rosa

The Villa Rosa Convent is situated in a quiet, exclusive suburb of well-kept villas, and a couple of embassies, away from crowds, traffic and the noise of the city. The convent is run by the International Order of Dominican Sisters and is around the corner from the 4th-century **church of Santa Prisca** and 0.5 kilometres from **Circus Maximus**, the stadium where the Romans staged their chariot races. The villa is on the **Aventine Hill**, one of the Seven Hills of Rome, with extensive views over the city. The single, double and triple guestrooms are spread over four floors and can be accessed by a lift. All guestrooms have private bathrooms. Breakfast is the only meal catered for. The sisters take holidays each August when the villa is closed down for the month. The convent has no car parking facilities and no credit cards are accepted. Many of the sisters are of Irish background and English is widely spoken here.

✉ Via delle Terme Deciane, 5 00153 Rome (RM)

🛏 from €45.00 pp, including breakfast

📞 +39 (0) **6 57 17 091**
📠 +39 (0) **6 57 45 275**

✉ villarosa2000@libero.it

☞ The nearest train station is **Circo Massimo** which is 600 metres from the convent.

✝ **Sunday Mass 0800 & 1900** (1900 in June) Church of Santa Prisca, Piazza Santa Prisca, 00153 Rome (RM)

👥 Open to both men and women

Open Houses
Rome Aventino

PLACES OF INTEREST ❦ It is thought that St Peter used the original **Church of Santa Prisca**, near the convent, to perform Baptisms. Excavations under the church, in the Via di Santa Prisca, have uncovered Christian artefacts, medieval frescoes, and a pre-Christian temple. The relics of St Prisca, who was beheaded during the 3rd century, are in a 9th-century crypt.

❦ At 1915 each day, during the Vespers evening prayer service Benedictine monks sing the Gregorian chant in the **Church of Sant'Anselmo** at **Piazza dei Cavalieri di Malta** on the **Aventine Hill**. If you arrive early you could browse in the monks' shop (closes at 1900 and all day Monday) which sells all kinds of non-religious items such as face creams, bubble bath, Trappist chocolate bars, wine and Benedictine liqueur. All are made by monks and nuns. Traditional religious objects are also on sale. The church is near the **Priorato dei Cavalieri di Malta** (*the Priory of the Knights of Malta*); there is a keyhole in one of the enormous wooden front doors of the priory through which the dome of **St Peter's** appears like a still life work of art.

❦ Further along the **Via di Santa Sabina** (which runs off the Piazza dei Cavalieri) and opposite the original and beautifully crafted front doors of the **Church of Santa Sabina**, (the church dates back to the 5th century) is a hole in the wall. Look through the opening to see an orange tree which is said to have descended from one planted by St Dominic in the 13th century. Further along the street enjoy one of the city's best views from the Giardino degli Aranci or 'Orange Garden' which was planted to honour St Dominic's orange tree. Near the garden is an ancient Roman road, the **Clivo di Rocca Savello**, which can be followed for 300 metres down to the River Tiber. There are views over the city for much of the way. Not far from here and outside the **Church of Santa Maria in Cosmedin**, near the **Circus Maximus**, visitors often need to queue to test an ancient Roman polygraph. The legend is that if a liar puts his hand in **La Bocca della Verità** (*Mouth of Truth*) which is set into a wall under the arches of the church, it will snap off his fingers.

❡ The **Baths of Caracalla**, on the Viale delle Terme di Caracalla, are all that remain of a Roman system of hot and cold baths and saunas dating back to 206AD. The baths are the atmospheric venue for a summer season of classical concerts, ballets and operas.

❡ The Protestant Cemetery, in the Via Caio Cestio and also known as the Non-Catholic Cemetery, is the burial place of English poets John Keats (1795–1821) and Percy Bysshe Shelley (1791–1822). Near both graves is the ancient (c12BC) impressive, pyramid tomb of an obscure Roman magistrate, Caius Cestius.

FOOD AND DRINK ❦ **Ristorante Consolini** (a few metres from the Ponte Sublicio on the Aventine side) is built on the site where Hercules is said to have murdered Vulcan's son Cacus for stealing his ox. With much less mayhem going on today, the chefs can concentrate on creating the delicious Roman food for which the restaurant is acclaimed. The views are good too.

✉ Via Marmorata, 28

☏ +39 (0)6 57 30 01 48   €€€€€

❡ In surroundings fit for an emperor, the **Ristorante Apuleius** is not far from the Villa Rosa convent. The menu is based on fresh seafood with a few meat dishes included. Julius Caesar would be quite at home eating amongst the marble pillars, Roman mosaics and inscriptions.

✉ Via del Tempio di Diana, 15

☏ +39 (0)6 57 28 92 29   €€€

❡ Emperor Julius Caesar and friends ate *Isicia Omentata*, an ancestor of the 'Big Mac' and sometimes seen on the menus of restaurants serving Roman-style cuisine.

Open Houses
Rome Campo dei Fiori

02

Casa di Santa Brigida

The **Convent of Santa Brigida** is located in a 15th-
century palace in the prestigious Piazza Farnese at the
foot of the **Palatine Hill**, close to the River Tiber. The
Piazza Farnese is one of Rome's most elegant squares
and the convent shares its address with the Palazzo
Farnese, the seat of the French Embassy in Rome.
Michelangelo designed the top floor of the building.

❧ Named after the founder of the order, St Bridget
(1303–1373), who was once resident here, the convent
is run in a smooth, efficient manner by the Brigittine
Sisters, members of an international Catholic Swedish
based order who welcome people of all faiths.

❧ The convent guestrooms have en suite bathrooms, a
telephone, central heating and air-conditioning. The
dining room is open for all meals, many of which are
served by the sisters. Facilities include a lift, a television
room and a spacious rooftop terrace. Paintings and
frescoes adorn the nuns' ornate chapel, where guests
can join the sisters in daily Mass. The convent is open
all year and restaurants, cafés and shops line the
neighbouring streets. The sisters are happy to offer
advice on places to eat, transport and tourist activities
in the area. The convent is well known within Italy and
bookings should be made well in advance.

✉ Piazza Farnese, 96
00186 Rome (RM)
Visitors' entrance is in
a side street at
Via Monserrato, 54.

🛏 from €150.00 pp,
including breakfast

☎ +39 (0) **6 68 89 25 96**
☎ +39 (0) **6 68 89 24 97**
📠 +39 (0) **6 68 89 15 73**

✉ *piazzafarnese@*
brigidine.org

☞ From the **Roma
Termini** train station
take bus number 64 to
the **Basilica of San
Lorenzo** in Damaso
which is 200 metres
from the convent.

✝ **Sunday Mass**
**1000, 1100, 1200
& 1800**
Basilica di Santa Maria
di sopra Minerva,
Piazza della Minerva,
00186 Rome (RM)

⛪ Open to both men and
women

PLACES OF INTEREST ❧ A popular tradition after an evening meal anywhere in Italy is to join the locals in a *passeggiata*, a relaxing evening stroll possibly invented to work off generous servings of pasta. A gelato in hand is almost essential.

❧ A traditional food market is held on the **Campo dei Fiori** every weekday until mid-afternoon. Once the stallholders pack up for the day, the bars, cafés and trattorias set up their tables, chairs and umbrellas. The statue in the centre of the Campo dei Fiori is of a former Dominican friar, Giordano Bruno (1548–1600). After a 7-year imprisonment he became the last man executed in Rome for heresy; his statue was erected on the site of the gallows.

❧ The **Basilica di Santa Maria di sopra Minerva**, in the Piazza della Minerva, is the burial place of Dominican friar and painter Fra Angelico (1387–1455) and St Catherine of Siena (1347–1380). St Catherine's embalmed head is kept separately in a church in Siena.

† Sunday Mass 1000, 1100, 1200 & 1800

❧ **Madama Lucrezia**, a 'talking' statue in the Piazza San Marco, occasionally wears an opinion around her sturdy neck.

❧ The Italian milliners **Troncarelli**, at Via della Cuccagna, 15, have been designing and hand-crafting hats for men and women since 1857. They sell a vast selection of stylish cappellos. Buy one to wear home.

Open Houses
Rome Campo dei Fiori

FOOD AND DRINK ☙ A short walk
from the **Piazza Farnese** is one of the
quirkiest eating places in Rome, **L'Eau
Vive** near the **Piazza San Eustachio**.
This affordable restaurant is run by a
community of Carmelite missionary
nuns called *Donum Dei*. The sisters
wait on the tables, serving traditional
French-style dishes and a select choice
of French wines. Much to the surprise of
many guests, the sister who is head chef
trained in Paris. The menu generally
includes lobster tails, Australian or New
Zealand beef, escargot, scallops and
French wines from Bordeaux.

❧ During the evening there is a short
halt in proceedings while the nuns
gather together in the dining room to
pray briefly and sing *Ave Maria*. Hymn
sheets are handed around and guests
are invited to join in the singing. The
sisters come from all corners of the
world and will sometimes perform a
dance in their national dress. Profits
from the restaurant are sent to the
order's missions in Kenya, Madagascar
and India. The frescoes on the ceiling of
the upper floor of the restaurant are well
worth a look. Closed in August.

❧ Sister Marie Michèle has shared her
'easy' roast turkey recipe, which often
features on the menu. See page 236.

✉ Via Monterone, 85, 00186 Rome (RM)

☎ +39 (0) 6 68 80 10 95
☎ +39 (0) 6 68 80 21 01
✆ +39 (0) 6 68 80 25 71

✉ eauvive@pcn.net   €€

❧ From L'Eau Vive, it is a pleasant amble
back to the convent through the lively
Campo dei Fiori. For a longer walk take
the side streets to the **Trevi Fountain**
and, if still feeling energetic, you could
walk on to the **Piazza di Spagna**, about a
kilometre away.

❧ And as it happens, the oldest and
arguably the best gelato shop in Rome is
not far away. The **Gelateria Giolitti** has
been serving gelato for 100 years. There
are umpteen wicked flavours to choose
from as well as ice cream cakes and
other yummy desserts.

✉ Via Uffici del Vicario, 40

☎ +39 (0) 6 69 91 243   €€

Fraterna Domus

The position of this convent makes it an excellent base from which to visit the major tourist sites of Rome. The convent is situated next door to the 9th-century **Church of Santa Lucia della Tinta** and close to the **River Tiber**. **The Piazza Navona**, the **Vatican**, the **Pantheon** and the **Spanish Steps** are all within walking distance.

¶ Fraterna Domus is run by an order of Catholic nuns, all of whom dress casually. The small size and simple furnishings of the guestrooms are offset by the air-conditioning, which is a real bonus during a sizzling Roman summer. All guestrooms have en suite bathrooms. An underground (pay) parking area is nearby. The number of steps and levels in the building may pose a problem for the elderly or the less mobile.

¶ The convent dining room is open for all meals, which are served by the nuns. The food is simple, but plentiful and inexpensive compared to many other restaurants in the area. Wine is served with lunch and dinner. The dining room is open to non-resident guests and mealtimes here are often animated occasions as the restaurant is a regular meeting place for many local residents and shopkeepers. The sisters take reservations.

OPEN HOUSE

✉ Cnr Via del Cancello &
Via Monte Brianzo
00186 Rome (RM)

🛏from €40.00 pp,
including breakfast

✆ +39 (0) 6 68 80 27 27
✆ +39 (0) 6 68 32 691

✉ fraternadomus@alice.it

☞ From **Roma Termini**
train station take bus
number 70 which
stops at Via Zanardelli,
near the convent.
From Termini it is a
2-kilometre taxi ride.

✝ **Sunday Mass**
Summer 0830, 1000,
1100, 1200 & 1900
Winter 0830, 1000,
1100, 1200, 1245
& 1830
Oratorio di San Filippo
Neri
Via del Governo
Vecchio, 134
00186 Rome (RM)

👥 Open to both men and
women

Open Houses
Rome Campo Marzio

PLACES OF INTEREST ✦ **Fraterna Domus** is located near the **Ponte Umberto I** and it is a short walk across this bridge to **Castel Sant'Angelo**, once the temporary home of endangered pontiffs, and now a museum. The **Vatican** is a few hundred metres further on.

❧ Sculptor Lorenzetto's (1490–1541) copy of Michelangelo's *Pieta* is in the **Church of Santa Maria dell'Anima** on the Piazza della Pace. The church is 500 metres from Fraterna Domus. The real thing can be found in the first chapel on the right inside the entrance to **St Peter's Basilica**.

❧ A valued client of the historic **Argentieri jewellery shop** and studio at Via Tor di Nona, 60, is the current Pope. Franchi Argentieri's highly skilled artisans create the Papal Piscatory ring for incoming Pontiffs. The Papal Ring is also known as the Ring of The Fisherman.

❧ The area is known for its antique, book and craft shops and a theatre which caters for non-Italian speakers. The **Teatro l'Arciliuto**, at Piazza Montevecchio, 5, is otherwise known as **The English Theatre** because all the performances of music and poetry are presented in English with translations in French, Spanish and German. **The Theatre Museum Burcardo** at Via del Sudario, 44 exhibits theatre memorabilia from the late 16th century. Collections include stage costumes, set designs and scripts.

❧ A branch of the oldest chemist shop in Italy, **l'Officina Profumo Farmaceutica di Santa Maria Novella** at Corso del Rinascimento, 47 is a purveyor of fine perfumes, soaps and bath products made from recipes passed down over the centuries. Whilst you are in the street you could cross the road to **Ai Monasteri** at number 72. First established in Rome in 1892, the shop sells products made by monks and nuns living in convents and monasteries throughout Italy. The range of goods is extensive and includes food, alcohol, bath and beauty potions and even grooming products for pets. The shop is near the **Palazzo Madama** where the Italian Senate sits.

❧ The Caleffi family continue the 110-year-old tradition of hand-making Italian shirts and ties in their shop **Caleffi** at Via Colonna Antonina, 53.

❧ **Antiquarius**, at Corso del Rinascimento, 63, trades in authentic rare maps, manuscripts and prints from around the world, some dating as far back as the 15th century.

FOOD AND DRINK ✦ The **Ristorante La Campana** claims to be the oldest restaurant in the city. It dates back to the 16th century and serves traditional Roman-style food such as artichokes, tripe, oxtail and ricotta cake with a few seasonal offerings. Local residents eat here which is a good indication of the quality and the price.

✉ Vicolo della Campana, 18

☎ +39 (0) 6 68 75 273   €€€€

❦ In the 1st century BC Romans came to the **Piazza Navona** to watch sporting events (not the man-eating type). Nowadays they come to eat, drink and people-watch from the prized tables of some of Rome's oldest restaurants. Amongst the most famous are the **Café Da Passetto**, the iconic **Tre Scalini** (of 'Death By Chocolate' ice cream fame— *tartufo* in Italian) and, just off the piazza, the **Café della Pace**. All three have been serving customers for over 100 years. However, overlooking Bernini's Fountain of the Four Rivers comes at a price.

✉ Café Da Passetto, Piazza Navona

☎ +39 (0) 6 68 80 65 69   €€€€€

✉ Tre Scalini, Piazza Navona

☎ +39 (0) 6 68 79 148   €€€€€

✉ Café della Pace, Piazza Navona

☎ +39 (0) 6 68 61 216   €€€€€

Casa Il Rosario

Located in the centre of ancient Rome, and just a few blocks from the **Roman Forum**, this Catholic convent is in an ancient building in a quiet and peaceful environment despite being in a busy area. The casa is run by nuns of the order of the Dominican Sisters of Charity and is within walking distance of the **Colosseum**.

❧ The simple, modest guestrooms at Casa Il Rosario are configured for single, double and triple occupancy and most have a private bathroom. A few rooms share a bathroom on the same floor. The guest areas are spread over four floors and are accessed by a small lift. One guestroom has wheelchair access and some rooms overlook an internal courtyard. Breakfast is served in the dining room on a 'help yourself' basis. Enjoy the sunshine and the views of the city or find a shady place to relax after a day's sightseeing, on the convent's rooftop garden terrace. Casa Il Rosario is open all year. No on-site car parking is available and credit cards are not accepted.

❧ The convent is in an area well serviced by cafés, restaurants and public transport.

✉ Via di Sant'Agata dei Goti, 10
00184 Rome (RM)

🛏 from €40.00 pp, including breakfast

📞 +39 (0) 6 67 92 346
📠 +39 (0) 6 69 94 11 06

✐ irodopre@tin.it

☞ From **Roma Termini** take the train to Cavour on Metro line B. The convent is 600 metres from Cavour station.

✝ **Sunday Mass**
0900, 1100 & 1830
Basilica di San Clemente
Via Labicana, 95
00184 Rome (RM)

♿ Discuss your needs in advance of arriving, ideally when booking.

⚥ Open to both men and women

PLACES OF INTEREST ❧ **The Palazzo del Quirinale**, once a summer residence for Popes, is now the official residence of the President of the Italian Republic. The *palazzo* is less than 1 kilometre from the convent.

❦ Near the convent and under the main altar of the 14th-century **Church of San Pietro in Vincoli** (or *St Peter in Chains*) in the piazza of the same name are the chains that are said to have bound St Peter when he was imprisoned around the year 67AD. Michelangelo's celebrated 'chipped' statue of Moses is also in the church. Theories abound as to the cause of the damage on the right knee. Some say the artist threw a hammer at it in a fit of rage because he considered the work so perfect that it should speak!

❦ Extensive excavations under the **Basilica of San Clemente, near the Colosseum**, have unearthed a 4th-century church and a house which may have belonged to St Clemente, who is buried in the basilica. The basilica is in the care of the Dominican Order who have opened the excavations to tourists and visitors. On St Clement's Feast Day on 23 November the saint's relics are carried through the local streets in a traditional religious ceremony.

❦ A chapel in the 4th-century **Basilica of Santa Croce in Gerusalemme** (in the Piazza Gerusalemme) houses relics, some of which are thought to be fragments of the **True Cross**, a nail used in Christ's Crucifixion and a sponge, believed to have touched the lips of Christ. The basilica is one of the seven pilgrim churches of Rome which the faithful visit to gain indulgences (forgiveness of sins).

❦ The **Domus Aurea** (*Golden House*, c64AD) in the Parco del Colle Oppio, was once the spacious palace of Emperor Nero. Parts of the building have been excavated and restored and guided underground tours are conducted on most days. The area is closed from time to time for further restoration.

Open Houses
Rome Colosseum

◀ The **Museo delle Mura**, (*Museum of the Walls*) in the Via di Porta San Sebastiano, 18, forms part of the **The Aurelian Wall** which was built to protect the city around 270AD. The museum, located within the wall's well-preserved towers, provides an insight into the history of the Aurelian Wall through models, maps and artefacts. Visitors to the museum are able to walk along sections of the old wall.

◀ Inspect designer handbags of dubious origins from any one of the many street sellers in the **Colosseum** area. The market on **Via Sannio**, behind the Piazza San Giovanni in Laterno, is open every morning except Sundays and specialises in clothes. The train station for this market is **San Giovanni**.

FOOD AND DRINK ◀ Not far from the Termini train station, the **Trattoria Severo 2000** is an unpretentious, family-run, neighbourhood trattoria serving pasta and pizza simply and well and at reasonable prices.

✉ Via Vicenza, 10

☎ +39 (0) 6 49 57 797   €€€

◀ On a scorching Roman summer evening you could take refuge at the **Ice Club**, a short walk from Casa Il Rosario. Don the gloves, hat and overcoat (provided), order a drink and even nibble on the ice-sculpted glass if you want.

✉ Via della Madonna dei Monti, 17

☎ +39 (0) 6 97 84 55 81   €€€

◀ Or you could meet some Irish folk at **Finnegan's Bar** and cool down with a pint of something cold.

✉ Via Leonina, 66

☎ +39 (0) 6 47 47 026   €

◀ When hunger strikes, the cheap and cheerful **Pizzeria Alle Carrette** is just a short stroll from the convent. If the authentic wood-fired pizzas don't hit the spot there is always the home-made desserts. Busy.

✉ Via della Madonna dei Monti, 95

☎ +39 (0) 6 67 92 770   €€€

05

Hotel Casa Kolbe

Casa Kolbe is situated in the Palatine area of the **Centro Storico** quarter, a quiet residential neighbourhood near the **Imperial Forum**, the **Circus Maximus** and the **Colosseum**. It is owned by the Conventual Franciscan Order of Friars, a branch of the First Order of St Francis. The monastery is named in honour of Polish Saint Maximilian Kolbe who was canonised in 1982 and who lived here from 1912 to 1919.

❡ Casa Kolbe is a simply appointed guesthouse within the walls of an old monastery which is set in large attractive gardens. The guestrooms are small and sparsely furnished; however, the necessities are provided and each room is air-conditioned. Guestrooms are fitted with a television and all have an en suite bathroom. All meals are available and are cheap, by Rome's standards. Breakfast is the customary Roman fare of coffee, bread rolls and jam. Wine is served at lunch and dinner. The ever obliging staff have a reputation for friendliness and nothing seems to be too much trouble. Facilities include a communal lounge room, bar, laundry and a small parking area is provided. Credit cards are accepted. The guestrooms overlooking the street can be noisy; however, they have a bird's eye view of the Roman Forum. Rooms at the rear of the building are quieter with some overlooking the garden.

✉ Via di San Teodoro, 44 00186 Rome (RM)

🏨 from €48.00 pp, including breakfast

☎ +39 (0) **6 67 94 974**
📞 +39 (0) **6 69 94 15 50**

☞ From **Roma Termini** take the train to Circo Massimo on Metro line B. Casa Kolbe is 1 kilometre from Circo Massimo station. Bus 170 from Termini stops at the Piazza della Bocca della Verità, near Casa Kolbe.

✝ **Sunday Mass** 0700, 0800, 0900, 1000, 1100, 1230 & 1900 The Church of Jesus, (Chiesa del Gesù) Via degli Astalli, 16, 00186 Rome (RM)

♗ Open to both men and women

Open Houses
Rome Palatino

A practical way to begin sightseeing is to take the Roman version of the 'hop-on–hop-off' bus, known as the **Archeobus**. The bus stops at important historical and artistic sites along the **Appian Way**, Rome's ancient road, built around 312BC. The Archeobus leaves from the **Piazza Venezia** every hour from 1000 until 1600. On Sundays the section of the road leading out of Rome is closed to traffic and, being lined with ruins, it makes for an interesting walk. From Rome, cyclists can follow some of the remaining tracks of the Appian Way, 560 kilometres down to **Brindisi** in **Puglia**. Ferry services operate on a regular basis between **Brindisi** and **Patras** and **Corfu** in Greece.

❡ To see the Christian sites of Rome, jump on the yellow open-topped **Roma Christiana** hop-on-hop-off bus, which stops at places in the city with a religious significance (including the **Vatican**). Establishing the bus service was a joint initiative of the Vatican and local government. Buses depart from the Termini train station daily, every hour from 0900 until 1900.

❡ The **Palatine Museum** in Via di San Gregorio on **Palatine Hill** is the repository for the ancient sculptures and historic artefacts found by archaeologists during excavations on the hill itself. The exhibition reflects the area from the time when the Palatine Hill was home to Rome's Emperors right up until the 19th century. According to folklore the twins Romulus and Remus, the founders of Rome, were discovered on the Palatine Hill by a she-wolf who mothered them (c771BC).

❡ The **Arch of Constantine** was built around the year 315BC and was a model for Napoleon's **Arc de Triomphe** in 1807 which is a little larger. The Arch of Constantine is situated at the end of **Via Sacra**, ancient Rome's 'high' street.

❡ Michelangelo designed the **Piazza del Campidoglio** on Capitol Hill at the request of Pope Paul III in 1536. He was the architect of the exterior of the piazza's palatial buildings and the unusual pattern on the cobblestones. The piazza can be reached from the **Piazza Venezia** via the **Monument to Victor Emmanuel II**.

❡ **San Gregorio Magno al Celio** (*Church of St Gregory the Great*) is on the **Caelian Hill**, one of the **Seven Hills of Rome**. Its magnificent parkland setting is an inviting setting for a picnic or a quiet stroll. On the walls of a small chapel within the church is a fresco of the Blessed Virgin which is said to have spoken to St Gregory (540–604AD). St Gregory became Pope Gregory I (Gregory the Great) in the year 590.

❡ In summer, take in a show by **The Miracle Players**. This English-speaking theatrical group, based in Rome, perform comedy theatre with icons of Ancient Rome as the subject matter. Past performances include *Cleopatra* and an irreverent *Caesar—More Than Just a Salad*. The shows take place in the Roman Forum, once the hub of ancient Rome and now overlooked by the Hotel Casa Kolbe.

FOOD AND DRINK ❡ Guests of the Casa Kolbe don't have to walk too far to find a pizza bar, café or a restaurant. The **Osteria del Campidoglio** (off the Via di San Teodoro) and the **Trattoria San Teodoro**, just a few doors away, are both good family-style eating places and not expensive. **Da Giggetto Trattoria** serves a Jewish version of Roman cuisine with degustation style four course house menus of varying prices.

✉ Osteria del Campidoglio, Via dei Fienili, 56
☎ +39 (0) 6 67 80 250 €€

✉ Trattoria San Teodoro, Via dei Fienili
☎ +39 (0) 6 67 80 933 €€

✉ Da Giggetto, Via del Portico d'Ottavia 21
☎ +39 (0) 6 68 61 105 €€€

❡ If making a reservation at the **Ristorante da Pancrazio**, request the 'underground room' which forms part of the ruins of the **Theatre of Pompey** where Julius Caesar was murdered. At the other end of the Theatre of Pompey the **Hostaria Costanza** also sits among the ruins of the theatre. Both restaurants serve Roman cuisine and neither are cheap.

✉ Ristorante da Pancrazio, Piazza del Biscione
☎ +39 (0) 6 68 61 246 €€€€€

✉ Hostaria Costanza, Piazza del Paradiso
☎ +39 (0) 6 68 61 717 €€€€€

Open Houses
Rome Prati

Casa Carmelitana San Alberto

Casa Carmelitana is owned by the order of the Sisters of Monte Carmelo (*Carmelitani*) and is situated in the **Prati** area of Rome, just a short distance from the **Vatican** and within easy walking distance of the historical centre. The convent is staffed by laity and run along hotel lines. The house has over 50 single, double, triple and quad guestrooms all with an en suite bathroom. Some double guestrooms are furnished with a king sized bed. A small fridge-bar, hairdryer, a telephone and satellite television reception are provided. Some rooms overlook the historical landmark **Castel Sant'Angelo**.

¶ Facilities include 24-hour reception, Internet access and a rarity in the centre of Rome, on-site parking for cars and coaches. The building is air-conditioned and centrally heated and some rooms have wheelchair access. The house restaurant serves traditional home-cooked Italian cuisine. Wine and other alcoholic drinks are available. A substantial buffet breakfast of tea, coffee, juice, breads, cereal, yoghurt, cold meats, cheese and pastries is served daily.

¶ The roof terrace has views over **St Peter's Basilica**. Conference facilities are available. Credit cards are accepted. A pick-up from the airport can be arranged.

OPEN HOUSE

✉ Via Alberico II, 44
00193 Rome (RM)

🛏 from €67.00 pp,
including breakfast

☎ +39 (0) 6 6840 191
+39 (0) 6 6840 192 00

✉ info@
domuscarmelitana.com

☞ From **Roma Termini** take the train to Ottaviano on Metro line A. The convent is approximately 1 kilometre from Ottaviano station. Or take Express bus 40 from Termini and get off at Piazza Pia, the last stop on the line. The convent is 500 metres away.

✝ **Sunday Mass**
0800, 0900, 1030
& 1830
Church of Santa Maria del Carmelo in Traspontina
Via della Conciliazione, 00193 Rome (RM)

♿ Discuss your needs in advance of arriving, ideally when booking.

⚥ Open to both men and women

PLACES OF INTEREST Castel Sant' Angelo on the banks of the **Tiber** was built originally as a mausoleum by Emperor Hadrian in 139AD. Later it became a refuge for Popes who were in danger; it was connected to the **Vatican** by a secret passageway, the **Passetto di Borgo**. For centuries the building was used as a prison. Both the prison and the former Papal apartments are open to visitors. Cross the **Ponte Sant'Angelo** back to the hubbub of Rome.

Escape the hubbub in the **Orto Botanico** (*Botanical Gardens*), off the Via Corsini, which during the 13th century, under Pope Nicolò III formed part of the Vatican Gardens. The gardens occupy land once used by monks to grow medicinal plants. Nearby is the **Teatro Verde** at Via Circonvallazione Gianicolense, 10, one of Rome's best loved puppet theatres where fairytales and children's stories rely on audience participation. Young visitors are encouraged to engage with the performers, visit the dressing rooms and inspect the props before the show. The shows are presented in Italian but all children are made welcome.

Bargain hunters may like to visit the **McArthur Glen factory** outlet in **Castel Romano**, 25 kilometres south of the centre of Rome. European brands are represented in this vast centre whose design is based on streets and piazzas of ancient Rome. The centre is best reached by car, but a free shuttle bus leaves from the Piazza della Repubblica.

✉ Via Ponte di Piscina Cupa

☎ +39 (0)6 50 12 21   open 1000–2100 daily

Oviesse, at Via Candia, 74, is one of a chain of department stores selling a wide range of men's, women's and children's clothing in the lower price bracket. Branches are across the city.

FOOD AND DRINK Casual tavernas specialising in pizza and pasta are well established in this area and the **Ristorante Cesare** is a popular choice for the hospitable atmosphere and the great pizzas. In winter, pizza topped with white truffle is often on the menu.

✉ Via Crescenzio, 13

☎ +39 (0)6 68 61 227   €€€

Most nights from 1900 the restaurant / nightclub **The Place**, near the Castel Sant'Angelo, serves upscale, international cuisine to the accompaniment of local bands and musicians.

✉ Via Alberico II, 27

☎ +39 (0)6 68 30 71 37   €€€€

For Irish hospitality try **Four Green Fields**, a friendly pub and restaurant with music, Guinness and a traditional atmosphere.

✉ Via Costantino Morin, 40

☎ +39 (0)6 37 25 091   €

Open Houses
Rome Spanish Steps

07

Maison d'Accueil St-Joseph

The Church of the Trinité-des-Monts (*Trinità dei Monti*) is perched at the top of the **Spanish Steps** and this 15th-century convent adjoins it. Until recently the convent was the headquarters of the international religious order of the *Sociéte du Sacré-Cœur* (Society of the Sacred Heart) which operated a guesthouse within the cloisters for families, young people and general tourists. The guesthouse was taken over in 2006 by the monks and nuns of the *Fraternités de Jérusalem* (Family of Jerusalem), a religious organisation established in France in 1975, which continues the long-established tradition of the Sacré-Coeur sisters of welcoming visitors.

❧ Sections of the inside of the convent have difficult access, making the accommodation here unsuitable for the elderly or the disabled. However, the position is worth any inconvenience. Most of the double, triple and quadruple rooms share a bathroom, with only a few having private facilities. No single rooms are available. Continental breakfast is the only meal served. The entrance to the convent is to the left of the building when facing the front of the church. Guests will be able to examine in detail the ancient frescoes adorning the cloister and refectory walls. Occasionally these artworks are put on public display.

❧ Young people are welcomed exclusively to the Maison d'Accueil St-Joseph between mid-January and mid-July and also during the month of October. At other times the guesthouse is open to all tourists and visitors.

OPEN HOUSE

✉ Trinité-des-Monts
Piazza Trinità dei
Monti, 3
00187 Rome (RM)

🛏 from €38.00 pp,
including breakfast

☎ +39 (0) **6 67 97 436**
📠 +39 (0) **6 67 81 007**

✎ *maison.accueil.rome@
jerusalem.cef.fr*

☞ From **Roma Termini**
take the train to
Spagna on Metro
Line A, the station
at the bottom of the
Spanish Steps. For
those who don't wish
to climb the 137-step
flight, the Trinatà dei
Monti can be reached
by taking the lift from
the station to the top
of the Spanish Steps.
The lift is just inside
the entrance to the
metro station.

✝ **Sunday Mass**
1130
Church of La Trinité-
des-Monts
Piazza Trinità dei
Monti, 3
00187 Rome (RM)

👥 Open to both men and
women

PLACES OF INTEREST ✦ With good reason, the **Spanish Steps** is one of the most visited attractions in Rome. The steps were built during the early 18th century to connect the 16th-century **Church of Trinità dei Monti**, at the top, to the square below. During the *Festa della Primavera* or Spring Festival, the steps are decorated with pots and urns blooming with multi-coloured azaleas. During the festival concerts of classical and sacred music are held in the church of Trinità dei Monti and also in the convent courtyard next door.

❡ **Catello d'Auria** at Via due Macelli, 55, is an elegant old shop selling gloves, stockings, socks and other lingerie. At the southern end of the street is the **Via del Tritone** where there are a number of shops selling quality handmade shirts and ties, including the historic **Camiceria Bazzocchi** at number 141. The shop has been in the same family for 100 years. For more choice try the upmarket **La Rinascente** department store on the Via del Corso at the **Piazza Colonna**. The **Il Discount delle Firme** at Via dei Serviti, 27 is cheaper, selling discounted handbags, shoes and perfume.

❡ Take a picnic to the **Villa Borghese**, a scenic park in the centre of Rome, behind the **Trinité-des-Monts** and with a mélange of lakes, flower beds, statues, fountains and a zoo which is the home of over 190 animal species. **The Borghese Gallery and Museum** inside the park, displays the collection of the once wealthy Cardinal Scipione Caffarelli (1576–1633). He was a nephew of Cardinal Camillo Borghese, who later became Pope Paul V (1605–1621). The Pope appointed Cardinal Scipione to the prestigious positions of private secretary and head of the Vatican Government.

FOOD AND DRINK ✦ The ristorante **La Tavernetta** serves a variety of home-made pasta dishes with a couple of lamb and fish options. The restaurant's clientele includes local families as well as tourists. An English menu is provided. If you crave a pizza the **Ristorante Pizzeria Fontanella** is next door.

✉ La Tavernetta, Via Sistina, 147

☎ +39 (0) 6 47 41 939   €€

✉ Ristorante Pizzeria Fontanella, Via Sistina

☎ +39 (0) 6 48 80 519   €€€

❡ **The Ristorante GiNa** offers a unique take-away service. The restaurant will provide a chic picnic basket and load it with delicious goodies of your choice for a picnic in the **Villa Borghese** or possibly on the **Spanish Steps** (if the guards on duty allow eating there). Plates, glasses, tablecloth and cutlery are included. Eat in if you prefer.

✉ Via San Sebastianello, 7A, Piazza di Spagna

☎ +39 (0) 6 67 80 251   €€€

Open Houses
Rome Spanish Steps

Casa Nostra Signora di Lourdes

The Casa Nostra Signora di Lourdes is situated in a street of chic boutiques, cafés, a number of small, fashionable hotels and a theatre, approximately 100 metres from the top of the **Spanish Steps** and the **Church of the Trinità dei Monti**. The Catholic sisters of the order of *Le Suore di Lourdes* (Sisters of Lourdes) who live here have been operating the guesthouse for more than 40 years.

❧ Guestrooms (single, twin and triple) are small but comfortable; most have marble floors and high ceilings. Some of the guestrooms have en suite bathrooms. The rooms on the **Via Sistina** side of the building can be subject to traffic noise but there are quieter rooms at the back overlooking an inner courtyard. Guests can choose between a wide, grand marble staircase and a small lift to reach the guestrooms and the rooftop terrace. There is a tiny television room behind reception on the ground floor. Guests are sometimes gently awakened by the nuns singing hymns during the morning Mass. When the singing stops, breakfast is ready. Crusty rolls, jam and delicious milky coffee are served by young postulants in a formal dining room where tables are meticulously laid with white linen and polished silverware. No other meals are available.

✉ Via Sistina, 113
00187 Rome (RM)

🛏 from €40.00 pp
including breakfast

☎ +39 (0) **6 47 45 324**
☎ +39 (0) **6 47 41 422**

🚉 From **Roma Termini** take the train to Barberini on Metro Line A and walk to the convent. The convent can also be reached from Spagna train station.

✝ **Sunday Mass**
0900 & 1030
The Church of Santa Susanna
Via XX Settembre, 15
00187 Rome (RM)
Masses are celebrated in English

⚥ Open to both men and women

PLACES OF INTEREST ❧ The Pallotine Fathers celebrate Sunday Mass in English in the **Basilica of San Silvestro in Capite**. The church is near the base of the **Spanish Steps**, about 500 metres from Casa Nostra Signora di Lourdes. A relic said to be of the head of St John the Baptist is kept in a chapel in the church.

✉ Basilica of San Silvestro, Piazza San Silvestro

✝ Sunday Mass 1000 & 1730

❡ Anglicans can attend Sunday English services at **All Saints Church**, off the Piazza di Spagna. The **St Andrew's Presbyterian Church** of Scotland conducts a service in English each Sunday.

✉ All Saints Church, Via del Babuino, 153

✝ Sunday Mass 0830 & 1030

✉ St Andrew's, Via xx Settembre, 7

✝ Sunday Mass 1100

❡ The crypt of the **Church of Santa Maria della Concezione** in the nearby Via Veneto contains thousands of creatively arranged bones and skulls of over 4000 deceased Capuchin monks. An even more ghoulish touch is a clock overhead, made almost entirely of bones, relentlessly ticking away as a reminder to visitors of the brevity of time on earth.

❡ A market for small antiques, books and prints is held in the **Largo di Fontanella Borghese** near the Piazza Borghese from Monday to Saturday. Antiques and artisans' shops line the pedestrian-only **Via dei Coronari** and **Via Margutta** and an antiques fair takes place on the Via dei Coronari over two weeks each May.

❡ The fashionable shops and boutiques in the side streets off the **Piazza del Popolo** are less well known to tourists, but popular with savvy Romans. The Piazza del Popolo is a gateway to the **Villa Borghese**.

Open Houses
Rome Spanish Steps

❧ **The Exhibition of Centopresepi** (*Exhibition of One Hundred Christmas Cribs*) at the Palazzo Ruspoli in the Piazza del Popolo, is presented each year under the auspices of the Vatican. The exhibition takes place from mid-December to the end of the first week in January, when hand-crafted antique cribs and Nativity tableaus go on display.

❧ The kids can have loads of educational fun at the **Il Museo dei Bambini** at Via Flaminia, 82, a hands-on children's learning centre focusing on the themes of communications, civilisation, the human body and the environment. The **Museo Nazionale delle Paste Alimentari** (*National Pasta Museum*), Piazza Scanderberg, 117 (near the Trevi Fountain) is dedicated to the history of pasta. Visitors can take home a sample box.

❧ The **Keats–Shelley Memorial House**, at Piazza di Spagna, 26, is the former home of John Keats and now a museum dedicated to the two great English poets—John Keats and Percy Bysshe Shelley.

FOOD AND DRINK ❧ The oldest café in Rome, the **Café Greco** (founded in 1760), is close to the Spanish Steps. The café has been attracting artists, writers and politicians for hundreds of years. Keats, Shelley, Liszt and Wagner frequented this café at various times. Tea lovers might prefer to take high tea at **Babington's Tea Rooms** (founded in 1893) situated at the foot of the Spanish Steps.

✉ Café Greco, Via Condotti
☎ +39 (0) 6 67 91 700   €€€€€
✉ Babington's Tea Rooms, Piazza di Spagna
☎ +39 (0) 6 67 86 027   €€€€€

❧ **The Lion Bookstore** is a well stocked English language bookshop with thousands of titles and a pleasant café in which to while away some time or share some gossip.

✉ Via dei Greci, 36
☎ +39 (0) 6 32 65 40 07   €

❧ The **TAD Conceptstore**, near the foot of the Spanish Steps, stocks everything from contemporary homewares to one-off clothing designs and accessories. Give the feet a break in the interior café which is an informal, relaxing space serving traditional café-type food.

✉ Via Del Babuino, 155A
☎ +39 (0) 6 32 69 51 22   €€€

Domus Nova Bethlem

Run by the Oblate Sisters of Baby Jesus, the guesthouse
is situated in the centre of ancient Rome on the
Esquiline Hill near the **Forum**, the **Colosseum** and
the **Termini** train station. The **Piazza dell'Esquilino**
and the **Basilica of Santa Maria Maggiore** (*Basilica
of St Mary Major*) are both on the next block. The
convent guesthouse consists of 24 single, double
and triple brightly furnished guestrooms, all with en
suite bathrooms. Guestroom facilities include air-
conditioning, a television and a telephone. Breakfast
is the only meal served and cafés and restaurants
are easy to find in this area. The Via Cavour is a busy
thoroughfare and the rooms facing the street can
be noisy. Guestrooms are available at the rear of the
building. The convent has a small inner courtyard and
car parking is charged at around €20.00 per day.
❡ The guesthouse is open all year and credit cards
are accepted. The Oblate Sisters also have a convent
guesthouse in Sorrento, Campania.

OPEN HOUSE

✉ Via Cavour, 85/A
   00184 Rome (RM)

🚃 from €58.00 pp,
   including breakfast

✆ +39 (0) 6 47 82 44 14
✆ +39 (0) 6 47 82 20 77
📠 +39 (0) 6 47 82 20 33

✐ domusnovabethlem@
   suorebambinogesu.it

☞ The convent is 700
   metres from **Roma
   Termini** train station.

✝ **Sunday Mass**
   0600, 0700, 0800,
   0900, 1000, 1100
   & 1830
   Basilica del Sacre Cuore
   Via Marsala, 42
   00185 Rome (RM)

👥 Open to both men and
   women

Open Houses
Rome Termini

PLACES OF INTEREST ❦ The **Via Merulana** which runs off the Piazza Santa Maria Maggiore (near the convent) leads from one great basilica to another. The **Basilica of Santa Maria Maggiore** is at one end and the **Basilica di San Giovanni in Laterno** (*Basilica of St John Lateran*) at the other.

❦ In a 16th-century building opposite the **Basilica of St John Lateran** are the stairs that Jesus is said to have walked up to be condemned by Pontius Pilate. The 28 marble steps must be ascended only on the knees. Those penitents who reach the top gain a plenary indulgence, otherwise known as a forgiveness of all sins. The steps are protected by a thick wooden covering, worn down by the knees of pilgrims. There are small, uncovered sections which can be touched; marks, protected by glass, are said to be the bloodstains of Jesus. The **Holy Staircase** and the relics of the Crucifixion in the **Basilica of Santa Croce in Gerusalemme** are believed to have been brought to Rome from Jerusalem in 326AD by St Helena of Constantinople (c248–329), mother of Emperor Constantine I (c272–337).

❦ Any plenary indulgence could well be annulled by the sin of greed in the leather stores along the **Via Nazionale** or at Italian shoe designer **Fausto Santini**'s flagship store at Via Frattina, 120.

❦ **Domus Nova Bethlem** is handy to a branch of UPIM, Italy's popular, low-cost department store chain where you can pick up a bargain in Italian shoes and clothes. UPIM is on the corner of Via Carlo Alberto and Piazza Santa Maria Maggiore.

❡ The **Museo Tipologico Internazionale del Presepio** (*International Museum of the Crib*) Via Tor de' Conti, 31A exhibits a permanent collection of Christmas cribs from all over the world and conducts courses for those who would like to learn how to make their own.

❡ The **Teatro dell'Opera** (*Rome Opera Theatre*) in the Piazza Beniamino Gigli is a highly acclaimed venue for opera and ballet. Ballerinas aged between 9 and 16 years can enrol in the Opera Theatre's School of Dance which has been conducting classes for over 70 years.

❡ Trains regularly depart for **Florence**, **Naples** and **Pompeii** from **Stazione Termini**. The towns can be visited from Rome in a (separate) day trip.

FOOD AND DRINK If attending the opera, you could have a pre-theatre dinner at the classy **Ristorante Rossini** in the Hotel Quirinale and then use the hotel's private entrance to move into the opera house. However, the restaurant's romantic, candle-lit ambience is conducive to lingering a while.

✉ Via Nazionale, 7

☎ +39 (0) 6 47 07 €€€€€

❡ **The Ristorante da Vincenzo** is another cosy family-run trattoria a stone's throw from Termini train station. Many of the delicious pasta and seafood dishes can be ordered in tasting portions and old Roman specialities such as Tripe Romano are sometimes on the menu.

✉ Via Castelfidardo, 4

☎ +39 (0) 6 48 45 96 €€€

❡ **Ned Kelly's Pub**, an Australian pub near The American College, serves Australian beer on tap and non-stop sport plays on the big screen. Value for money pub meals and snacks are available. Open 'til very late.

✉ Via delle Coppelle, 13

☎ +39 (0) 6 68 32 220 €

Open Houses
Rome Trastevere

Casa di Santa Francesca Romana

Casa di Santa Francesca Romana is situated near the **Church of St Cecilia** in Trastevere and has been owned by the Catholic Church since the 19th century. The convent guesthouse is run by lay staff. During the 15th century the house was the childhood home of St Francesca Romana.

❦ Today, the casa extends hospitality to individuals, couples, groups and families. The guestrooms here are all en suite and all rooms are air-conditioned. A mini-bar, telephone, hairdryer and satellite television are provided. Some guestrooms have a balcony with views over the immediate neighbourhood. Single, double, triple and quad rooms are available. Facilities include a lift and an interior garden courtyard providing a quiet, shady place to relax. The convent dining room is open for all meals. The guesthouse is open all year round and credit cards are accepted. This is a large complex with six conference rooms of various sizes available for meetings and conventions. The convent chapel has seating for 150 people. The convent is on a quiet street with neighbourhood trattorias and pizzerias close by.

OPEN HOUSE

✉ Via dei Vascellari, 61
00153 Rome (RM)

🛏 from €58.00 pp,
including breakfast

☎ +39 (0) **6 58 12 125**
📠 +39 (0) **6 58 82 408**

⌨ *istituto@sfromana.it*

☞ From **Roma Termini**
take the train to
Circo Massimo on
Metro line B, which
is 1 kilometre from
the convent. Or from
Roma Termini take
bus H or bus number
170.

✝ **Sunday Mass**
1000
Church of Santa Cecilia
in Trastevere
Piazza di Santa
Cecilia, 22
00153 Rome (RM)

⚭ Open to both men and
women

PLACES OF INTEREST ❦ Getting lost is a perfect way to discover the colourful **Trastevere** district. A labyrinth of medieval laneways, this traditional Roman neighbourhood is famous for its craft and artisan shops and teems with artists, musicians, actors and writers.

❧ A lively nightlife and countless restaurants, cafés and bars typify the area. A traditional religious festival, the Festa di Noantri, is celebrated in mid-July when the whole of **Trastevere** turns into a boisterous, mega street market.

❧ A statue representing the Madonna del Carmine, which was found in Trastevere by fishermen some centuries ago, leads a procession of enthusiastic locals and pilgrims from the **Church of Sant'Agata** in Trastevere to the **Church of San Crisogono**, where it is honoured for 8 days before being returned, via a procession, to its permanent home, the Church of Sant'Agata. The procession is a part of the Festa dei' Noantri.

❧ Rome's largest prison, the **Regina Coeli**, is in Via della Lungara in Trastevere. It is built on the site of the former **Church and Monastery of Santa Maria Regina Coeli**, founded in 1654. The church, also known as the Church of San Francesco di Sales, has been preserved and is now inside the walls of the prison. Pope John Paul II celebrated Mass here for the inmates in July 2002.

❧ The 5th-century **Church of St Cecilia** in the Piazza di Santa Cecilia is dedicated to the patroness of music. The bath in which an attempt was made to execute Cecilia can be seen in the **Chapel of the Bath**; she later died from the injuries that were inflicted upon her.

❧ The artisans at **Joseph Debach Shoes** at Vicolo del Cinque, 19, skilfully create unusual shoes and sandals; each pair is hand-crafted with a 'look at me' quality.

❧ A flower and vegetable market is held in the **Piazza San Cosimato** each weekday morning and the **Porta Portese**, one of Rome's flea markets, is held in Trastevere, between Ponte Sublicio and Ponte Testaccio on Sunday mornings.

FOOD AND DRINK ❦ In Roman times the Via dei Vascellarie was a street of artisans' and potters' studios, reflected today in the wooden ceiling and stone walls of the **Ristorante Asino Cotto** (translation is *cooked ass*). However, the only really unexpected offering on the avant-garde menu is a delicious Chocolate Mousse with Celery Syrup.

✉ Via dei Vascellari, 48

☎ +39 (0) 6 58 98 985 €€€€

❧ **Le Mani di Pasta** has a loyal clientele of local residents—who may be addicted to the Gorgonzola ice cream.

✉ Via dei Genovisi, 37

☎ +39 (0) 6 58 16 017 €€€

Open Houses
Rome Vaticano

11

Casa La Salle

Casa La Salle is owned by a community of Roman Catholic De La Salle Christian Brothers who pursue the order's mission of providing education for the underprivileged. The community's estate in Rome is the headquarters of the order and a section has been set aside for accommodating overnight guests. The guesthouse is run in a professional manner along hotel lines. Casa La Salle is located approximately 3 kilometres west of **St Peter's Basilica**.

❡ The casa has 250 single and twin rooms, all with en suite bathrooms. All guestrooms are serviced daily; a direct dial telephone service and an Internet connection are provided. A guestroom for the disabled is also available. The dining room is air-conditioned and all meals are served. Individual travellers as well as large groups can be catered for and use of function rooms and conference facilities can be provided. Take-away lunches and special meals can be arranged. Guests can spend time strolling or relaxing in the expansive gardens surrounding the building. Twenty-four-hour reception is provided and accommodation is offered all year round. The relics of the founder of the order, St John Baptist de la Salle, are in the chapel within the complex.

✉ Via Aurelia, 472
00165 Rome (RM)

🏨 from €44.00 pp,
including breakfast

☎ +39 (0) 6 66 69 81
📠 +39 (0) 6 66 00 0384

✉ prenotazioni@
casalasalle.com

☞ From **Roma Termini**
take the train to
Cornelia on Metro
line A. On reaching
Cornelia follow the
signs to the Piazza
Irnerio/Via Aurelia exit.

✝ **Sunday Mass**
Summer: 0830, 1100,
1200 & 1930
Winter: 0830, 0930,
1100, 1200 & 1800
Basilica Nostra Signora
di Guadalupe
Via Aurelia, 675
00165 Rome (RM)

♿ Discuss your needs in
advance of arriving,
ideally when booking.

⚥ Open to both men and
women

PLACES OF INTEREST ❧ **The Vatican**, one of the seven pilgrim churches of Rome, has its own post office and issues the Vatican stamps, which make an attractive change on a postcard home. Cards must be posted within the **Vatican City**. The Vatican also mints its own coins. The Vatican Pharmacy can make up prescriptions and the pharmacy sells certain pharmaceutical drugs not available in other parts of Italy.

❧ **The Vatican Christmas Concert** is traditionally held in the **Pope Pio Auditorium** in the Vatican each December with the proceeds going to the missions. Instigated at the wish of the late Pope John Paul II in the late 1980s, concerts in recent times have been cancelled by Pope Benedict XVI. In the past some performers have used the opportunity to express controversial personal opinions which may have had something to do with it.

❧ Inside the **Church of the Sacro Cuore del Suffragio** at Lungotevere, 12 in Prati is an unusual room known as the **Museo delle Anime dei Defunti o del Purgatorio** (*Museum of the Souls in Purgatory*), where the items on display are said to confirm the existence of an 'after-life'.

❧ Back in the 'present' the **Via Cola Rienzo**, which runs off the **Piazza del Risorgimento** near the Vatican, is lined with trendy clothes boutiques, jewellery and leather shops and a COIN department store. The shops in this area are much cheaper than those in downtown Rome. Streets such as the **Via Condotti** (off the Piazza di Spagna) and the **Via Veneto** (behind the Trinita dei Monti) are two of Rome's most sophisticated and expensive, lined with exclusive boutiques and stores, including **Ferragamo**, **Louis Vuitton**, **Furla**, **Valentino** and **Armani**.

❧ The **Isola Tiberina** (*Tiberina Island*) is a small island in the River Tiber and a miniature version of the Ile de France in Paris. The island lies between the **Ponte Garibaldi** and the **Ponte Palatino** which can be accessed via the **Ponte Cestio** or the **Ponte Fabricio**. The island is an oasis of calm away from the noise of the traffic and is a tiny city in itself with shops, a church, bars and cafés. An outdoor cinema festival is held on the island from mid-June to August.

Open Houses
Rome Vaticano

FOOD AND DRINK ❧ An inexpensive bite can be enjoyed at **La Pilotta da Mario**. Pizza and fresh, home-made pasta dominate the menu, with a couple of meat dishes listed as well. The service is friendly and the atmosphere warm.

✉ Via di Porta Cavalleggeri, 35, off Via Aurelia

☎ +39 (0) 6 63 26 43   €€

❡ **Franchi** is one of the city's best delis and **Castroni**, a gourmet grocery store next door, makes great Italian-style coffee. Pick up something delicious for a picnic or just to eat on the run.

✉ Via Cola di Rienzo, 200

❡ Another option is the **Mercato Rionale**, the local food market in the Via Cola di Rienzo near the Unità Square.

❡ **Ristorante Sora Lella** on Tiberina Island has been run by the same family for over 60 years. Somewhat rustic and welcoming in style, the restaurant serves traditional and modern Italian cuisine at moderate prices. Choose from the *a la carte* menu or from the degustation options which include a typical five course Roman-style tasting menu, and a vegetarian choice.

✉ Via Ponte Quattro Capi, 16

☎ +39 (0) 6 68 61 601   €€→€€€€

Casa Procura

Casa Procura is situated 1 kilometre from the **Vatican**, in a modern building where the peaceful atmosphere offers an escape from the hurley-burley outside. The house is run by the religious order of the Pallottine Missionary Sisters, an international Catholic congregation of nuns who have their headquarters in Rome and convents on every continent.

❡ The sisters have created a welcoming and convivial atmosphere where guests are encouraged to make themselves at home. The airy, simply furnished single and double guestrooms have en suite bathrooms and many have a balcony overlooking the dome of **St Peter's Basilica**. Other guestrooms share a bathroom on the same floor. Breakfast is the only meal available. Facilities include a small television room and a breakfast room. The sisters can often arrange tickets to the Pope's General Audience (each Wednesday) and to other religious events. Check-out on day of departure is 0900. No credit cards are accepted.

✉ Viale delle Mura Aurelie, 7ʙ
00165 Rome (ʀᴍ)

🛏 from €50.00 pp, including breakfast

📞 +39 (0) **6 39 36 351**
📠 +39 (0) **6 39 36 69 43**

✐ *info@procuramission ariepallottine.it*

☞ From **Roma Termini** take bus number 64 and get off at the Via di Porta Cavalleggeri.

✝ **Sunday Mass**
0700, 0830, 1000, 1100 & 1200
Church of San Gregorio ᴠɪɪ
Via del Cottolengo, 4
00165 Rome (ʀᴍ)

🎴 Open to both men and women

Open Houses
Rome Vaticano

PLACES OF INTEREST ❧ A room in the **Palazzo della Cancelleria** (*Palace of the Chancellery*) in the Piazza della Cancelleria is decorated with an enormous fresco of Pope Paul III by artist Georgio Vasari (1511–1574). Referred to as the '100 day painting' by Vasari's fellow artists, it was painted in a record 100 days. Reputedly, when he heard about this, Michelangelo commented: 'It looks like it'. The Papal Chancellery was built by Cardinal Raffaele Riario in the late 15th century, partly financed by the Cardinal's gambling winnings at cards.

❡ If you enjoy football you could watch a game at the **Stadio Olimpico** (*Olympic Stadium*) in Viale del Foro Italico, the home ground of the Roma and Lazio teams. In late 2007, the Vatican became the major sponsor of a local football club, AC Ancona. The club was purchased by the Vatican's sporting division in a bid to clean up Italian football.

❡ The **Castello Odescalchi** (*Odescalchi Castle*), a 15th-century lakeside castle in Bracciano, 55 kilometres north of Rome, was the wedding venue of actor Tom Cruise and Katie Holmes in November, 2006. The Cruise–Holmes wedding was not the first celebrity nuptials to take place in the castle chapel. In 1979 actress Isabella Rossellini married film director Martin Scorsese here. The castle and the small holiday town of **Bracciano** can be reached by train from Rome's Ostiense train station on the Viterbo line.

❡ The **Corsini Gallery**, at Via della Lungara, 10, is a small, state-owned gallery exhibiting works by Rubens, Caravaggio and Van Dyck, and early paintings by regional Italian artists. The paintings are the collection of Cardinal Neri Corsini (1685–1770), nephew of Pope Clement XII (1730–1740); the collection also includes artworks amassed by Pope Clement when he was Cardinal Lorenzo Corsini.

Hadrian's Villa and the **Tivoli Gardens** are approximately 30 kilometres east of Rome. Numerous attractions including statues, mosaics, magnificent gardens and fountains form part of Emperor Hadrian's extravagant abode. Details are available at any tourist office and pick-ups from most major hotels can be arranged.

The Villa Madama, in the Via di Villa Madama, is about 4 kilometres north of the convent. Once a sumptuous Roman villa designed by the painter Raphael (1483–1520) for the former Archbishop of Florence and then Cardinal, Giulio de Medici (1478–1574), it is now used by the government. However, the gardens of the estate are open to visitors.

FOOD AND DRINK ❦ Take the **Tram-ristorante**, Rome's mobile sightseeing restaurant. Groups of 28 or more can experience a unique style of dining whilst seeing the sights from the comfort of a restored tramcar.

✎ *cpasogno@romeguide.it*　　€€€

The Ristorante La Vittoria, near the convent, is the type of restaurant everyone should have as a 'local'. It is not fancy, no panoramic view, but friendly and welcoming with good honest home-style cooking at affordable prices. It is sometimes possible to hear the services at St Peter's when sitting at the tables outside.

✉ Via delle Fornaci, 15

☏ +39 (0) 6 63 18 58　　€€

The Ristorante L'Antico Porto near Castel Sant'Angelo is long established. The restaurant specialises in all types of seafood and the menu includes pasta with seafood, lobster, prawn and fish dishes and a handful of selections to keep the carnivores at bay.

✉ Via Federico Cesiums, 36

☏ +39 (0) 6 32 33 661　　€€€€

Open Houses
Rome Vaticano

Casa Santa Maria alle Fornaci

Casa Santa Maria alle Fornaci is owned and run by the Trinitari Fathers, members of an international Catholic congregation of priests, nuns and laity. The padres in Rome have opened their house to pilgrims and tourists visiting the city, be they individuals, groups or families. The establishment is situated just 500 metres from the **Vatican** in an area of Rome dominated in ancient times by brick kilns, the remains of which can still be seen in buildings in the area today.

❦ The casa is run in the style of a hotel. The convent's 50 guestrooms are small and simply furnished and all have an en suite bathroom and air-conditioning. Rooms are available in single, double and triple configurations and can be accessed by a lift. Breakfast is the only meal served. Facilities include a television lounge and a computer and fax machine are available for the use of guests. The guesthouse is open all year and credit cards are accepted here. There are no facilities for car parking.

OPEN HOUSE

✉ Piazza di Santa Maria alle Fornaci, 27 00165 Rome (RM)

🛏 from €48.00 pp, including breakfast

📞 +39 (0) 6 39 36 76 32
📠 +39 (0) 6 39 36 67 95

✉ cffornaci@tin.it

☞ From **Roma Termini** take the suburban line train to **San Pietro** from where it is a short walk to the convent. Or take bus number 64 from Via Einaudi in front of Roma Termini which stops at the San Pietro train station.

✝ **Daily Mass**
0900, 1000, 1100, 1200 & 1700
Sunday Mass
0900, 1030, 1130, 1215, 1300, 1600 & 1730 St Peter's Basilica Vatican City State 11020 (VA)

⚭ Open to both men and women

PLACES OF INTEREST ✒ **Papal Audiences** are usually held inside the Vatican complex on Wednesdays at approximately 1030. In July and August the Holy Father holidays at his summer residence in **Castel Gandolfo**, where the General Audience is held during this time.

❡ Free tickets to the Papal Audience are available from the **Office of the Prefecture of the Pontifical Household** next to the Basilica of St Peter. To locate the office enter from the Portone di Bronzo, the large bronze doors under the colonnades on the right hand side when facing the basilica. The office is open from 0900 to 1300 on Monday and from 0900 to 1800 on Tuesday. Tickets can be arranged by contacting the Office of the Prefecture of the Pontifical Household on the numbers below. Your local parish priest may be able to arrange tickets for you or, if staying in a convent in Rome, you could also check with the nuns there. Tickets can also be requested for Pontifical ceremonies.

☎ +39 (0) 6 69 88 48 57
📠 +39 (0) 6 69 88 58 63

❡ To save waiting in long queues, another option is to book tickets to the **Vatican Museums, Gardens, Sistine Chapel and Papal Audiences** in advance using a local tour company. Many have English-speaking guides and reservations staff. Your travel agent could arrange this for you. *MyVaticanTour.com* is the tour company officially endorsed by the Vatican. Guided tours of the Museums, Gardens and Sistine Chapel are also conducted by the Vatican and can be arranged by faxing the number below. Entrance to the Vatican Museums is free on the last Sunday of each month between 0900 and 1345. No tickets are needed to attend the **Papal Blessing in St Peter's Square** each Sunday at noon.

✉ Guided Tours of the Museums, Gardens & Sistine Chapel
📠 +39 (0) 6 69 88 51

❡ To arrange a tour of the **necropolis** beneath the Vatican, including a visit to the tomb of St Peter, contact the **Vatican Excavations Office** with your request. Bookings should be made 8 weeks in advance. **The Vatican Grottoes**, where past Popes are buried, including Pope John Paul II, are open daily from 0700.

Vatican Excavations Office
☎ +39 (0) 6 69 88 53 18
📠 +39 (0) 6 69 87 30 17
✉ scavi@fsp.va

Open Houses
Rome Vaticano

❧ **Confessions** (*Sacrament of Penance*) are heard in a number of different languages in St Peter's Basilica between 0700–1230 and 1600–1800 Monday to Saturday and between 0700–1300 and 1600–1800 on Sunday. During winter the afternoon confessions commence at 1500.

❧ To obtain a **Certificate of Papal Blessing** to hang in your home or as a gift for a birthday, First Communion, wedding or other celebration then visit the **Papal Blessings Office** on the Via del Pellegrino to the right of the Piazza San Pietro. Certificates take some weeks to process but can be posted on. Prices vary according to size, etc and start at around €35.00. A Papal Blessing can also be ordered through your local parish priest.

❧ The Vatican has an information office for pilgrims and tourists which can be contacted in the following ways:

✑ upt@scv.va

☎ +39 (0) 6 69 88 44 66

☎ +39 (0) 6 69 88 48 66

📠 +39 (0) 6 69 88 51 00

❧ Send supportive messages to Pope Benedict:

✑ benedictxvi@vatican.va

✉ His Holiness, Pope Benedict xvi
Apostolic Palace
00120 Vatican City (va)

FOOD AND DRINK ❦ The **Vatican Museum Caféteria** has a large informal-style eating area which is located near the Vatican Museums. The caféteria offers a wide choice of hot and cold food such as pizza, sandwiches, soups, pasta, salad, cakes and pastries.

✉ Vatican Museum Caféteria   €€

❧ During the days when he could venture out for a casual meal, (ex) Cardinal Joseph Ratzinger would often eat at the **Cantina Tirolese**, an hospitable Austrian restaurant and wine cellar. The Pope's favourite table was number 6.

✉ Via Vitelleschi, 23

☎ +39 (0) 6 68 13 52 97   €€€

❧ If Tuscany isn't on the travel itinerary the next best thing could be tasting it at the **Ristorante L'Antica Griglia Toscana**. While there are no vineyards, olive groves and medieval hill towns on the horizon, there is Florentine steak, pappardelle and plenty of Chianti Classico.

✉ Via dei Gracchi, 86

☎ +39 (0) 6 32 00 903   €€€€

Open Houses
Rome Vaticano

Hotel Casa Bonus Pastor

Casa Bonus Pastor is a modern 3-star hotel owned
by the Vatican and staffed by both religious and lay
people. It is situated in large grounds in a park behind
the **Vatican Museums**, where in a previous life it was a
gracious old palace.

❡ The casa is run along hotel lines and has 200 modern,
air-conditioned guestrooms all with an en suite
bathroom, hairdryer, satellite television, direct dial
telephone and a digital safe. The hotel has a bar and
restaurant on the fifth floor with sweeping views over
the city. The restaurant serves home-style Italian cuisine
and is open for all meals. There is a lift to all floors, a
24-hour reception service and plenty of parking. The
casa has wheelchair access and credit cards are accepted.

✉ Via Aurelia, 208
00165 Rome (RM)

🛏 from €65.00 pp,
including breakfast

☎ +39 (0) **6 69 87 12 82**
✆ +39 (0) **6 69 87 14 35**

✉ bonuspastor@glauco.it

☞ Take bus number
46 from the Piazza
Venezia or bus number
49 from Piazza Cavour
which stop near the
hotel.

✝ **Sunday Mass**
1100 & 1900
Church of Madonna del
Riposo
Via Aurelia, 327
00165 Rome (RM)

♿ Discuss your needs in
advance of arriving,
ideally when booking.

⚭ Open to both men and
women

Open Houses
Rome Vaticano

PLACES OF INTEREST ❧ Check your watch when you hear the cannon shot fired from the **Piazzale del Gianicolo** on Gianicolo (*Janiculum*) **Hill**. This takes place every day at precisely midday and stems from a custom first begun in 1847 at Castel Sant'Angelo. The cannon was moved to its present location in 1904.

❧ From the **Porta San Pancrazio** in Trastevere the **Passeggiata del Gianicolo** leads to the Piazza Giuseppe Garibaldi near the top of the **Gianicolo Hill**, (and on to the Vatican) from where the domes and sculpted church spires reveal the grandeur of the city. (While the hill offers some of the best views of Rome it is not one of the 'official' Seven Hills.) The public park and gardens on Gianicolo offer a blessed escape from the noise and commotion of the city. During August a program of theatre, music and dance is held in the piazza.

❧ The cavernous emporium the **Cereria Di Giorgio**, in Via San Francesco di Sales at the bottom of the **Gianicolo Hill**, stocks candles of all shapes, colours and sizes. The company supplies the Vatican and many of Rome's churches as well as off-the-street customers.

❧ Climbing the **Cupola of St Peter's Basilica** is a sweaty, 323-step ascent. There is a lift for the less energetic. Either way, the spectacular views from the top make it all worthwhile.

❡ The **ruins of Ostia Antica**, Rome's ancient maritime port, are just a Metro or boat ride away. Take the Metro to station Ostia Antica where, during the summer months, musical and theatrical shows are presented in the ruins of the old Roman theatre. Each Friday, Saturday and Sunday at 1000 a boat departs from the Ponti Marconi in Rome for Ostia Antica.

❡ The master perfumers of the Durante family create the most desirable fragrances, oils, soaps and perfumed candles. All are on sale at the **Pro Fumum Durante**, at Viale Angelico, 87, one of the family's four fragrance shops in Rome.

❡ The **Trionfale food and flower market** in Via Andrea Doria sells only the highest quality produce and seasonal specialities. It is located near the Ottaviano Metro station, within walking distance of the Vatican. Pick up some tasty snacks to stock up the refrigerator or select a garden-fresh lunch.

FOOD AND DRINK ❡ Restaurants in the Vatican area can be touristy, overpriced and sub-standard. However, priests and religious eat at restaurants too and as they know this area well and have limited funds it could be a good (and economical) idea to follow their lead.

❡ However, it is not unusual to find a cleric or a cardinal dining in the refined surrounds of the **Taverna Giulia**. This is an upscale restaurant serving Ligurian cuisine where pasta, herbs, pesto and foccacia are staples and a heavyhanded use of garlic and olive oil is the norm.

✉ Vicolo dell'Oro, 23

☎ +39 (0) 6 68 69 768   €€€€

❡ For something cheaper and serving traditional Roman fare try the **Ristorante Il Matriciano** where the quality is much higher than the price.

✉ Via dei Gracchi, 55

☎ +39 (0) 6 32 12 327   €€

❡ Vatican staffers can often be found tucking into the seafood, pasta and risotto offerings at the **Osteria Venerina**, between the Vatican and Castel Sant'Angelo.

✉ Via del Mascherino, 80

☎ +39 (0) 6 45 44 84 33   €€€

15

Hotel Casa Tra Noi

The Hotel Casa Tra Noi is run by the Catholic religious order the Tra Noi Movement, and is situated in the **Vatican City** area less than 1 kilometre from **St Peter's Square** and near the fringe of the **Villa Doria Pamphili**, the largest park in Rome. The single, double and triple guestrooms all have en suite bathrooms, a telephone for inbound calls and air-conditioning.

❧ The restaurant serves reasonably priced Italian home-style cuisine and all meals are available on a 'meal plan' basis if required. The hotel has a bar serving alcohol, soft drinks, tea and coffee.

❧ Ideal for groups and meetings, the convention hall holds 250 people. The hotel is an uphill walk from the railway station, which may be a problem for the less mobile. Tra Noi has its own secure, private car park. Credit cards are accepted.

❧ The area around the Hotel Casa Tra Noi is not well serviced by restaurants, cafés or shops.

✉ Via di Monte del Gallo, 113
00165 Rome (RM)

🏨 from €63.00 pp, including breakfast

📞 +39 (0) **6 39 38 73 55**
📠 +39 (0) **6 39 38 74 46**

📧 tranoi@tiscali.it

🚆 From **Roma Termini** take the suburban line train to **San Pietro**. The convent is approximately 1 kilometre from San Pietro station.

✝ **Sunday Mass**
1000 & 1200
(may change during August)
Church of Sant'Onofrio
Piazza Sant'Onofrio, 2
00165 Rome (RM)

⚥ Open to both men and women

PLACES OF INTEREST ✔ Well used by locals walking their dogs, joggers and workers taking time out, the **Villa Doria Pamphili** is the largest park in Rome.

❧ Within the vast estate of grottos, statues, villas, gardens and gushing fountains is the **Museo di Villa Doria Pamphili**, in the Villa Vecchia at Via Aurelia Antica, 183; it is dedicated to the history of the Roman villa.

❧ The residence of the Russian Ambassador, **Villa Abamelek**, is also situated in the park and is the setting for concerts and cultural events during the summer.

❧ The medieval town of **Anagni**, 70 kilometres east of the Vatican, has a rich religious heritage and was the preferred summer abode of Popes before **Castel Gandolfo** became popular. During the 13th and 14th centuries Anagni produced four Popes, the last being Pope Boniface VIII (1294–1303). It is a matter of conjecture that Pope Boniface came to the throne by dishonestly persuading Pope Celestine V to renounce his Papacy. Celestine resigned and is said to have made the prediction:

> *You have stolen the chair like a fox: your temper will rule in it like a lion; but you will die like a dog.*
>
> THE ENGLISH REFORMATION, FRANCIS CHARLES MASSINGBERD (1800–1872), JOHN W. PARKER, LONDON 1857.

Boniface did indeed die a broken man after being held in prison by another enemy, Phillip IV of France. While the **Papal Palace** in Anagni can be visited, the interior of the 11th-century **Anagni Cathedral** and the classical Byzantine frescoes in the cathedral crypt are more awe-inspiring.

Open Houses
Rome Vaticano

❧ The **Auditorium Parco della Musica** in the Flaminio area of Rome is often the venue for performances of the prestigious **National Academy of St Cecilia** and for visiting international classical music groups. In summer the Academy performs outdoors at the **Baths of Caracella** or at the **Villa Giulia** which was once the palace of Pope Julius III (1550–1555). The **National Etruscan Museum** is inside the Villa Giulia, which is located on the north-western edge of the Villa Borghese.

❧ A tall, bronze figure of St Peter stands on a pedestal in **St Peter's Basilica** and is attributed with some uncertainty to 13th-century sculptor Arnolfo di Cambio (c1245–c1302).

❧ It is believed that the statue holds the keys to The Kingdom of Heaven and it is a time-honoured tradition for pilgrims to touch the statue's bronze right foot, in the hope that St Peter will open the gates for them. Not surprisingly the statue's foot has become worn down over the centuries.

❧ Religious curios and inexpensive *objets d'art* are on sale at the **Vatican Emporium** at Via del Mascherino, 42, which carries a varied range as well as gifts and souvenirs. Similar shops in the Vatican area are **Comandini** at Borgo Pio, 151 and the **Savelli** shop at Via Paolo VI, 27. They all offer a post-home service.

FOOD AND DRINK ❧ Each Thursday, Friday and Saturday evening at 2100 the cruise boat *Agrippina Maggiore* departs from the wharf at Ponte Sant'Angelo on a sightseeing voyage down the **River Tiber**. Nibbles and wine are served during the 2-hour journey.

☎ +39 (0) 6 97 74 54 98   €€€

❧ Take the kids to try one of the 40 varieties of pizza at the **l'Isola della Pizza**, near the Vatican. This informal, easy-going restaurant has been a favourite with the local residents for more than 20 years. Eat indoors or on the terrace.

✉ Via degli Scipione, 45

☎ +39 (0) 6 39 73 34 83   €€€

❧ Enjoy the 'craic' of the Irish! **Morrison's Irish Pub**, where the Guinness on tap is said to be as good as that found in Ireland.

✉ Via Ennio Quirino Visconti

☎ +39 (0) 6 32 22 265   €

Campania & The Amalfi Coast

ONE OF EUROPE'S MOST POPULAR holiday destinations, Campania is world renowned for its breathtaking vistas along the **Amalfi coastline**. **Naples**, just over an hour by train from Rome, is the gateway to the legendary resorts of the region that stretch from **Castellammare** in the north to **Amalfi** and **Salerno** in the south. Offshore, the glamour of the **Isle of Capri** beckons.

Each year countless tourists are attracted to the ruins of the Roman towns of **Herculaneum** and **Pompeii**, devastated in 79AD by the eruption of **Mt Vesuvius**.

Others head for the Grecian temples of **Paestum** further south. These days, urban sprawl is slowly pushing farms and vineyards up the slopes of Vesuvius, just as they were centuries ago. Indeed, some of the local grape varieties—Fiano, Aglianico and Greco—stem from those of ancient times.

During the 4th century Emperor Constantine the Great ensured the spread of Christianity throughout Italy when he rejected Paganism and the mighty Roman Empire turned towards more Christian beliefs. Monasteries and convents were established throughout the country and many of those in **Campania** still actively follow the long-established tradition of offering pilgrims and other travellers a home-away-from-home.

Open Houses
Campania & The Amalfi Coast Capri

16

Villa Helios

Villa Helios was built in the early 20th century and is run by a religious foundation, a local parish and the Franciscan Sisters of the Sacred Heart who donate all the profits of the guesthouse to charity. The villa is in the centre of **Capri**, and overlooks the **Mediterranean Ocean**. The renowned **Piazza Umberto I**, the main town square, is at the end of the Via Croce. Located in a quiet area, the villa's accommodation is spread over two floors. ¶ All guestrooms have en suite bathrooms, air-conditioning and many have a panoramic view over the **Bay of Naples**. There is a television lounge on the ground floor and a small chapel once used by the original occupants, the Sisters of Santa Elisabetta, is upstairs. The villa is surrounded by lush gardens and an orchard. There is a 5-night minimum stay in summer.

✉ Via Croce, 4
80073 Capri (NA)

🛏 from €55.00 pp,
including breakfast

📞 +39 (0) **81 83 70 240**
📠 +39 (0) **81 83 70 240**

✉ info@villahelios.it

☞ Capri is only accessible by boat. Ferries, hydrofoils and water taxis run regularly from the ports of **Naples, Positano, Amalfi** and **Sorrento**. On reaching Capri there is a funicular as well as taxis to take visitors up the hill to the Piazzetta Umberto I. The villa is a few minutes' walk from here.

✝ **Sunday Mass**
0800, 1030 & 1200
Ex Cathedral of San Stefano
Piazza Umberto I
80073 Capri (NA)

♿ Discuss your needs in advance of arriving, ideally when booking.

⚥ Open to both men and women

PLACES OF INTEREST ❧ The Isle of Capri is divided into two areas with Capri on one side and Anacapri on the other. Capri is probably best known for its **blue grotto**, (there is a green grotto as well) and tours to the cave depart regularly from the **Marina Grande**. The town of Anacapri can be reached in a few minutes by bus from the Piazza Umberto I. A chair lift scales up from Anacapri to the island's highest point, Mt Solaro.

❧ The **Church and Hermitage of Santa Maria a Cetrella** on **Mt Solaro** is dedicated to sailors and fishermen and was established during the 15th century and used at various times by Franciscan and Dominican monks as a place of retreat. The church has been restored and it is now open for visitors, though not every day. Occasional religious services are conducted in the church.

❧ Writer Graham Greene (1904–1991) once lived and wrote in the **Villa Il Rosaio** in Via Ceselle in Anacapri near the pinnacle of **Mt Solaro**. One of his favourite haunts was the ever-popular trattoria, da Gemma at Via Madre Serafina, 6, behind the Piazza Umberto. Graham Greene's signed photograph, along with those of other celebrity guests, mostly Hollywood movie stars who once dined here, adorn the walls.

❧ The **Carthusia I Profumi di Capri** (*Carthusian Perfumes of Capri*) in Via Camerelle stocks the local perfumes which were originally created by the monks of the Carthusian Monastery of San Giacomo in Capri during the 14th century. The perfumery has a factory shop on Via Federico Serena. The monks' original methods and recipes are still used today. The medieval monastery is open to visitors.

Open Houses
Campania & The Amalfi Coast Capri

❦ At the end of a special meal why not indulge in a little of the locally made Limoncello liqueur. Work off any excesses on one of the scenic pathways which run for miles all over the island. Maps of walking trails can be obtained from the local tourist office. Near the **Villa Helios** is the path along the Via Krupp which winds its way to the **Marina Piccola**, a 4-kilometre round trip. British singer (Dame) Gracie Fields (1898–1979) lived for more than 30 years at **Villa Canzone del Mare** (*Song of the Sea*) near the marina. After her death the house was purchased by the Swarvoski family, of crystal fame.

❦ Explore the caves, coves and beaches of the Capri coastline in a *gozzi*, a traditional wooden fishing boat, which can be hired on the marina.

❦ Take home a pair of bejewelled handmade sandals from the **Canfora Boutique** on Via Camerelle near the **Piazzetta Quisisana** where a family of craftsmen have been adding sparkle to jaded feet for over 60 years. Sandal 'к' was a favourite of Jackie Onassis.

❦ *Capri* means *goats* in English.

FOOD AND DRINK ❦ Established around 1870, the **Trattoria da Gemma** is still operated by the descendants of the family who entertained author Grahame Greene and his literary friends in the 50s, 60s and 70s. Unlike Grahame Greene, today's guests can dine on the terrace if they choose and enjoy the seafood, the pasta, and the Caprese-style pizza along with the view.

✉ Via Madre Serafina, 6

☎ +39 (0) 81 83 70 461   €€€€

❦ The **Limoncello di Capri**, at Via Roma, 79, stocks this tangy, refreshing drink made from locally grown lemons. Delectable, creamy Limoncello chocolates are also sold here. There is another Limoncello shop in Anacapri.

✉ Via Roma, 79

☎ +39 (0) 81 83 75 561

❦ **Ristorante La Canzone del Mare** is situated oceanside at the Marina Piccola in the bathing centre originally established by English singer Gracie Fields. The restaurant is open for long lunches (and a swim or two) between May and September. Try the local tri-coloured speciality of the island, Insalata Caprese (Capri salad).

☎ +39 (0) 81 83 70 104   €€€€€

Open Houses

Campania & The Amalfi Coast Pagani

OPEN HOUSE

Monastero di Santa Maria della Purita

A Catholic monastery has occupied this site since the 12th century. The Monastery of Santa Maria della Purita lies in a garden of citrus trees, next to the Church of the Sanctuary of the Child Jesus of Prague, where a wooden statue of the Infant Jesus of Prague has stood above the altar for 4 centuries. The monastery and guesthouse is under the control of the religious order the **Piccoli Discepoli della Croce** (*Little Disciples of the Cross*) and is situated 18 kilometres inland from **Salerno**, within easy motoring reach of the **Amalfi Coast** and the villages around the **Gulf of Salerno**.

❧ The accommodation offered to pilgrims and tourists is in modestly furnished guestrooms of single, double and multiple configuration. All guestrooms have an en suite bathroom. The homely monastery restaurant caters to simple tastes in Italian cuisine with an emphasis on healthy food. All meals are available if required. Lunch and dinner are served with wine (optional) and guests are sometimes offered a glass of home-made Limoncello to finish off.

❧ There is a sheltered, shady garden area where guests can relax or have meals. Facilities include a library, a chapel and on-site parking (limited). Musical and other cultural events are held in the monastery, mainly in summer.

✉ Corso Padovano, 71 84016 Pagani (sa)

🏨 from €28.00 pp, including breakfast

📞 +39 (0) **81 91 63 85**
📠 +39 (0) **81 91 63 85**

✉ *puritas@tiscalinet.it*

☞ Take the train to Pagani station which is almost 1 kilometre from the convent or to Nocera Inferiore which is approximately 2 kilometres away.

✝ **Sunday Mass**
0700, 0800, 0900, 1000, 1100, 1200 & 1800
Basilica of Sant'Alfonso Maria de Liguori 84016 Pagani (na)

⚭ Open to both men and women

Open Houses
Campania & The Amalfi Coast Pagani

PLACES OF INTEREST ❦ **Pagani** is
situated at the foot of **the Latteri
Mountains**, 24 kilometres north of the
town of Ravello. It is a few hundred
metres from the entrance to the Napoli–
Salerno autostrada.

❧ The Alfonsiano Museum and the
**Basilica of Sant'Alfonso Maria de'
Liguori**, in **Pagani**, are shrines to
St Alphonsus Liguori (1696–1787),
founder of the Catholic Redemptorist
Order. St Alphonsus is buried in the
basilica. Nearby, in the 11th-century
Sanctuary of Mater Domini in **Nocera**,
the King of Naples and Sicily, Charles I
D'Anjou (1227–1285), son of Louis VIII of
France, is entombed. Charles' autocratic
rule as King of Sicily was responsible
for the 1282 Easter uprising known as
the 'Sicilian Vespers' when the people
of Sicily successfully revolted against
the French. The uprising is said to have
begun at the time Vespers was due to
commence in the Church of the Holy
Spirit in **Palermo**.

❧ **Ravello**, south of Pagani, is known as
a town of music and during the **Ravello
Festival of Classical Music** concerts
are performed outdoors against the
panoramic backdrops and historical
settings of the Amalfi Coast. The festival
is held through the summer each year
and some events take place amongst
the Grecian temples at **Paestum**, 60
kilometres south of **Pagani**. The well-
preserved remains of three mammoth
Greco-Roman temples dating back to
6BC still dominate the archaeological
site at **Paestum**.

❡ **Salerno**, located on the Gulf of Salerno, has for centuries been a town of ceramists—a tradition which continues today. The Museum of Ceramics, in the **Villa Guariglia** in the ancient Etruscan town of **Vietri sul Mare**, displays a permanent collection of pottery and stoneware from the 17th century and beyond. Visiting exhibitions are hosted and summer concerts are held in the gardens of the estate.

❡ The stone pathways of the **Villa Cimbrone Gardens**, at Via Santa Chiara, 26, **Ravello** lead past temples and fountains, sculptures and rose gardens to the *terrazzo dell' infinità* and to what has been described by American novelist Gore Vidal (b 1925) as 'the most beautiful view in the world'. Equally as alluring is the picturesque medieval town of **Atrani**, which is perched on a rocky outcrop just a few minutes' stroll along the coastal walking path from the larger and more touristy hub of **Amalfi**. Atrani is less than 1 kilometre from Amalfi along the coastal walking path.

FOOD AND DRINK There are a number of pizzerias and family-style restaurants in the **Via Tramontana** and around the **Piazza Sant'Alfonso** in Pagani. However, if you are heading for the Amalfi area, the waterfront of the tiny town of **Atrani** is lined with eating places. You could try the **Ristorante Pizzeria Le Arcate** where the seafood pizzas are equal to the stunning sea views.

📞+39 (o) 89 87 13 67 €€€

❡ A few kilometres west of Paestum the **Tenuta Vannulo** organic buffalo farm, near the town of **Capaccio**, produces a rich, tasty buffalo mozzarella. Visitors can wander around the vast estate, inspect the buffalo, watch mozzarella being made and buy a chunk to take away.

✉ Via Galileo Galilei

📞+39 (o) 828 72 47 65

❡ A food market is held in the main square in the town of **Nocera Inferiore**, near **Pagani**, each Monday morning.

Casa per Ferie la Culla

La Culla is an 18th-century Italian villa atop a small hill approximately 1.5 kilometres from the centre of **Sorrento**. Run by an order of Catholic Oblate Sisters who also have a convent guesthouse in Rome, the two-storey building is bordered by wide, covered arched terraces and loggias, all with panoramic views over the **Bay of Naples** and to **Mount Vesuvius**. Many of the upstairs, front-facing guestrooms have the same spectacular outlook. The guestrooms are spacious and comfortable and all have en suite bathrooms. Rooms are cleaned every day, but guests are requested to make their own beds. All meals are available but reservations are necessary. The villa is set back from the road and is very quiet.

❧ La Culla is a popular holiday house for many Italian families during school holiday periods as the beach is within walking distance. A small, outdoor, vine-covered seating area off the courtyard provides a shady corner in which to relax. There is a bus stop outside the convent. Car parking on the convent grounds is extremely limited.

✉ Corso Italia, 377
80097 Sorrento (NA)

🛏 from €35.00 pp

☎ +39 (0) **81 87 81 797**
✆ +39 (0) **81 87 81 797**

✉ laculla@libero.it

☞ Take the train to **Sorrento** and take a taxi to the convent which is 1.5 kilometres from Sorrento station.

✝ **Sunday Mass**
1000 & 1115
Church of Santissima Trinità
Via Gennaro Maresca
Piano di Sorrento
80063 Sorrento (NA)

⚕ Open to both men and women

PLACES OF INTEREST❧ The privately run **Circumvesuviana commuter train** originates in Naples and terminates at **Sorrento**, from where buses leave regularly for **Amalfi**, 30 kilometres east. The bus is an inexpensive way to see the local sights and the views are astonishing. To extract maximum value out of the tiny fare sit on the ocean side. But don't look down—and hang on tight as you lurch around the hairpin bends! The drivers seem to be in training for the next Grand Prix.

❦ You can get off the bus at any of the little towns that take your fancy. But try not to miss **Positano**, even though it's a dozens-of-steps hike down to the beach and back. Be warned that this steep route is lined with designer boutiques, some selling locally made one-off creations and the walk can prove to be as hard on the pocket as it is on the legs.

❦ The Circumvesuviana travels north to **Ercolano**, the station before **Pompeii** where taxis wait to take tourists up to **Mt Vesuvius**. A road runs almost to the top of Vesuvius but to view the crater you need to walk the last 200 metres or so. The Circumvesuviana also stops at Pompeii station, just steps from the famous ruins. It's a pleasant, easy walk in theory, but you may find yourself running the gauntlet of souvenir sellers.

❦ The Annual **Sorrento Summer of Music Festival** from July to September is held behind the much-photographed, medieval arches of the Convent of St Francis in **Sorrento**, home to a community of Franciscan friars. The convent cloisters have their origins in the 8th century. The festival attracts international guest artists who perform classical and chamber music and jazz.

❦ Take home some Mediterranean flavour from the locally owned **Louise** shop at Via dei Mulini, 22, **Positano**. It features some of the most brightly coloured women's shirts and blouses on the coast. Styles range from elegant to casual.

Open Houses
Campania & The Amalfi Coast Sorrento

FOOD AND DRINK ✉ The recipient of 2 Michelin stars, the **Ristorante Don Alfonso**, run by the Laccarino family, is on a magnificent estate near the centre of the town of **Sant'Agata sui Due Goti** in the hills behind Sorrento, approximately 30 minutes by car from La Culla; or you could take the bus which leaves every half an hour from Sorrento train station. The restaurant specialises in contemporary Mediterranean cuisine and the olive oil—as well as the herbs, vegetables and fruit served in the restaurant—are all produced on the Alfonso family farm. The wine list includes the best Italian labels and if you are too weary to drive back to the convent you can always stay the night.

☎ +39 (0) 81 87 80 026   €€€€€

❦ **Vizi & Sfizi** in Sorrento stock an enticing selection of locally produced food, wine and gourmet gifts and offer a post-home service.

✉ Via Fuoro, 22

☎ +39 (0) 81 87 73 854

❦ The **Ristorante Vela Bianca** in Sorrento overlooks the bay and the yachts moored in the marina below. This is a warm, welcoming and stylish restaurant with an innovative menu based around pasta and seafood.

✉ Via Marina Piccola, 5

☎ +39 (0) 81 87 81 144   €€€€

❦ The **Sorrento Cooking School**, in Sant'Agnello, near Sorrento, conducts 4-hour cooking classes in English after which participants share their creations at the dining table.

✉ Viale dei Pini, 52

☎ +39 (0) 81 87 83 255

Tuscany

TUSCANY'S ETRUSCAN ROOTS are a source of endless fascination to art and history buffs. But ruins and priceless artworks aside, the many best-selling memoirs detailing Tuscan daily life have only made the region increasingly popular. **Medieval hill towns** may be busier than ever but Tuscany also has over 200 kilometres of coastline, lively seaside cities, beaches and thermal springs. Marble is mined in this region and the area is crisscrossed with hiking paths and pilgrim trails.

Wine is the lifeblood of the region and while Tuscany might be famous for Chianti (the genuine article has a black rooster on the neck of the bottle), the walled, hilltop town of **San Gimignano**, perched above ancient vineyards, produces one of Tuscany's oldest wines, the crisp and delicious white, Vernaccia. Those partial to a dessert wine will prefer Tuscany's Vin Santo or 'holy wine'; a classic sweet wine, although of debatable religious significance, it is produced throughout the province. Try it with biscotti in the dining room of a monastery or convent guesthouse.

Open Houses
Tuscany Cortona

Casa Betania

The convent is almost a kilometre from the town's main Piazza Repubblica, in a peaceful hillside location just outside the city's ancient Etruscan walls. It is run by the Catholic order of the Poor Sisters of the Sacred Stigmata of St Francis of Assisi as a place of welcome for singles, couples, groups and families who are visiting the hill town of Cortona. Tourists and those wishing to spend a few days in a calm, peaceful atmosphere can take advantage of the sisters' hospitality.

❡ The house was renovated in 2002 and many of the airy and spacious, single, double and triple guestrooms now have en suite bathrooms. Other rooms share a bathroom on the same floor. All meals are available and local restaurants and cafés are not too far away. The convent garden is scattered with tables and chairs and overlooks the villages and farms of the Chiana Valley. Parking is available.

✉ Via Gino Severini, 50
52044 Cortona (AR)

🛏 from €30.00 pp,
including breakfast

📞 +39 (0) 575 63 04 23
📠 +39 (0) 575 63 04 23

✉ info@
casaperferiebetania.com

☞ The nearest train stations are Camucia, 5 kilometres south of the convent and Terontola which is a further 7 kilometres south of Camucia. Local buses leave both stations for the centre of Cortona. A taxi is usually available.

✝ Sunday Mass
Summer: 1030 & 1700
Winter: 1030 & 1630
Santuario Le Celle
Località Le Celle
52044 Cortona (AR)

Open to both men and women

PLACES OF INTEREST ✦ **Cortona** is the home of author Frances Mayes who wrote the best-selling memoir *Under the Tuscan Sun*. The house at the centre of the book is *Bramasole* on the Viale Passerini on the eastern outskirts of the town. To get to the house, walk past the Tennis Club, and up the viale Passerini for 1 kilometre. *Bramasole* is on your left. It is believed that after a public swimming pool was built below the property, Frances purchased another house in the hills behind *Bramasole* which she and her husband Ed plan to restore.

❡ **Cortona** is 40 kilometres north of **Pienza**, the village used in the filming of scenes from the movie *The English Patient*. Scenes were filmed on **Pienza's Piazza Pio II** and in the hilltop **Monastery of Sant'Anna** in Camprena, (see Additional Accommodation) 6 kilometres from Pienza. The interior of the **Church of San Francesco** in **Arezzo** was also used. Arezzo is 28 kilometres north of Cortona.

❡ The isolated 13th-century **Santuario Le Celle**, embedded into the craggy ledges of **Monte Sant'Egidio**, 3.5 kilometres from Cortona, is where St Francis of Assisi (1182–1226) lived towards the end of his life. His monastery and the cell which he once occupied can be visited.

❡ In a custom stemming from medieval times, the town of **Castiglion Fiorentino**, a small hilltop settlement of Etruscan origin 11 kilometres north of Cortona, celebrates with a *Palio* (horse race around the main town square) on the third Sunday in June.

Open Houses
Tuscany Cortona

❡ The collection of the local **Diocesan Museum** in **Cortona's Piazza del Duomo** includes two works by Dominican friar and painter Fra Angelico (c1395–1455) including one of his three versions of the *Annunciation*. Fra Angelico lived at the convent during the time he was a novice (priest).

❡ The **Stations of the Cross** on the outskirts of Cortona are a series of mosaics representing Christ's journey to Calvary by Italian artist Gino Severini (1883–1966) and line the (steep) route of the **Via Margherita**. The line of Stations end at the **Church of Santa Margherita**. The incorrupt body of St Margherita of Cortona lies near the main altar.

⚜ Sunday Mass 0800, 1000
    Summer: 1700; Winter: 1600

❡ The **Tuscan Sun Festival**, held each August in Cortona, is a 2-week long festival of music and art embracing food and wine classes, book readings and even health and beauty activities and events. Classical music is the major theme of the festival which attracts some of Europe's most talented musicians.

FOOD AND DRINK ✎ Cortona has a range of restaurants to suit all pockets. The elegant restaurant **Osteria del Teatro** would befit a special occasion.
✉ Via Maffei, 2
✆ +39 (0) 575 630 556   €€€€

❡ The family-owned **Trattoria Dardano** in the old town has a casual, mellow atmosphere and a menu of Tuscan favourites.
✉ Via Dardano, 24
✆ +39 (0) 575 60 19 44   €€€

❡ Alternatively, sit under the Tuscan stars at **La Tufa** on the town's outskirts, a well-priced family restaurant and pizzeria.
✉ Ossaia di Cortona, 67
✆ +39 (0) 575 67 77 17   €€

❡ The well-known residence of Frances Mayes has been honoured with a luscious red wine, 'Bramasole', produced by the local vineyard **La Braccesca** and sometimes available in the local restaurants.

❡ **Cortona** has a weekly market each Saturday morning and **Camucia**, 2 kilometres away, has a regional market each Thursday.

20

Casa per Ferie Villa la Stella

Villa La Stella is owned by the international Catholic religious order, the *Missionari Oblati di Maria Immacolata Italian* (Italian Missionary Oblates of Mary Immaculate) and is situated 2 kilometres south of the ancient Etruscan hilltop village of **Fiesole** and 4 kilometres from the centre of **Florence**. It is believed the poet Dante Alighieri (1265–1321) wrote to his beloved friend, Beatrice Portinari, under a myrtle tree in the gardens of Villa La Stella.

❡ Over the centuries the building has been enlarged and restored and the villa now has 42 guestrooms all with en suite bathrooms and a telephone. There are 16 single rooms, four of which are suitable for the disabled as well as twin, double, triple and quad rooms. A lift accesses all three levels and a number of ground floor guestrooms open out into the convent's landscaped gardens. Breakfast is the only meal served and facilities include a dining room, chapel, a laundry service and a television room. Tea and coffee making facilities are provided. The house has a large car park.

✉ Via Jacopone da Todi, 12
50133 Fiesole (FI)

🚪from €55.00 pp

☎ +39 (0) **55 50 88 018**
📠 +39 (0) **55 55 22 756**

✒ *villalastella@omi.it*

☞ From **Santa Maria Novella train station** take bus number 7 for the 20-minute, 5-kilometre trip to Fiesole. Get off at bus stop number 7 on the Via San Domenico and cross the road to the Via Jacopone da Todi.

✝ **Sunday Mass**
Summer: 1030, 1200 & 1800
Winter: 1030, 1200 & 1730
Cathedral of San Romolo
Piazza Mino da Fiesole
50014 Fiesole (FI)

♿ Discuss your needs in advance of arriving, ideally when booking.

⚭ Open to both men and women

Open Houses
Tuscany Fiesole

PLACES OF INTEREST ❧ The 13th-century Monastery and **Church of San Francesco** on the Via Francesco occupies the most elevated position in Fiesole, and is said to have been built in such a position so as to be closer to Heaven. The monastery's museum is open to the public and its collection includes artefacts relating to the history of the order as well as Roman and Etruscan objects found locally. Sections of the monastery including cells once used by the monks are also open to visitors.

❧ More Etruscan discoveries are on view at the **Archaeological Museum** which is built on the site of ancient ruins, including a Roman theatre. The town's **Roman Theatre** is the venue of plays and concerts during the summer. The **Bandini Museum** in Via Duprè exhibits a collection of Florentine paintings and sculptures from the 12th and 13th centuries onwards. The attractive surrounds of the little town provide an ideal setting for a quiet picnic, perhaps while pondering the architecture of **Florence** in the distance.

❧ Sit and 'people watch' from one of the street-side cafés in the **Piazza Mino** in the centre of Fiesole which is especially busy on weekends and public holidays. After a couple of leisurely espressos you could explore the grounds of the **Villa Peyron** at Via di Vincigliata, 2, approximately 2.5 kilometres from the Piazza Mino. The design of the villa's fastidiously maintained terraced gardens has an element of laid-back Tuscan flair meets formal English perfection. The designer of the garden, wealthy landowner Paul Peyron, donated the grounds to the state in 1998.

❡ **The Fiesolana Summer Festival** is held in Fiesole's ancient amphitheatre between June and September with performances of opera, dance and classical music. Cinema, art and literature are also part of the festival.

❡ Keen golfers could play a round at the **Poggio dei Medici Golf Club and Resort** at Via San Gavino, 27, in Scarperia, 30 kilometres north of Fiesole. The club is an exclusive 18-hole par-73 course which has been the venue for the Italian Ladies' Golf Open for over 15 years.

❡ A little closer to Fiesole is the **Villa Demidoff Park**, in the Via Bolognese in Pratolino. The vast estate was once privately owned by a Russian aristocrat but is now open for the public to enjoy. Walking trails, ruins, sculptures, water features and a restored 16th-century villa are part of the attraction.

FOOD AND DRINK ✈ Each Saturday a **produce market** is held on the **Piazza Mino**, so named after local sculptor Mino da Fiesole (c1429–1484) whose work can be admired in the 11th-century Romanesque **Cathedral of St Romulus** in a corner of the piazza.

❡ Bars, cafés and eating places are spread around the Piazza Mino and one of the nicest is the **Ristorante Perseus**, which serves local Tuscan specialities like *Ribollita* (bread soup) and wild boar. The atmosphere is rustic and charming and a garden area is used in summer.

✉ Piazza Mino, 9R

☎ +39 (0) 55 59 143 €€€

❡ Florence is visible in the distance from the stylish dining room and outside terrace of the **Ristorante La Reggia**. Diners can choose the finest regional cuisine from an upscale, inventive menu and a good drop of wine from the seriously well-stocked cellar.

✉ Via San Francesco, 18

☎ +39 (0) 55 59 385 €€€€€

❡ The restaurant at the **Poggio dei Medici Golf Club** befits a special occasion. However, a relaxing and casual lunch can be had in the restaurant garden overlooking the first tee.

☎ +39 (0) 55 84 350 €€→€€€€

Open Houses
Tuscany Fiesole

21

Convento di San Domenico

Founded in 1406, the Convento di San Domenico is in a busy little enclave on the main road from **Florence** to the village of **Fiesole**. The monastery is run by Catholic Dominican friars who are custodians of a wealth of artistic treasures created by Italian artists in the 15th and 16th centuries. One of the contributors was Fra Angelico, a former Dominican monk and artist who lived for a time in the monastery. His paintings titled *Crucifixion* and *Madonna and Saints* can be seen on the walls inside.

❧ An unused section of this ancient monastery has been set aside to accommodate overnight guests in simply furnished single and double rooms. All guestrooms share toilets and bathrooms. The guestrooms are a little spartan and still have the neat, uncluttered appearance of a monk's cell. However, the genuine warmth and friendliness of the friars more than makes up for the lack of mod cons. No meals are served but there is a pizzeria, bar and a café in the piazza outside the convent and more eateries in **Fiesole** proper, 1 kilometre further up the hill (by way of a very steep and winding road). However, a bus stop is outside the monastery.

❧ The friars have strict rules about arrival and departure times. Arrivals are only permitted between 0900 and 1400 or between 1700 and 2000. Departures must be before 0900.

✉ Piazza San Domenico, 4 50016 San Domenico di Fiesole (FI)

🛏 from €28.00 pp

☏ +39 (0) 55 59 230
☏ +39 (0) 55 59 79 188

✎ vincap@tin.it

☞ From the **Santa Maria Novella train station** take bus number 7 to Fiesole and get off at the San Domenico stop. Fiesole is 8 kilometres north-east of Florence.

✝ **Sunday Mass**
1100 & 1900
Church of San Domenico di Fiesole
Piazza San Domenico, 4
50016 Fiesole (FI)

♿ Discuss your needs in advance of arriving, ideally when booking.

⚥ Open to both men and women

PLACES OF INTEREST ❧ On weekends the former Etruscan village of **Fiesole** is a popular day escape for Florentines where they can relax in a street-side café and admire their city from afar.

❦ The fertile hills of Fiesole are thick with olive trees and many a grand villa. The imposing **Villa di Maiano** on the Via del Salviatino was transformed into the Pensione Bertolini for the movie *A Room with a View*. The villa has expansive views and many indoor scenes were filmed there. The movie won an Oscar® for art direction and set decoration in 1987.

❦ The columned façade of the **Hotel Villa San Michele** (once the Monastery of San Michele) stands out high on the hills of Fiesole; it was designed by Michelangelo. The hotel is now a favourite destination of Italian honeymooning couples.

❦ The **Convento / Santuario di Monte Senario** in Bivigliano, 20 kilometres north of Fiesole, was established in 1245 by seven 'holy men' from Florence, said to have been chosen by Our Lady, and who founded the now international religious order, the Servants of Mary (*Servites*). Servite friars still occupy the monastery today and the relics of the holy men lie in the convent church. The friars produce *Gemma d'Abete* (Pine Tears), an aromatic liqueur made from pine resin which is on sale in the monastery shop.

✝ Sunday Mass 0800, 1000, 1130 & 1730

❦ Take the bus from outside the **Monastery of San Domenico** up the hill to **Fiesole** for a wide choice of cafés, bars, trattorias and interesting shops. The local tourist office in Via Portigiani can supply maps of local themed walking routes, most of which originate in the Piazza Mino.

❦ The **Villa della Petraia**, at Via della Petraia, 40, and **Villa di Castello**, at Via di Castello, 47, are both situated in the enclave of Castello, on the outskirts of Fiesole. The palatial **Italianate gardens** of both villas were originally established by the Medici family and later owned by the Ginori family of porcelain fame. The villas are open to visitors (gardens only, not the interiors). The Villa Petraia was a favoured residence of King Vittorio Emanuele II (1820–1891). The 15th-century Villa di Castello is where Carlo Lorenzini (1826–1890), who wrote under the name of Carlo Collodi, penned the ever-popular children's story *Pinocchio*. Guided or independent tours can be taken of both gardens which are 1 kilometre apart.

Open Houses
Tuscany Fiesole

The **Richard Ginori Ceramic Outlet**, at Viale Giulio Cesare, 19 Sesto Fiorentino retails the famous Ginori porcelain at reduced prices. The Medici family were avid collectors of the brand. The **Ginori Museum of Porcelain** (*Museo di Doccia*) is at via Pratese, 31, around the corner from the outlet, and displays thousands of pieces of china and earthenware from the early 19th century onwards.

The **Sanctuary of Madonna delle Grazie del Sasso** is a place of pilgrimage near the village of **Santa Brigida** on the scenic outskirts of Fiesole. The Virgin Mary is said to have appeared to two shepherd girls around 1480 instructing them to build a church in her name. The rock on which Mary is said to have stood is under the altar of the sanctuary church which is built on the site of her appearances.

FOOD AND DRINK The **Villa Maiano's La Terrazza** restaurant near Fiesole is open for lunch and dinner and much of the produce served is grown on the estate, including 20,000 olive trees. Olive oil tastings can be arranged and are held in rooms which were once part of a Benedictine monastery.

✉ Via Benedetto da Maiano, 11

☎ +39 (0) 55 59 432 €€€€

Plenty of shady picnic spots can be found in the rolling hills of Fiesole and **Vinandro** can provide the necessities. This quaint, old-fashioned deli sells local cheese, smoked ham and salami, bread and a good selection of local wines.

✉ Piazza Mino, 33

☎ +39 (0) 55 59 121 €€

A local brother and sister team run the small but cosy **Ristorante I'Polpa** on the Piazza Mino in Fiesole. The duo bring their favourite family recipes to the dining table and happily share cooking hints with their guests.

✉ Piazza Mino

☎ +39 (0) 55 59 485 €€€

Open Houses
Tuscany Florence

Casa Santa Nome di Gesu

The convent is run by the Francescane Missionarie di Maria (*Franciscan Missionaries of Mary*) and is within the confines of a 15th-century palace in the **Oltrarno** area. The convent boasts stone floors, high ceilings, decorative staircases, a potpourri of antique furniture and upper floor views over the attractive piazza.

❡ The large, spotlessly clean guestrooms are simply furnished and available in single, double and triple configuration with some family sized rooms containing four or five beds. There are various choices of rooms with sink, shower or bathtub and share bathrooms and toilets are on each level. The front-facing guestrooms overlooking the piazza can be noisy, especially in summer. The rooms to the rear overlook the nuns' garden and are much quieter. The building has no lifts and is not air-conditioned. Fans are provided in each room. Breakfast is the only meal served but dining out won't be a problem as there are many well priced restaurants and pizzerias in the area. Guests can relax in the lovely convent garden, browse through a book in the library or watch TV in the lounge room. Central Florence is a 20–30-minute walk away.

❡ The sisters don't speak much English but there is usually someone on reception who does.

OPEN HOUSE

✉ Piazza del Carmine, 21 50124 Firenze (SC)

🛏 from €48.00 pp, including breakfast

✆ +39 (0) 55 21 38 56
📠 +39 (0) 55 28 18 35

✉ info@fmmfirenze.it

☞ Take Bus D from the Santa Maria Novella train station which stops near the Piazza del Carmine.

✝ **Sunday Mass**
Summer 0800, 1000, 1200 & 1800
Winter 0800, 1000, 1200 & 1730
Church of Santa Maria del Carmine
Piazza del Carmine 50124 Florence (FI)

⚭ Open to both men and women

Open Houses
Tuscany Florence

PLACES OF INTEREST ❧ Don't be deceived by the unprepossessing façade of the **Church of Santa Maria del Carmine** in the Piazza del Carmine which camouflages a prized collection of Renaissance art. The church is best known for its **Brancacci Chapel** where a series of scenes from the life of St Peter are painted in detailed wall frescoes. The frescoes were begun by Italian artists Masolino da Panicale (1383–c1440) and Thomas Cassai, better known as Masaccio (1402–1429) and completed by Filippino Lippi (c1457–1504).

❧ Filipio Brunelleschi's (1377–1446) elaborate, Renaissance royal residence the **Palazzo Pitti**, home of the Medici and the Bourbon dynasties, is in the Piazza Pitti, not far from the convent. Across from the Pitti Palace is **Casa Guidi**, the apartment occupied in Florence by poets Elizabeth (1806–1861) and Robert Browning (1812–1889). They lived here from 1847 until Elizabeth's death in 1861. The apartment is on the first floor of the Palazzo Guidi at Piazza di San Felice, 8.

❧ Cross the river and you will find **Florence's central market** which is situated near the **Church of San Lorenzo**. It is closed on Sundays and public holidays. The food section is undercover in the Via dell'Ariento and on the street outside, endless rows of stalls trade in leather items. The **Mercato Nuovo** (*New Market*) in the Piazza di Mercato Nuovo is always full of people and stalls and display stands stocked with leather belts, handbags, wallets and coats. A wild boar (*il porcellino*) guards the marketplace and a quick pat on the snout guarantees a return visit to the city. A market for food, clothes, leather and shoes is held in **Cascine Park** on the western outskirts of the city every Tuesday morning.

❧ **Dante's House**, at Via Santa Margherita, 1, is now a museum in honour of Italian writer Dante Alighieri who was born in Florence in 1265 and lived in the city until his exile in 1301, after a dispute with the taxation office and another with Pope Boniface VIII. Dante died in Ravenna 20 years later, having never returned to his birthplace. The Church of **Santa Margherita de' Cerchi** is next to Dante's house and where the body of his lifetime infatuation, Beatrice Portinari (1266–1290), is buried.

❡ **The Monastery of Certosa**, in **Galluzzo**, 5 kilometres south of the centre of Florence, (on the road to Siena) was established during the 14th century as an art school for Florentine students. Occupied by the Carthusian Order up until the 1950s, this enormous complex is now the home of Cistercian monks. Certosa is a full working monastery where the monks manufacture perfume, Eau de Cologne, grappa and a number of medicinal liqueurs. All are on sale in the monastery shop. The monks conduct guided tours of the complex (every Tuesday to Sunday from 0900 to 1200 and from 1500 to 1800) including visits to the **Basilica di San Lorenzo**, a picture gallery (Napoleon helped himself to much of the precious artwork) and cells once occupied by the monks.

⳨ Sunday Mass 1000 & 1100

FOOD AND DRINK ⳾ Sit under the ancient arches and linger awhile on the terrace of the smart, upmarket restaurant **La Loggia**. Most people come for the gourmet Tuscan cuisine but the breathtaking views over the city are worth the trip alone.

✉ Piazzale Michelangiolo, 1

☎ +39 (0) 55 23 42 832　　　€€€€€

❡ Restaurants, trattorias and pizzerias are not hard to find around the **Piazza del Carmine**. In the piazza itself the trendy **La Dolce Vita** wine bar is a favourite with the 'in' crowd.

✉ Piazza del Carmine

☎ +39 (0) 55 28 45 95　　　€€€€

❡ The **Trattoria Napoleone** is open for dinner only and presents a well priced menu of Tuscan favourites including *Zambone* (pork trotters), Florentine beefsteak and pizza.

✉ Piazza del Carmine, 24

☎ +39 (0) 55 28 10 15　　　€€€€

❡ If, after a long day, you don't have the energy to brave the streets for a bite you can have your Italian eating experience **delivered** to your door.

Pizza Taxi

☎ +39 (0) 55 43 43 43

Pizza Pronto

☎ +39 (0) 55 71 67 67

Open Houses
Tuscany Florence

23

Convitto Della Calza

The Convitto Della Calza is situated near the **Pitti Palace** and the **Boboli Gardens** in the **Oltrarno** district, one of the most historical areas of **Florence**. The convent was founded by the Jesuits in the 15th century. It is now owned and run by the Catholic Archdiocese of Florence. The convent is a virtual art gallery with ancient frescoes lining many of the walls.

❧ The Convitto Della Calza is run along hotel lines and offers comfortable, clean and well-furnished accommodation in single, double and triple guestrooms. All 32 air-conditioned guestrooms have en suite bathrooms, Internet connection, telephone, hairdryer, safe and televisions; some have wheelchair access. The building has been completely renovated and, because of its size, the complex is popular with groups. State-of-the-art conference facilities and equipment are available. Anything from a cup of coffee to a full-scale gala dinner can be arranged. However, individual pilgrims and tourists are also welcome and are well catered for. A restaurant and bar are open for all meals and drinks. Reception is open 24 hours and credit cards are accepted.

❧ The convent is 2 kilometres from the centre of the town and while there is no on-site car parking, discounted parking for guests is available in the **Piazza della Calza**.

✉ Piazza Della Calza, 6
50125 Florence (FI)

🏨 from €50.00 pp,
including breakfast

☎ +39 (0) **55 22 22 87**
📠 +39 (0) **55 22 39 12**

✉ calza@calza.it

☞ From **Santa Maria Novella** station bus numbers 11, 36 or 37 travel to the Piazza della Calza. The convent is 2 kilometres from the Santa Maria Novella station and a pleasant walk (without luggage) across the **Ponte Vecchio** and through the artistic **Oltrano Quarter.**

✝ **Sunday Mass 0930, 1100, 1200 & 1800**
Basilica di Santa Croce
Piazza Santa Croce
50125 Florence (FI)

♿ Discuss your needs in advance of arriving, ideally when booking.

⚥ Open to both men and women

PLACES OF INTEREST ❧ A bonus for guests of the **Della Calza** is that they have access to the artistic creations left behind on the walls by the artists of various religious orders who once occupied the building. One of the most highly regarded works of art is a fresco of *The Last Supper* by Franciabigio (1482–1525).

❧ The convent is close to the Via Senese, the main road leading from Florence to Siena and also to Rome. A round trip to **Siena, Monteriggioni** and **San Gimignano** can be easily done in a day, especially during summer when the days are longer.

❧ Florence is renowned worldwide for art, culture and especially for music. Concerts, operas and ballets are presented throughout the city all the year round. **The Maggio Musicale Festival of Opera**, a major event, is held annually in May and June at the Teatro Communale and other theatres in the city, attracting distinguished philharmonic and symphony orchestras and renowned ballet companies from all over Europe.

❧ Much of the movie *A Room With a View* was filmed at locations in Florence, including the **Church of Santa Croce** and the **Hotel degli Orafi** at Lungarno Archibusieri, 4 near the Ponte Vecchio where guests can book the actual 'room with a view' used in many of the scenes.

❧ **Oltrarno** is known as an artisans' quarter and a number of craft schools are situated in the area. The **Arti Orafe Jewellery School** at Via dei Serragli, 104/124 is the headquarters of the Florentine School of Goldsmithery and courses (short and long) are conducted here for novice jewellery designers. Introductory and intensive courses of various lengths are conducted at **The Darkroom** at Via Cantagalli, 1R, a school for students seeking a career as a professional photographer.

Open Houses
Tuscany Florence

❡ The **Casa Buonarroti Museum**, at Via Ghibellina, 70, Florence, is dedicated to the great Michelangelo (Buonarotti) and many of his works are on display here along with the extensive artistic collection of the Buonarotti family. Dedicated to another artistic medium, the **Museo Zoologico La Specola** (*Specola Zoological Museum*) at Via Romana, 17, exhibits a collection of wax 'human bodies' exposing in full colour, veins, arteries, bones and organs. Some 'bodies' date back three centuries. Not for the squeamish.

❡ The majesty of Florence can be fully appreciated from the **Piazzale Michelangiolo**, which overlooks the city. If you have an aversion to queues you could always study the bronze replica of the statue of Michelangelo's *David* in the centre of the piazzale, instead of the real thing—although connoisseurs of fine art will almost certainly be appalled.

FOOD AND DRINK ❧ The **Trattoria Omero**, not far from the Piazzale Michelangiolo, serves not only scrumptious Italian food but has a delicatessen attached where you can buy home-cooked produce (hams, pasta, sauces, cheese, bread, wine) to take away.
✉ Via del Pian dei Giullari,
✆ +39 (0) 55 22 00 53   €€€

❡ A little closer to the convent, the **Trattoria Boboli** is one of the city's numerous low profile, unpretentious restaurants serving simple, orthodox Italian cuisine, including a thick, lip-smacking *Ribollita*.
✉ Via Romana, 45R
✆ +39 (0) 55 23 36 401   €€€

❡ You probably won't find too many locals at **Harry's Bar** on the **Lungarno Amerigo Vespucci**, an institution in Florence with foreigners and film stars who like to sip their Bellinis on the terazza and watch the sun go down over the Arno. The original Harry's Bar, once patronised by Ernest Hemingway and his *literati* cronies, is in Paris. Replicas of the real thing can now be found in New York, Singapore, Venice, Los Angeles, Munich, Hong Kong and of course, Florence.
✆ +39 (0) 55 23 96 700   €€€€€

Open Houses

Tuscany Florence

Istituto Gould /
Foresteria Valdese

The Istituto Gould / Foresteria Valdese is run by a partnership of Italian Evangelist Protestant Churches (*Chiese Evangeliche Protestanti*), and is situated in a 17th-century Florentine palace on the south bank of the **River Arno**, 500 metres from the **Ponte Vecchio**. The institute is 1 kilometre south of **Santa Maria Novella train station**.

❧ The centre's 40 simply furnished guestrooms are available in single, double, triple and quadruple configurations. Most guestrooms have en suites while others share a bathroom. Rooms are not serviced and guests are asked to make their own beds. Breakfast and dinner are available for groups only but there are numerous restaurants, bars and cafés in the immediate area. The house is open all year and has wheelchair access. It is important to pre-arrange arrival details. The reception desk opens on Monday to Friday at 0845 and closes at 1930 with a 2-hour break for lunch between 1300 and 1500. On Saturday reception opens at 0900 until 1800 with a 1-hour lunch break at 1300. However, reception is closed all day Sunday. There is a car park 300 metres away.

OPEN HOUSE

✉ Via de' Serragli, 49
50124 Florence (FI)

🛏 from €32.00 pp

📞 +39 (0) **55 21 25 76**
📠 +39 (0) **55 28 02 74**

✉ *foresteriafirenze@ diaconiavaldese.org*

☞ From **Santa Maria Novella** station take bus number 36 or 37 which stop near the Via Serragli. The institute is 1 kilometre across the river from Santa Maria Novella station.

✝ **Sunday Service 1030**
Evangelical Valdese Church
Via Micheli, 26
50121 Florence (FI)

♿ Discuss your needs in advance of arriving, ideally when booking.

⚤ Open to both men and women

Open Houses
Tuscany Florence

PLACES OF INTEREST ❧ The institute is located in the quieter **Oltrarno** quarter of artisans' shops, authentic Florentine cafés and art galleries, and lies near two magnificent gardens—the Medici family's **Boboli Gardens** and the more contemporary **Torrigiani Gardens**.

❧ Surrounded by a park of oak trees and cypresses, Florence Nightingale's (1829–1910) birthplace, the **Villa La Colombaia** at Via di Santa Maria a Marignolle, 2 on the southern outskirts of Florence, was the home of the well-to-do English Nightingale family. Since 1957 the villa has been a convent occupied by the religious order of the Sisters of the Adorers of the Precious Blood. The convent is often visited by those curious about the life of this famous nurse.

❧ Bargain hunters could visit the clothing factory outlet near the town of **Rignano sull'Arno**, 30 kilometres east of Florence. **The Mall Factory Outlet Centre** is at Via Europa, 8, **Leccio Reggello**, 10 kilometres from Rignano and the stores here include Emmanuel Ungaro, Fendi, Zegna, Giorgio Armani, Gucci, La Perla, Ferragamo, Valentino and Yves St Laurent. Take a bus from near the Santa Maria Novella train station directly to the centre.

❧ **The Prada outlet** is in another area further south of Rignano sull'Arno, at **Levanella**, near Montevarchi. Take the train from Santa Maria Novella in Florence to Montevarchi and a taxi to the outlet which is a short drive away.

❧ **The Ferragamo Museum**, in the Palazzo Spini Feroni, at Via dei Tornabuoni, 2, Florence, exhibits a collection of Ferragamo-designed shoes and footwear worn by various public personalities, and sketches and shoe designs from the 1920s onwards.

❡ The **Oltrarno Street Festival** of music and arts is held in the **Piazza della Passera** each year through the month of July. Performances cover a range of music genres including jazz, blues and rock and many are free of charge. During the festival the local cafés, restaurants, bars and shops stay open well into the night as the street entertainment draws large crowds.

❡ Golfers could have a few holes at the **Ugolino Golf Club**, where the Italian Open was played in 1983. Visitors must have a minimum handicap of 36 and produce a membership card of their home club. Ugolino is near **Impruneta**, 11 kilometres south of Florence.

❡ **Impruneta** has a reputation for terracotta products. Kilns and pottery shops can be found all over town. A favourite earthenware creation is the Chianti rooster—which comes in all sizes.

FOOD AND DRINK ❡ The **Ristorante Villa Pitiana**, part of a country estate in **Reggello**, conducts tasting programs of the local wine, cheese, olive oil and salami for small groups of time poor travellers. The tastings are held over a 2-hour period. Half-day cooking classes are led by the restaurant's head chef.

✉ Via Provinciale per Tosi, 7

☎ +39 (0) 55 86 02 59   €€€

❡ **Trattoria La Casalinga** is a much-frequented meeting place of local students and poor artisans of the Oltrano area. Now that tourists have discovered the cheap and generous servings, the place is always busy.

✉ Via dei Michelozzi, 9ʀ

☎ +39 (0) 55 21 86 24   €

❡ Also cheap and cheerful, the **Trattoria da Ginone** caters for meat eaters and vegetarians and won't burn a hole in the wallet.

✉ Via dei Serragli, 35ʀ

☎ +39 (0) 55 21 87 58   €

Open Houses
Tuscany Florence

Istituto Oblate Dell'Assunzione

The convent is run by the sisters of the Oblate dell'Assunzione Religiose Missionarie (*Oblate Missionary Sisters*) and is within the walls of a spacious Florentine villa on a narrow street lined with suburban shops and only a few blocks from the **Duomo**. Ring the bell and push open the huge wooden doors and you will find yourself in an airy foyer looking through to a surprisingly large, well-kept, informal garden courtyard. The convent's guestrooms are on the floors above and can be accessed by a lift.

❦ The guestrooms are simply though thoughtfully furnished and most have en suite bathrooms. A light Continental breakfast is available, but no other meals are served. Guests can join the nuns in their tiny chapel for the daily celebration of Mass. The convent is open all year. There is no car parking. The order has a convent in **Sorrento** where tourists are also welcome to stay overnight.

✉ Borgo Pinti, 15
50121 Florence (FI)

🏨 from €42.00 pp, including breakfast

✆ +39 (0) 55 24 80 582
✆ +39 (0) 55 23 46 291

☞ The convent is almost 2 kilometres from the **Santa Maria Novella train station** and a taxi can be taken from here. Without luggage it is a pleasant and interesting walk through the city centre, past the Duomo and along to the Borgo Pinti.

✝ **Sunday Mass**
0730, 0900, 1030, 1200 (*accompanied by Gregorian chants*) & 1800
Cathedral of Santa Maria del Fiore (Duomo)
Piazza del Duomo
50121 Florence (FI)

⚭ Open to both men and women

PLACES OF INTEREST ❦ **The Convent of San Marco** (c1437) in the Piazza san Marco is 600 metres from the Borgo Pinti. Renaissance artist Fra Angelico (1400–1455) painted most of the frescoes inside the convent, including many of those on the walls of the monks' cells. One of Fra Angelico's best known works and two of his three interpretations of *The Annunciation* are on view.

❦ A painting hangs in the **Basilica della Santissima Annunziata** (*Church of the Annunciation*) in the Piazza della Santissima Annunziata, Florence, and is said to have been commenced by a Servite monk in 1252 who abandoned the project before completion. Legend has it that the now perfect painting was finished by an angel.

† Sunday Mass 0700, 0800, 0900, 1000, 1100, 1200, 1300, 1800 & 2100

❦ **The Officina Profumo Farmaceutica di Santa Maria Novella** (*Perfume and Pharmaceutical Workshop of Santa Maria Novella*) at Via della Scala, 16, Florence was established in the 13th century by Dominican friars as part of the monastery built on this site. The 'chemist' shop was used to create herbal remedies for the monastery fraternity. Four centuries later the monks opened their showroom to the public, which had expanded to offer perfumes, lotions and various elixirs made by the monks. One of the ancient apothecary's most famous clients was the Queen of France, Catherine Medici (1519–1589) who was a fan of the monks' *Aqua di Colonia* (Eau de Cologne) which is still sold today and made to the original formula.

❦ **The Cathedral of Santo Stefano** in **Prato**, 20 kilometres north of Florence, harbours an unusual relic, the *Sacra Cintola*, more commonly referred to as The Virgin's Girdle. The *Cintola* is said to have been dropped by Mary to St Thomas as she ascended into Heaven. The belt is displayed from the pulpit of the cathedral on Easter Sunday, 1 May, 15 August, 8 September and Christmas Day. On these days crowds of locals gather in the piazza in front of the cathedral to view the sacred relic.

Open Houses
Tuscany Florence

❧ The **Grotta Giusti Spa Centre**, at Via Grotta Giusti, 1411a, in Monsummano Terme, near **Prato** is a complex of health-giving, sauna-type caves known for their varying temperatures. As a guide to what to expect they are named *Paradise*, *Purgatory* and *Hell*.

❧ One of the most magnificent Jewish temples in Europe can be found in Florence. **The Great Synagogue** in Via Luigo Carlo Farini was founded in the 19th century and is a prominent landmark in the city. Within the complex, the **Museo Ebraico** (*Jewish Museum*) illustrates the history of the Jewish people in Florence.

✡ Service times vary, call for details
☏ +39 (0) 55 24 5252
☏ +39 (0) 55 24 1811

❧ The **Sant'Ambrogio morning market** (food, flowers and clothes) is held each weekday morning in the **Piazza Ghiberti**, Florence. If you are still in the mood for shopping, the flea market in the Piazza dei Ciompi, 100 metres away, is open daily from 0900 until 1900 (Closed Sunday and Monday during winter.)

FOOD AND DRINK ❧ **Ristorante La Giostra** is owned by the Austrian Prince Dimitri Kunz d'Asburgo Lorena and his family. Not far from the convent, this is a warm, romantic restaurant where the food is lovingly prepared and served with care and enthusiasm—as is the wine.

✉ Borgo Pinti, 12R
☏ +39 (0) 55 24 13 41   €€€€€

❧ **Ristorante Ruth** is an informal kosher restaurant situated near the Great Synagogue. The menu is based on pasta, fish and vegetables and kosher cheese is used on the pizzas.

✉ Via Farini, 2A
☏ +39 (0) 55 24 80 888   €€€

❧ A **Kosher fast food** and take-away shop is also near the synagogue.

✉ Via dei Pilastri, 7A R   €€€€€

❧ Ancient stone walls surround the town of **Lucca**, 70 kilometres west of Florence. It is possible to walk or cycle along the top of these walls which surround the 'old town'. The **San Colombano Café** is situated within the ramparts and is a convenient stopover for a cappuccino or a cold drink. The separate **Ristorante San Colombano** serves meals in Lucchese style including Farro soup, *Tortelli*, *Matuffi* (polenta with a meat sauce and parmigiano) and *Buccellato* (Lucchese dessert cake).

✉ Baluardo San Colombano, 10
☏ +39 (0) 583 46 46 41   €€€

Villa Agape

Villa Agape is a large 16th-century monastery perched on a hill overlooking Florence and situated just 5 kilometres from the centre of the city. There is a bus stop near the convent. Since the 15th century the villa has been owned by various religious orders and private citizens including the Duchess Anne of Orléans (1906–1986), widow of Prince Amedeo, 3rd Duke of Aosta (1898–1942) who landscaped the magnificent gardens. The Duchess left the villa to the *Suore Stabilite della Carità* (Sisters of Charity) in her will.

⸙ The sisters run this convent guesthouse on a hotel-style basis with the assistance of outside staff. All 50 guestrooms have en suite bathrooms and the convent dining room is open for all meals. A bonus for guests is the villa's classical Italianate and English-style gardens which were designed by the Duchess and from where the skyline of **Florence** can be seen in the distance. The sisters often host lunches for groups of garden enthusiasts. Meeting rooms are available and are large enough to host small conferences. There is on-site car parking.

⸙ Gladys and Charlie Maclean, grandparents of Scottish novelist Charles Maclean, owned the Villa Agape during 1922–1948, when it was named Villa Arrighetti.

> *At the bottom of the garden, I discover the iron gates to the viale, where in May 1938 Gladys stood and watched Hitler and Mussolini drive by in a convertible on their way to San Miniato. She refused to wave; instead, she turned to her companion, Miss Good, and said, "Darling, if only we had a bomb. Imagine…"*
>
> CHARLES MCLEAN 'MASTERCLASS'
> *TRAVEL AND LEISURE* MARCH 2006

✉ Via Torre del Gallo, 8
50125 Florence (FI)

🛏 from €50.00 pp

📞 +39 (0) 55 22 00 44
📞 +39 (0) 55 23 37 012

✉ villaagape@
suorestabilite.com

☞ From the **Santa Maria Novella station** take bus number 12 or 13 and get off at the intersection of Viale Galileo Galilei and Via del Giramontino from where it is a 10-minute (uphill) walk to the convent.

† **Sunday Mass**
0800 & 1100
Church of Saints Stefano and Caterina of Pozzolatico
Via Vecchia di Pozzolatico, 1
50125 Florence (FI)

⚭ Open to both men and women

Open Houses
Tuscany Florence

PLACES OF INTEREST ❧ Florences'
Arcetri Observatory and the **Galileo Galilei Institute** are in Largo Enrico Fermi, near the Villa La Stella. The **Villa Il Gioiello** in via del Pian dei Giullari where Galileo lived and subsequently died, is within walking distance.

❧ The **Monastery of Badia a Passignano** in the hamlet of **Tavarnelle Val di Pesa**, 25 kilometres south of Florence, was founded by Bishop Sichelmo of Florence (964–985) in the year 890 and occupied by the Benedictine monks of the Vallombrosan Congregation from 1049. The monastery has always been a centre of spirituality and learning—astronomer Galileo Galilei once taught here. A much acclaimed interpretation of *The Last Supper* by Florentine painter Domenico Ghirlandaio (1449–1494) enhances a wall in the refectory. The monastery can be visited only on Sunday afternoons when the monks arrange guided tours. The monks extend an invitation to young people contemplating monastic life to spend a week with them to experience life within the cloisters.

✝ Sunday Mass 1100

❧ When you finally get to Florence you will be sure to recognise the **Ponte Vecchio**, surely one of the most photographed bridges in the world. It is lined with tiny shops selling a vast range of gold jewellery (although of varying quality). Some go to the bridge to follow an old romantic tradition. Lovers can lock in their love forever by scratching their names on a padlock, fastening it to a horse tether or a railing on the bridge and throwing the key into the River Arno below. Locks can be purchased from the souvenir shops near the bridge.

❧ The Gothic **Basilica of Santa Croce** on the **Piazza Santa Croce** is one of Florence's best-known churches. This grand structure is a treasure house of frescoes, paintings and sculptures by artists including Giotto (1267–1337), Michelangelo (1475–1564) and Donatello (1386–1466). Michelangelo and astronomer Galileo Galilei (1564–1642), along with many other illustrious Florentines, are buried here.

✝ Sunday Mass 0930, 1100, 1200 & 1800

❡ The revered **Florentine Leather School** is situated within the Santa Croce complex and is open to the public. Visitors come here to observe the craftsmen at work and purchase or just admire their fastidiously hand-crafted creations. Santa Croce and the adjoining monastery were founded by the Franciscan Order and some believe by the great St Francis himself.

❡ Squeezed in amongst the leather outlets in the Santa Croce area, **Bartolucci** at Borgo dei Greci, 11A/R, is a unique shop packed to the rafters with hand-crafted pinewood pieces. Take home a true-to-size motor bike (with or without sidecar), clocks, model aircraft or wooden Pinocchios in a multitude of sizes.

❡ Everything anyone could possibly wish for in a kitchen is sure to be somewhere in **Dino Bartolini**'s culinary accoutrement shop at Via dei Servi, 30, Florence; just the place to pick up that temperature-controlled butter dish.

❡ The talented **Berti Brothers**, at Via del Padule, 23D, Scandicci, 10 kilometres south-west of Florence, are mosaic artists in the traditional Florentine style. Some of the unusual items they create are framed, semi-precious, stone mosaic 'paintings' of Florentine scenes, hand-crafted lamps, plates, tables and a range of decorative items for the house.

FOOD AND DRINK ❧ The medieval **monastery of Passignano**, south of Florence, stands out above the tiny village of **Tavarnelle Val di Pesa**. Nearby, the chefs of the **Osteria di Passignano** conduct hands-on afternoon cooking classes for tourists and visitors. The lessons include a wine tasting in the cellars of the ancient abbey and when the food is ready the class sits down to dine.

✉ Via Passignano, 33

☏ +39 (0) 55 80 71 278   €€€

❡ See how the professionals do it at the Michelin-starred **Onice** restaurant in the Villa La Vedetta. Indulge in a fine dining experience amongst luxurious surroundings, adventurous food, caring service and top Italian wines.

✉ Viale Michelangiolo, 78

☏ +39 (0) 55 68 16 31   €€€€€

❡ Back in the city, join the locals at the **La Pentola d'Oro Firenze**, where tables are shared and the atmosphere is lively; however, the main attraction is the cheap and delicious Tuscan cuisine.

✉ Via di Mezzo, 24–26R

☏ +39 (0) 55 24 18 08   €

Open Houses
Tuscany San Gimignano

27

Convento Sant'Agostino

The Convento Sant'Agostino is a working monastery situated in a quiet piazza at the edge of the walled hilltop town of **San Gimignano**, 40 kilometres north of Siena. The Order of St Augustine built this property around 1280AD, and to the present day Augustinian monks work and worship here.

❧ The monastery operates as a parish church, and is not primarily a commercial *pensione*. Since only a limited number of guestrooms are available, booking is necessary. As the number of visitors at any one time is small, the two ladies who work in the kitchen treat guests as part of the monastery family. Guests are expected to observe the monastery timetables and there are no exceptions.

❧ There is an interesting anecdote, the authenticity of which has not been verified. Until quite recently, an Augustinian brother, Fra Romolo OSA, was well known as sacristan of the church. Apparently he refused to make an exception and closed the church door to exclude HRH Prince Charles, Prince of Wales when he arrived late. It was the monastery's scheduled afternoon closing time and it was dinnertime for the friars.

❧ For information on the availability of accommodation contact the Prior of the Augustinians at San Gimignano. Send a letter well ahead of time, written in either English or Italian.

✉ Piazza
Sant'Agostino, 10
53037 San Gimignano
(SI)

💶 price to be negotiated

📞 +39 (0) **577 90 70 12**
📠 +39 (0) **577 94 03 83**

🚌 From Florence take the bus from the stop near the Santa Maria Novella train station to **Poggibonsi** where it is necessary to change to a bus to San Gimignano. Buses run approximately every half an hour from Florence and from Poggibonsi. Tourist buses depart Florence daily for day trips to Siena and San Gimignano.
Cars are not allowed in San Gimignano and must be parked in allocated areas outside the walls of the town. Take care as the parking police in San Gimignano have a reputation for being the most vigilant in Italy.

✝ **Sunday Mass**
0800, 1100 & 1800
Church of
Sant'Agostino
Piazza
Sant'Agostino, 10
53037 San Gimignano
(SI)

✾ Open to both men and women

PLACES OF INTEREST ❦ Acclaimed frescoes in the **Sant'Agostino monastery church** depict events in the life of St Augustine and were painted in 1465 by Italian Renaissance artist Benozzo Gozzoli (1420–1497).

❦ Staying in **San Gimignano** is like being on a medieval film set. Two movies, *Brother Sun, Sister Moon* (about St Francis of Assisi), and *Tea with Mussolini* were filmed there. As there are no large hotels in the town, tour bus groups do not stay overnight.

❦ The **Museum of Religious Art** off the **Piazza Duomo** exhibits artworks on loan from local convents, monasteries and churches in the local area. The museum is near the town's Duomo, the **Basilica di Santa Maria Assunta**, which is also well endowed with ancient art. Behind this museum, near the town fortress is the **Vernaccia Wine Museum** where visitors can discover all about viniculture in **Chianti** and possibly sample a few good drops.

❦ Take a stroll around the streets and alleyways of **San Gimignano** when most of the tourists have left to get a real feel for the town. Tourists start arriving around 1100 and have usually departed by 1500 to make the trip back to **Florence**. You could walk the town's ancient wall which is about a 6-kilometre trek or climb one of the village's medieval towers for stupendous views over the Tuscan countryside. The highest tower, the **Torre Grossa**, stands at 60 metres.

❦ On a hot summer day you could join the queue to either of the gelaterias in San Gimignano's main square, both of which sell delicious, authentic home-made Italian gelato. Stroll past the unique side-street shops, and possibly to **Leoncinis** in the Via San Giovanni, which has an enticing collection of local pottery for sale, as do many of the town's shopping outlets.

❦ **Black truffle hunts** take place in Tuscany in the summer months and the rarer white truffle can be hunted between September and December. The local tourist office in San Gimignano can arrange truffle hunting excursions.

❦ **The Sanctuary of the Madonna of Pancole**, 5 kilometres from San Gimignano on the road to Certaldo, is a place of pilgrimage to a site where the Madonna is said to have appeared in the 1660s. The church that was subsequently built was destroyed by the Nazis but a 15th-century painting of the Madonna and Child by Pier Francesco Fiorentino (c1444–1498) remained undamaged and now hangs in the new church.

Open Houses
Tuscany San Gimignano

❧ Former British Prime Minister Tony Blair has enjoyed family holidays staying at the *Villa Cusona* on the Fattoria di Cusona rural estate between San Gimignano and Tavarnelle. It is possible to visit the **Fattoria di Cusona** vineyard by appointment. No visitors are permitted to enter the grounds of the villa, the summer residence of the noble Strozzi family, of Medici bloodlines.

FOOD AND DRINK ❧ Authentic Vernaccia and Chianti wine can be enjoyed at the family-owned **Fattoria Il Palagio** vineyard in Castel San Gimignano, 12 kilometres from the main town. The owners also grow grapes and olives at the **Fattoria Abbazia Monte Oliveto** vineyard (about 1 kilometre out of San Gimignano) where well-trained rows of Vernaccia grapevines surround a 14th-century abbey once owned by Olivettan monks. There is a small wine shop at the abbey vineyard which also sells fruity, home-grown olive oil. **Castel San Gimignano** is situated between **San Gimignano** and **Volterra**.

Fattoria Il Palagio
☎ +39 (0) 577 95 30 04
Fattoria Abbazia Monte Oliveto
☎ +39 (0) 577 90 71 36

❧ Ten kilometres north of San Gimignano in the medieval town of **Certaldo Alto** the charming country-style restaurant **Osteria del Vicario** lies within the walls of a 13th-century monastery. To dine on the much acclaimed Tuscan cuisine at one of the outside tables, with the towers and city walls of San Gimignano in the distance is a uniquely Tuscan experience.
✉ Via Rivellino, 3
☎ +39 (0) 571 66 82 28   €€€€€

❧ In San Gimignano the **Osteria delle Catene** rarely disappoints with an eclectic menu offering an unusual interpretation of traditional Tuscan cuisine. Wines from local vineyards are served here.
✉ Via Mainardi, 18
☎ +39 (0) 577 94 19 66   €€€€€

❧ **Markets in San Gimignano** are held on Thursday and Saturday mornings in the Piazza del Duomo.

Hotel Alma Domus

Alma Domus is owned by the Dominican Sisters of
St Catherine of Siena who run this busy guesthouse
with the help of local parishioners. The convent is
situated next to the Sanctuary of **St Catherine of Siena**,
the former house where St Catherine (1347–1380) was
born. On a hill above the convent is the **Basilica of
San Domenico** where a side chapel and altar has been
dedicated to the saint.

❧ The sisters offer single, double and triple rooms, most
with en suite bathroom and some with air-conditioning.
Some guestrooms are quite large and those on the
higher levels have balconies (request when you make
the booking) with spectacular views over rooftops and
up to the town's medieval Duomo. An unusual feature
of the bathrooms is the wall mounted shower head
which comes without shower curtain and allows water
to splash around the room—a minor inconvenience for
the price, the position and the view. The convent has
a lift and there is on-street parking nearby. The sisters
don't provide meals but there is a restaurant opposite
the convent which is open for breakfast and cafés and
trattorias in the immediate area.

✉ Via Camporeggio, 37
53100 Siena (SI)

🛏 from €45.00 pp,
including breakfast

☎ +39 (0) 577 44 177
☎ +39 (0) 577 44 487
☎ +39 (0) 577 47 601

🚌 Siena can be reached
by bus or train from
train station **Santa
Maria Novella** in
Florence. The train
station in Siena is on
the outskirts of town;
the bus station is closer
to the centre of the
town. Alma Domus
is 500 metres from
the bus station and
a steep, uphill walk.
A taxi is available at
the bus station or take
bus number 1, 3, 6, 18
or 30.

✝ **Sunday Mass**
**0900, 1030, 1200
& 1800**
Basilica di San
Domenico
Piazza San Domenico
53100 Siena (SI)

⚥ Open to both men and
women

Open Houses
Tuscany Siena

PLACES OF INTEREST ‹ Medieval, walled **Siena** is one of the best-preserved towns in Italy. Motor vehicles are banned in many streets, making the town easy to negotiate on foot despite the hills. The town's ornate Gothic cathedral rivals the Duomo in **Florence**.

‹ The heart of the town is the **Piazza del Campo**, lined with medieval buildings and colourful outdoor cafés and doubling as a race-track twice each year. If you are in Siena on 2 July or 16 August the irregularly shaped piazza is the venue of the **Palio** (horse race) when each district (*contrada*) of Siena sends a representative to ride in the traditional bare-backed race. The riders have to race their horses three times around the piazza as crowds of thousands cheer them on. In the days preceding the Palio, Siena takes on a carnival atmosphere with street parties, celebration, music and feasting. Each of the 17 districts has its own **Contrada Museum** which portrays the district's history and Palio victories. The Siena Palio is a religious festival dating back to medieval days. The first race is dedicated to the Madonna di Provenzano in honour of an appearance of the Virgin Mary in the 17th century and the second to the Madonna dell'Assunta, a Patron Saint of Siena. Both are said to have performed miracles on behalf of the people of Siena.

‹ In the **Church of San Domenico** near **Alma Domus** is an altar containing relics of St Catherine of Siena. Whilst most of her remains are buried beneath the altar of the **Church of Santa Maria sopra Minerva** in Rome, the embalmed head of St Catherine can be seen on the altar of a side chapel in the church in Siena.

‹ **The Abbey of San Galgano** in the Val di Merse, between Siena and Massa Marittima in the south, is a 12th-century Gothic Cistercian abbey and church, which has been partially restored after being vacant since 1789. The monks now live in the **Hermitage of Montesiepi**, near the ruins of the original abbey. The body of St Galgano is buried in the hermitage where another relic, a 'sword in the stone', can be seen firmly wedged in rock. Some 9 centuries earlier, St Galgano thrust the sword into stone to mark his rejection of worldly pleasures. Only the handle of the sword, in the shape of a cross, is visible. The abbey is near **Monticiano**, 33 kilometres south of Siena.

‹ A weekly food and bric-a-brac market is held in the **La Lizza Park** in Siena on Wednesday mornings from 0800. The park is about 500 metres from the **Piazza del Campo**.

FOOD AND DRINK ❧ Restaurants and cafés on the **Piazza del Campo** can be expensive and the food can be ordinary; however, there is nothing quite like sitting and having a drink and watching the passing parade on this famous piazza. Off the Campo there are dozens of pizzerias, osterias and trattorias to choose from.

❡ Take the willpower along too if you venture into **The Pasticcerie Nannini**, the ultimate Sienese *pasticceria* (pastry shop). All of Siena's sweet traditional specialities are on sale—almond pastries, chocolate bicuits, creamy custard with pine nuts and home-made gelato. Another branch, the **Conca D'Oro**, is nearby.

Pasticcerie Nannini

✉ Via Massetana Romana, 42

☎ +39 (0) 577 45 533 €€€

Conca D'Oro

✉ Via Banchi di Sopra, 24

☎ +39 (0) 577 23 60 09 €€€

❡ Learn more about Sienese cuisine on a day-long Italian cooking class at the **Lella Ciampoli Cooking School** in Siena or dine at the restaurant named after St Catherine, the **Ristorante Grotta di Santa Caterina Siena—Da Bagoga**, where the specialities include *Spaghetti Puttanesca* (made with garlic, onion, olives, capers, anchovies, and tomatoes) and *Pappardelle ai Porcini* (ribbon pasta with a mushroom sauce).

Lella Ciampoli Cooking School

✉ Via Fontebranda, 69

☎ +39 (0) 577 46 66 09

Da Bagoga

✉ Via della Galluzza, 26

☎ +39 (0) 577 28 22 08 €€€

❡ A morning market is held in **Monteroni d'Arbia**, 12 kilometres south of Siena, each Tuesday between 0800 and 1300.

Spiritual Retreats
Rome

Hotel Divino Amore
Casa Del Pellegrino

The convent and hotel, part of a sanctuary and pilgrimage site known as the **Santuario Madonna del Divino Amore** (*Sanctuary of the Mother of Divine Love*), are situated approximately 12 kilometres south of the centre of Rome and are overseen by an apostolate of local priests and nuns. A miracle is believed to have occurred here in 1740AD when a local man was saved from an attack by wild dogs through the intercession of the Madonna. Word of the miracle soon spread and in 1745, to cope with the ever increasing number of pilgrims who were beginning to visit the site, a church was erected. **The Madonna del Divino Amore** is credited for the preservation of Rome during World War II. In the early 1990s the original sanctuary was re-constructed in another area on the property and was consecrated by Pope John Paul II in 1999. Pilgrims continue to visit both sanctuaries to participate in pilgrimages, religious processions and numerous liturgical services. Pope Benedict XVI visited the sanctuary for a prayer service in May 2006. The original sanctuary is still well maintained and attracts thousands of pilgrims each year.

❡ The sanctuary's hotel, also known as the 'house of the pilgrim', is a large complex which can accommodate up to 400 guests at any one time. The air-conditioned single and twin guestrooms have colour television and en suite bathrooms. The hotel, which is run professionally, is situated in spacious grounds alongside the sanctuary's 18th-century church. There is plenty of car parking. Staff are multi-lingual and a bar and restaurant are open for drinks and all meals. Credit cards are accepted.

✉ Via del Santuario, 4
00134 Castel di Leva
Rome (RM)

🛏 from €45.00 pp,
including breakfast

✆ +39 (0) 6 71 35 19
✆ +39 (0) 6 71 35 15 15

📧 casadelpellegrino@
virgilio.it

☞ From the Piazza San Giovanni in **Laterno** take bus number 218. Or from the **Laurentina** metro station take bus number 702 or 044. The buses stop near the sanctuary.

✝ **Sunday Mass**
0600, 0700, 1300 & 1900 *in the Old Sanctuary,*
0800, 0900, 1000, 1100, 1200, 1600, 1700 & 1800h *in the New Sanctuary.*
A Eucharistic procession from the New Sanctuary to the ancient crypt of the Old Sanctuary takes place during the 1800 Mass.
Santuario Madonna del Divino Amore
Castel di Leva, 00134
Rome (RM)

⚤ Open to both men and women

PLACES OF INTEREST ❧ **The Santuario della Madonna del Divino Amore** is one of the seven pilgrim churches of Rome. Every Saturday night, from Easter until the end of October, an evening pilgrimage departs from the city, with visitors and tourists welcome to participate. The pilgrimage departs at midnight from the **Piazza di Porta Capena** (near the Circus Maximus and the Circo Massimo train station) and reaches the **Sanctuary of Madonna del Divino Amore** in the early hours of Sunday morning (around 0500). The 12-kilometre route is followed (on foot) along the **Via Appia Antica**, on to **Via Ardeatina** and past the **Catacombs of St Callisto** to the sanctuary.

❡ From the convent it is only an 18-kilometre drive to the small town of **Frascati**, famous for its white wine. At weekends the town fills with visitors escaping the congestion of Rome, so for a quieter time, visit during the week. **Castel Gandolfo**, a hilltop town overlooking **Lake Albano** and the Pope's summer residence, could be visited on the way. Established by Pope Urban VIII in 1623, the Papal Palace is stunningly positioned overlooking the lake. Concerts and musical events are often held within the palace grounds.

❡ To celebrate the annual harvest, the town hosts a Peach Festival in late July. It is a tradition that during this festival the Mayor and the villagers of the town present the Pope with an offering of peaches. **Castel Gandolfo** is 8 kilometres from **Frascati** and 25 kilometres from the centre of Rome.

❡ Some 10 kilometres away in **Morena**, heading towards Rome, is the unusual gallery of the **Association of Art and Decoration** at Gioia Tauro, 57. The gallery specialises in *trompe l'oeil*, false marbles and painting on glass. Courses and lessons can be arranged.

❡ **The Museum of the Resistance** and the **Ardeatine Catacombs**, at Via Ardeatina, 174, are a memorial to 335 Roman citizens who were murdered by the Nazis in 1944. In 1997 after being extradited from hiding in Argentina, former Nazi captain and war criminal, Erich Priebke, who ordered the massacre, was finally sentenced to life imprisonment. He remains the oldest prisoner in Europe.

Spiritual Retreats
Rome

¶ The Park Traffic School (*Parco Scuola del Traffico*) at Piazza Barcellona, 10, is a unique driving school for children aged 4 to 18 years. Children are taught the rules of the road on a specially designed track. Scale model electrical cars and motorcycles with working engines are used. The school is 10 kilometres south of Rome and 2 kilometres from Castel di Leva.

¶ The Rome Gladiator School (*Scuola Gladiatori Roma*), at Via Appia Antica, 18, conducts 1-day gladiatorial courses. Swords and armour are provided, but thankfully lions have not been available since the 6th century.

FOOD AND DRINK ❧ The restaurant in the **Hotel Divine Amoro** serves a wide range of Italian food; however, for a change, good, cheap pizza and pasta are available all day except Monday at the **Il Merlo Parlante**, approximately 3 kilometres from the sanctuary.

✉ Via Federico Cassito, 45

☎ +39 (0) 6 71 35 41 91   €€

¶ The **Hostaria Antica** was first established in 1796. The restaurant is situated among the ruins of the Appian Way, and guests occupying the tables in the trattoria's courtyard will dine amongst the catacombs of the slaves of Emperor Augustus.

✉ Via Appia Antica, 87

☎ +39 (0) 6 51 32 888   €€€€

¶ Alongside the lake in **Castel Gandolfo**, 25 kilometres south-east of Rome and 200 metres from the Pope's summer residence, is **Bucci's Ristorante**, perched above the lake with one of the best panoramas in the town. Happily, the food is as good as the view.

✉ Via de Zecchini, 31

☎ +39 (0) 6 93 23 334   €€€€

30

Comunitá Monaſtica di Camaldoli

SPIRITUAL RETREAT

The Benedictine monastery of Camaldoli is situated in the **Casentine Forest** between the borders of **Tuscany** and **Romagna**. Run by the monks of the Camaldolese Congregation of the Order of St Benedict, the monastery is open to those who prefer time out from normal daily life to share a short period of time in solitude, prayer and celebrations of the Liturgy with the monastic community. Family prayer weeks are held in August.

❧ Accommodation consists of single and multiple rooms, some of which have en suite bathrooms. All meals are catered for and there is a library for guests and a monastery shop. The monastery is sometimes the venue for musical and cultural events.

❧ The monks own a number of farmhouses in close proximity to the monastery which are also used to accommodate guests. The houses have been restored and renovated and are self-contained. The accommodation they provide would be suitable for groups, tourists and families on holiday. To enquire about holiday accommodation or to make a booking contact:

✆ +39 (0) 575 371 691
✆ +39 (0) 575 371 1691
✉ info@camaldoliospitalita.it

✉ 52010 Camaldoli (AR)

💶 price to be negotiated

✆ +39 (0) 575 55 60 12
✆ +39 (0) 575 55 60 01

✉ monastero@camaldoli.it

🚗 From **Florence** take the train to **Bibbiena** and a bus from Bibbiena to the monastery. Buses to Camaldoli are not regular (check times with the monastery before travelling. For information telephone 0575 55 60 13) and the monastery is more easily accessed by car. The monastery is 75 kilometres east of Florence by road.

✝ **Sunday Mass**
1130
Hermitage of Camaldoli,
52010 Camaldoli (AR)
1130
Monastery of Camaldoli
52010 Camaldoli (AR)

⚭ Open to both men and women

Spiritual Retreats
Tuscany Camaldoli

PLACES OF INTEREST ❧ If you would rather not venture outdoors, spend some time in the monastery library browsing through a few of the 35,000 volumes. You could always pay a visit to the 16th-century **monastery apothecary** where the monks make aromatic liqueur, jams, herbal tea and even cosmetics and skin care products. All are on sale.

❦ Explore the **Casentine Forest** by following any of the walking and hiking paths leading off from around the monastery. A visitors' centre and a park information point can be found in the **Camaldoli village** where maps of the trails are available. The *'alberi e bosco'* (trees and forest) 2-kilometre walking trail begins and ends at the monastery and weaves through the blue spruce and chestnut forests which have been planted by the monks.

❦ The **Sacro Eremo** (*Holy Hermitage*) where the monks known as the Camoldese Hermits live in total seclusion is almost 100 metres above the monastery.

❦ Take a scenic drive through the mountains and valleys to **Chiusi della Verna**, 33 kilometres south-east of Camoldoli and visit the **Sanctuary of La Verna**, a favourite place of pilgrimage for followers of St Francis of Assisi.

❦ **Casentine wool** is used in creating the traditional (and warm and fashionable) Casentino coat, versions of which can be purchased in the wool factories and shops of **Stia**, 20 kilometres west of **Camaldoli**. Orange and green have been the traditional colours of a Casentine coat; however, these days a wide variety of blends, hues and designs are available. Try the TACS Mill at Via Sanarelli, 49 and in the Piazza Tanucci, or Tessilnova at Via Giovanni Sartori, 2. Cashmere sweaters, mohair rugs and a huge variety of woollen products are on sale in shops throughout the town.

❦ **The Church of Santa Marie delle Grazie** on the Via Santa Maria is on the northern outskirts of **Stia** and is cared for by the Vallombrosan monastic community. The church was built at the place where the Madonna is said to have appeared to a peasant woman in 1428.

† Sunday Mass

Summer: 1600; Winter 1700

❡ The **Monastery of Vallombrosa** in Via San Benedetto was founded in the 11th century, and is the headquarters of the Vallombrosan Congregation of the Order of St Benedict. HRH Prince Charles, Prince of Wales, visited the abbey in 2002 to view the Museum of Sacred Art, the medieval ceiling frescoes and the monks' choir stalls. Galileo Galilei was once a student here. The monks manufacture perfume, liqueur, bath products, honey, confectionary and jam, all of which can be purchased in the monastery shop. **Vallombrosa** is 45 kilometres north-west of **Camaldoli**.

⳨ Sunday Mass 0800, 0945, 1100, 1700 & 1800

❡ During the 11th century the **Terme di Bagno di Cetica** (*Thermal Waters of Cetica*) in **Castel San Niccolò** was the meeting place of the founder of the Vallombrosan religious order, St Giovanni Gualberto, and the founder of the Camaldolese order, St Romuald. Both men blessed the waters which have since been reputed to have restorative properties, especially for digestive problems. The spa complex is only small and the waters are a constant 8°C all year round.

FOOD AND DRINK ❦ The **Ristornate La Pergolina** can be found 6 kilometres south of the monastery in the medieval village of **Partina**, where the chefs make the most of local produce which includes white truffles, mushrooms and pecorino cheese. Guests can dine in the formal, candle-lit inside rooms or in the warmer weather in the casual ambience of the summer terrace.

✉ Via Santa Rita, 54

☎ +39 (0) 575 56 19 54 €€→€€€€

❡ The hilltop **Ristorante Torricella** in the hotel of the same name is on the outskirts of the town of **Poppi**, 15 kilometres from Camaldoli. The restaurant looks out over the **Casentine hills** and up to the **Poppi Castle**. The lengthy menu includes rabbit, duck, meat and pasta dishes and wines mostly from Tuscan vineyards.

✉ 1416 Ponte a Poppi

☎ +39 (0) 575 52 70 45 €€€

❡ **Bibbiena** has a weekly market each Thursday morning. A Monday afternoon market is held on the Strada di Casentini in **Castel San Niccolò**, 20 kilometres south-west of Camaldoli.

Spiritual Retreats
Tuscany Chiusi della Verna

31

Santuario della Verna

The Sanctuary of La Verna is a Catholic monastery of the Order of Friars Minor of the Franciscan Order, disciples of St Francis of Assisi (c1181–1226) and where St Francis of Assisi once lived and prayed. While at **La Verna** in 1224, St Francis received the Stigmata in the form of Christ crucified.

❡ The monastery is a place of spirituality and pilgrimage and the friars who live here welcome guests to spend some time in rest, prayer and guided or self-directed retreat. The monastery has 72 single, double and triple rooms, all with heating and en suite bathrooms. There is no daily room cleaning service. Separate accommodation in out-buildings on the property is available to large groups.

❡ The dining room, known as the Refectory of the Pilgrim, can cater for up to 400 guests and all meals are available. A bar sells wine and soft drinks and a selection of liqueurs manufactured by the monks. Day visitors are welcome to make use of the dining facilities and the bar.

❡ Every day, twice a day, at 1400 and 2400 the friars make a pilgrimage along the Corridor of the Stigmata to pray in the chapel where St Francis received the Stigmata.

✉ Via del Santuario, 45 52010 Chiusi della Verna (AR)

🛏 from €42.00 pp (single), including breakfast

☎ +39 (0) 575 53 41
☎ +39 (0) 575 34 210
📠 +39 (0) 575 59 93 20

✉ la.verna@libero.it

☞ Take the train or bus to **Bibbiena** which is 3 kilometres from the sanctuary and walk from here. A bus service (irregular) leaves from Bibbiena and stops near the sanctuary. Check times before departing. The sanctuary can also be accessed by car.

✝ **Sunday Mass**
0800, 1000, 1100, 1215, 1630 & 1800
Santuario della Verna
Via del Santuario, 45
Chiusi della Verna
52010 (AR)

⚥ Open to both men and women

PLACES OF INTEREST ❧ **La Verna** is an isolated monastery but pilgrims have been flocking here for centuries to follow the footsteps of St Francis. The friars are especially busy every 14 September the anniversary of the day St Francis received the Stigmata, when even more visitors than usual congregate at the site. Pilgrims can worship in the **Chapel of the Stigmata** and the 13th-century **Church of Santa Maria degli Angeli**, the first church ever built on the estate. Many make the short pilgrimage to the Sasso Spico, the rock under which St Francis prayed and on to the cave where he slept.

❡ Centuries-old beech forest and woodlands of silver fir cloak the slopes leading up to the monastery and paths and walking trails slip off into the woods. A track heads from the monastery down to the village of **La Beccia**, about 100 metres away. Another trail leads from the monastery, through the fir forest up to the summit of **Monte Penna**, a testing trek which ends at a tiny chapel and awesome 360-degree views. The Chiusi della Verna Visitors Centre, Parco Martiri della Libertà, 21, can supply detailed maps of walking and hiking routes through the **Casentine National Park**.

❡ The **Santuario di Santa Maria del Sasso** forms part of a Dominican monastery and is situated near the town of **Bibbiena** on the site where the Madonna is said to have appeared to Caterina, a local 7-year-old girl, in 1347. The crypt where the appearances occurred is open daily between 0700 and 1200 and 1500 and 1800.

✝ Sunday Mass 0830 & 1030

❡ The medieval village of **Caprese Michelangelo**, 10 kilometres south of Chiusi La Verna, is the birthplace of the great sculptor and artist Michelangelo Buonarotti. The house where Michelangelo was born in 1475 is now a museum displaying reproductions of his works.

❡ Since Etruscan times the town of **Arezzo**, 38 kilometres south of Chiusi della Verna, has been steeped in the production of gold jewellery. The local jewellery shops cater for all tastes and budgets but an antique market, held on the first weekend of every month, could be just the place to find that needle in a haystack. Jewellery, furniture, paintings, prints and other artworks are on sale.

Spiritual Retreats

Tuscany Chiusi della Verna

❧ The town of **Sansepolcro** has been a centre for Italian lace for 200 years. The **Spazio del Merletto** (*Lace School*) conducts classes in lace-making. Students can also visit the lace museum **Museo de Merletto** which is in the same building. Every even-year in September and October the Sansepolcro Lace Festival attracts lacemakers and enthusiasts from all over Europe. The town is 30 kilometres south of Chiusi della Verna.

❧ **The Smugglers' Walk**, a 20-kilometre route departing from the villages of **Chitignano** and **Anghiari**, is an annual event held on the last Sunday of August which revives an ancient tradition of swapping Anghiari tobacco for Chitignano gunpowder. The exchange takes place on the **Ponte alla Piera**, halfway between the towns. Participants can leave from either place and take part in the local festivities on completion of the walk, including smoking home-rolled cigars. Chitignano is 10 kilometres south of Chiusi della Verna.

❧ Each day of the week you can visit the market of a different neighbouring town. Monday in **Pieve Santo Stefano**, Tuesday in **Sansepolcro**, Wednesday in **Anghiari**…the towns come alive on market day! These markets offer local produce, clothing, household goods, etc, and are a great opportunity to experience provincial Italy.

FOOD AND DRINK ❦ Friendly, family run inns and hotels can be found throughout the **Chiusi della Verna** district and most have restaurants attached. The **Ristorante Da Giovanna** and the restaurant of the **Hotel Letizia** (within walking distance of the sanctuary), are open to the public. There are two small restaurants in the village of **La Beccia**.

Ristorante Da Giovanna

✉ Via San Francesco, 3

☎ +39 (0) 575 59 92 75 €€€

Hotel Letizia

✉ Via Roma, 26

☎ +39 (0) 575 59 92 06 €€€

❧ **Eating at the Ristorante La Nena** is akin to eating in someone's home. The small uncluttered dining room is simply outfitted and a small menu of fish, meat and game is complemented by an extensive wine list.

✉ Via Giacomo Matteotti, 10, Anghiari

☎ +39 (0) 575 78 94 91 €€€

❧ Near **Chitignano**, the rustic, farmhouse-style **Osteria Panta Rei** serves Italian-style comfort food in somewhat folksy surroundings. Ingredients are sourced locally and the salami, pasta and desserts are home-made.

✉ La Casa, 70

☎ +39 (0) 575 59 15 00 €€

Spiritual Retreats
Tuscany Chiusure

Monastica di Monte Oliveto Maggiore

Chiusure is a peaceful hilltop hamlet alongside the ruins of an ancient castle. The 14th-century monastery is on the outskirts of the village, surrounded by a thick cypress forest. Over the centuries, hospitality has been a tradition of the Congregazione Benedettina Olivetana (*Congregation of the Benedictine Olivetans*) who live here. The monastery guesthouse offers single, double and family guestrooms which are available to those seeking spiritual renewal. The monastery restaurant is open for all meals.

❡ The walls of the monastery and the church, which is built in the shape of a Latin cross, are embellished with art dating from the 15th century. The cloisters are lined with frescoes and a 16th-century library houses the monks' collection of precious books and manuscripts. The monks now work on restoring these ancient volumes and parchments.

❡ The original monastery pharmacy is used by the monks to produce honey and liqueurs which are on sale in the monastery gift shop along with olive oil and wine and other items made by the community. The monks sing the Gregorian chant during Vespers at 1815 on weekdays and at 1830 on Sunday and public holidays. The monastery closes each day between 1200 and 1500.

✉ 53020 Chiusure (SI)

💶 price to be negotiated

📞 +39 (0) 577 70 76 52
📠 +39 (0) 577 70 76 44

✉ foresteria@
monteolivetomaggiore.it

☞ Take the train to
Asciano, 8 kilometres
north of the monastery
or to Buonconvento,
9 kilometres south of
the monastery and a
taxi from either town.
The monastery is best
accessed by car as a
taxi might not always
be available. To call a
taxi, dial 0577 80 60 94
or 0577 80 65 03.

† Sunday Mass
Summer: 0800, 1100
& 1730
Winter: 0800, 1100
& 1700
Abbey of Monte
Oliveto Maggiore
53020 Chiusure (SI)

🐝 Open to both men and
women

Spiritual Retreats
Tuscany Chiusure

PLACES OF INTEREST ✦ **Chiusure** is in an area of hot, sulphurous thermal springs and the town of **Rapolano Terme**, 17 kilometres north, is the thermal centre of Tuscany. St Catherine of Siena once took to the waters for therapeutic reasons at an ancient thermal pool in the town of **Bagno Vignoni**, 25 kilometres to the south of Chiusure. The pool can still be seen but is now closed for bathing.

❡ If travelling north, the Italian shoe and leather manufacturer **Pratesi** has a factory outlet at Via Dante Alighieri, 83, in Ambra, near Bucine, 33 kilometres north of Chiusure and sells discounted leather shoes, handbags, belts and jackets. The outlet is closed on Sunday and open from 0900 every other day. The factory closes for lunch between 1230 and 1500.

❡ **The Abbey of Sant'Antimo**, in Castelnuovo dell'Abate, near Montalcino and 20 kilometres south of Chiusure dates back to the year 814 and is occupied by the Catholic Order of Premonstratensian Canons. Explore the ancient abbey by following any of the four marked walking routes and discover the medieval art and history of Sant'Antimo. The friars sing the Gregorian chant during evening Vespers at 1900 (1830 onSundays and Holy Days).

⊹ Sunday Mass 0930 & 1100 *(times vary)*
⊹ Vespers 1900, *except* Sundays & Holy Days 1830

❡ **The Museo d'Arte Sacra** (*Museum of Sacred Art*) in the Piazza Fratelli Bandiera in Asciano exhibits religious paintings, sculptures and artworks which have come from churches and monasteries in the area. Works by Segna di Bonaventura (1298–1358) and Ambrogio Lorenzetti (1290–1348) and other painters of the Sienese School hang in the museum.

❦ **The Nature Train** departs from Siena and passes between **Asciano** and **Monte Antico**, stopping at **Monte Oliveto Maggiore** and at villages and hamlets (on request) along the route. Passengers can jump off to do some sightseeing and rejoin the train later. The train departs from the Siena train station and operates on Sundays in May, June, September and October, with three departures daily. Other departures link with festivals and cultural events in the district and include the Truffle Train, Olive Oil Train, Etruscan Train and the Chestnut Train.

FOOD AND DRINK ❦ Almost 6 kilometres south of Chiusure, the village of **San Giovanni d'Asso** produces wine and olive oil and a famous white truffle. A white truffle market and auction takes place in the town each November. The hilltop villages around **Chiusure** all produce their own unique variation of olive oil, wine, salami and cheese.

❦ The walled town of **Buonconvento**, 9 kilometres south of Chiusure, has a weekly market each Saturday morning in the Piazza Gramsci. While you are in Buonconvento you could have a bite at the **Ristorante I Poggioli** for a local version of fresh, simple cuisine at unpretentious prices and a modest list of the rich, ruby red wines of Montalcino.

✉ Via Tassi

☎ +39 (0) 577 80 65 46 €€

❦ At **Ristorante Il Conte Matto**, in Trequanda, 10 kilometres east of Chiusure, diners can opt for a Tuscan degustation menu from four or five variations and prices and choose a wine from hundreds of labels.

✉ Via Maresca 1, Trequanda

☎ +39 (0) 577 66 20 79 €€€

Spiritual Retreats
Tuscany Bagno a Ripoli

33

Convento dell'Incontro

The Convento dell'Incontro was founded by St Leonard
of Port Maurice (1676–1751) in the early 18th century
and is owned by the Provincia Francescana dei Frati
Minori (*Franciscan Province of the Friars Minor*). The
guesthouse is run by a voluntary Catholic religious
group linked to the order, the l'Associazione Obiettivo
Francesco (*Association of the Intentions of Francis*). The
convent is east of Florence, approximately 12 kilometres
from the centre of the city, and is sometimes used by the
Florentine Franciscan friars as a place of rest and retreat.
The convent is situated in large grounds in a woodsy area
near the village of **Villamagna**.

❡ The guesthouse has been in operation since the year
2000 when a large section of the convent was renovated
for the purpose of providing accommodation. Single,
twin and multiple guestrooms are available and all share
a bathroom on the same floor. Guests can spend time in
self-directed retreat in the calm and tranquillity of the
convent and the surrounds. A small chapel inside the
convent is dedicated to St Leonard. Tourists can also
stay overnight here. The convent has a large, on-site car
parking area.

✉ Via dell'Incontro, 1
50012 Villamagna
Bagno a Ripoli (FI)

▦ price to be negotiated

☎ +39 (0) 55 65 19 122

✐ info@
conventoincontro.it

☞ The convent is 1.5
kilometres from the
village of **Villamagna**
on the south-eastern
outskirts of **Florence**.
The convent is
easily reached by
car from Florence
and is signposted in
Villamagna.

✝ **Sunday Mass**
1730 (*may vary*)
Convento dell'Incontro
Via dell'Incontro, 1
50012 Villamagna,
Bagno a Ripoli (FI)
1030
Parish Church of San
Donnino a Villamagna
Piazza di
Villamagna, 10
50012 Villamagna
Bagno a Ripoli (FI)

⚭ Open to both men and
women

PLACES OF INTEREST ❧ The convent is in an area of endless vineyards and horse stables advertising trail rides and riding lessons. **Villamagna** is only 18 kilometres from the factory outlets of **Rignano sull'Arno**. (See page 188)

❧ Mapped and signposted footpaths and hiking trails branch off from the town of **Pontassieve**, 10 kilometres north-east of Villamagna. The trails pass medieval churches and the ruins of old castles and from some vantage points Florence can be seen in the distance. A trail runs from Pontassieve to the village of **Rosano** where the 11th-century **Abbey of Santa Maria di Rosano** is occupied by an enclosed order of Benedictine nuns. Pope Benedict XVI often visited the monastery when he was a cardinal and on becoming Pope granted the Rosano nuns responsibility for the contemplative community of religious who pray in the **Vatican Gardens**. This community, which changes every 5 years, is made up of religious of all nations who pray constantly for the intentions of the Pope.

❧ Each Good Friday, hundreds of pilgrims and local residents don elaborate, Roman style costumes to take part in a centuries-old tradition re-enacting the Passion of Christ in the annual **Easter Procession**, which takes place in **Grassina**, 10 kilometres south of **Villamagna**. The event is now so popular that onlookers must reserve seats to attend.

❧ **Bagno a Ripoli's Open Museum** is a series of three themed driving routes weaving around the local area and encompassing the region's art, history, culture, people and environment. Maps and further information can be obtained from the Office of Culture at Via Fratelli Orsi, 18, in Bagno a Ripoli.

Spiritual Retreats

Tuscany Bagno a Ripoli

❧ A 6-kilometre return walking route commences at the **Giardino Il Ponti in Bagno a Ripoli** and trails past local vineyards, farms, hamlets and wayside shrines. The path leads past the tiny **Church of Vicchio** in which the 15th-century Tabernacle of Rimaggino was crafted for the sole purpose of protecting a fragment of the Holy Cross, said to have been found in the Holy Land by St Helen and taken to Rome. The relic still remains in the Tabernacle today.

❧ If you are travelling north of Florence, the **Pratesi** shop in Via Montalbano, **Casalguidi** on the outskirts of Pistoia, 50 kilometres north-west of Villamagna, stocks an exclusive range of discounted linens and household goods. Closed on Sunday.

❧ Every Wednesday morning a market takes place in **Bagno a Ripoli** at the **Giardino dei Ponti** (*Garden of the Bridges*) where concerts and local festivities are also held. **Pontassieve** has a Wednesday market in the Piazza Vittoria Emanuele II and on Saturdays in the Piazza Mosca. The village of **Pelago** 6 kilometres further on has a market each Thursday.

FOOD AND DRINK ❧ The **Osteria da Melo**, near the monastery in Rosano, is a family-style restaurant with a warm, cosy interior and a small outdoor dining area. The chef hails from Sicily and the menu lists Tuscan and Sicilian dishes. Open Tuesday to Saturday and for lunch on Sunday.

✉ Via di Rosano, 198

☏ +39 (0) 55 65 19 000   €€€

❧ The rather bland exterior of the **Sante Osteria** in **Bagno a Ripoli** disguises a first-class seafood restaurant. Fish and all manner of crustaceans are served along with pasta and rice dishes and barbequed Florentine beef is also on the menu. A small outdoor area can be used in summer.

✉ Via di Vacciano, 37

☏ +39 (0) 55 64 61 591   €€€

❧ The **Fattoria Le Sorgenti** estate in **Bagno a Ripoli** produces a popular and robust Tuscan red called Scirus. They also produce their own olive oil. The views over Florence are an extra treat.

✉ Via di Docciola, 8

☏ +39 (0) 55 69 60 04

Spiritual Retreats
Tuscany Siena

Hermitage of Lecceto

Secluded in a dense forest of oak trees 7 kilometres west
of **Siena**, this isolated monastery is run by a community
of contemplative Augustinian nuns. Augustinians
have lived here since the 14th century. The holy sisters
have opened a section of the monastery for overnight
guests who come to spend time in self-directed prayer
and retreat. The monastery radiates an atmosphere of
peace and piety and its surroundings are conducive to
prayer and meditation. Accommodation is available for
overnight guests in twin and multiple guestrooms on a
share bathroom basis. Use of a fully equipped kitchen is
provided.

❡ Guests may be invited to join the nuns in the
liturgical ceremonies of the community. Overnight stays
at the monastery are by prior arrangement only. For
information contact the sisters at the hermitage by letter,
written in either English or Italian, well ahead of time. It
is thought that St Catherine of Siena paid regular visits
to the monastery and St Catherine's Well, where the
saint is believed to have rested after walking from **Siena**,
is in the convent grounds.

✉ Strada di Lecceto, 6
53100 Siena (si)

💶 price to be negotiated

📞 +39 (0) 577 34 93 93
📠 +39 (0) 577 34 93 72

☞ The monastery is quite
remote and well off
the tourist and public
transport trails, though
easily accessed by car
from **Siena**.

✝ Sunday Mass
0800, 1100, 1215
& 1900
Cathedral of Siena
(Duomo)
Piazza del Duomo
53100 Siena (si)

Open to both men and
women

Spiritual Retreats
Tuscany Siena

PLACES OF INTEREST ❧ You could take a day trip to **San Gimignano**, 45 kilometres north of Siena, and on the way stop for lunch—and for some photos of the splendid views— at the tiny, walled, hilltop village of **Monteriggioni**. Wine lovers could make a short diversion to the Rocca del Macie winery in **Castellina** in the heart of the **Chianti Classico** region to sample some of the award-winning red wine (a post-home service is available). Visitors to the winery are greeted by a giant black rooster, confirmation of a vineyard producing genuine Chianti.

❧ From **San Gimignano** you could take the long way back to Siena and pick up some hand-woven cashmere scarves, shawls or blankets from the **Azienda Agricola la Penisola** (*Agricultural Company of Penisola*) at **Radda** in Chianti, one of Tuscany's cashmere goat farms. Radda is 40 kilometres east of San Gimignano and 30 kilometres north of Siena.

❧ The village of **Colle di Val d'Elsa** lies between Siena and San Gimignano and is probably best known to connoisseurs of fine hand-crafted crystal as 'the Italian Bohemia'. Each year in September the town hosts an exhibition of the works of local crystal craftsmen. However, all year round visitors can wander into the artisan workshops in the town and browse for pieces to take home. Friday is market day in Colle di Val d'Elsa.

❧ Back in Siena at the **Dante Alighieri Language School** at Via Tommaso Pendola, 37, students are busy learning to speak Italian. Students can combine a language course with cooking lessons or with an art, opera or drama course. Courses are open to tourists and run for one day or, for those who can't bear the thought of leaving Siena, up to 32 weeks.

❡ If you have never played a musical instrument the **Accademia Musicale Chigiana**, at Via di Città, 89, in Siena conducts short courses in violin, piano, guitar and conducting, not only for students of music, but also for those who are interested in learning how to play an instrument but who have had no previous training. The **Siena Jazz School** at the Fortezza Medicea in the Piazza della Libertà in Siena conducts short courses in vocal training for those with no singing experience whatsoever. Introductory courses in jazz and modern music are also on the calendar.

❡ Siena's **Summer Festival of Jazz** is organised by the Siena Jazz School and takes place over two weeks each summer (usually in July / August) with concerts held at indoor and outside venues around the town.

FOOD AND DRINK The **Enoteca Italiana di Siena** in the Fortezza Medicea is a showcase for the best of Italian wine. Over 1000 different wines from all over the country are stored here and visitors can sample different varieties, buy bottles to take away and in summer enjoy a meal in the garden of the Restaurant Millevini. Tours to the local vineyards can also be arranged here.

✉ Via Camollia, 72

☎ +39 (0) 577 24 71 21　　　　　　€€€

❡ The town square in medieval **Monteriggioni** is flanked by an ancient church, tourist shops and a couple of cafés and bars. One of the more pleasant places to dine is in the garden of the **Ristorante Il Pozzo**, off the town square.

✉ Piazza Roma, 2

☎ +39 (0) 577 30 41 27　　　　　　€€€

❡ Take home a taste of Tuscany from the **Fattoria Castello di Monteriggioni**, also located on the square where local wines and olive oil are on sale.

✉ Loc. Castello, Monteriggioni

☎ +39 (0) 577 306 015

❡ **Panforte di Siena** is said to have been created by Siennese monks around 1000AD and is a sweet speciality of Siena. Take some home—perfect with coffee, or anything!

Lazio & Rome

❧ Each Good Friday evening in Rome the Pope leads the **Via Crucis**, a procession re-enacting the Way of the Cross. The procession, which commences at the **Colosseum** at 2100, ends on **Palatine Hill** and attracts throngs of pilgrims. Former Franciscan Friar St Leonard of Port Maurice (1676–1751) was an advocate of the tradition and his relics now lie in the 17th-century Church of San Bonaventura, part of a friary on the Via Bonaventura on Palatine Hill. The body of St Bonaventura (1221–1274), a former disciple of St Francis of Assisi, is also entombed in the church.

❧ The **Basilica of Maria Maggiore** on the Esquiline Hill is one of Rome's renowned pilgrim churches. According to legend, the basilica was built on the site of a miraculous August snowfall. The festival of Madonna delle Neve (*Our Lady of the Snow*) is celebrated at Santa Maria Maggiore every year on 5 August when, during Mass, white rose petals, representing snow, float down on the altar during High Mass. The Sforza Chapel, within the basilica, was designed by Michelangelo in 1564 and completed by Giacomo della Porta (c1537–1602).

❧ The **Via Francigena** (*Highway to Heaven*), as mentioned in the Austrian pilgrimage section, commences at Canterbury in England and weaves through France and Switzerland to the burial place of St Peter, in the Vatican in Rome. The trail passes through the Italian towns of Santhià and Vercelli in Piedmont, Pavia in Lombardy and follows the 'boot' of Italy down through Tuscany and on to Bolsena, Viterbo, Sutri, over the Monte Mario hill and finally into Rome (the Italian trail is approx. 700 km).

❧ The immense, impressive **Abbey of Montecassino** lies off the main highway between Rome and Naples. The abbey was established in 529 by St Benedict of Nursia, one of the Patron Saints of Europe. St Benedict died in Montecassino and is buried alongside his twin sister, St Scholastica, beneath the high altar in the abbey basilica. The abbey is open every day except between 1230–1530. There are no eating or drinking facilities for day visitors to Montecassino but cafés and restaurants can be found in the town of Cassino, close by.

† Daily Mass 0900, 1030 & 1200

❧ The Italian section of the **Via Slavica** pilgrimage route from Vienna commences in the historical old Roman city of Aquileia (established in 181BC) in Northern Italy, not far from the Slovenian border. The trail continues on through the regions of Veneto and

Umbria to the Vatican in Rome. This once popular but neglected trail is presently being re-established.

❧ **The Santuario della Madonna del Divino Amore** is one of the seven pilgrim churches of Rome. A miracle is believed to have occurred here in 1740AD when a local man was saved from an attack by wild dogs through the intercession of the Madonna. Word of the miracle soon spread and in 1745, to cope with the ever increasing number of pilgrims who were beginning to visit the site, a church was erected. The Madonna del Divino Amore is credited for the preservation of Rome during World War II. Every Saturday night, from Easter until the end of October, an evening pilgrimage departs from the city, with visitors and tourists invited to participate. The pilgrimage leaves at midnight from the **Piazza di Porta Capena**, (near the Circus Maximus and the Circo Massimo train station) and reaches the Sanctuary of Madonna del Divino Amore in the early hours of Sunday morning. The route followed (on foot) is along the Via Appia Antica, on to Via Ardeatina and past the Ardeatine Catacombs and the Catacombs of St Callisto to the sanctuary.

❧ **The St Francis** (of Assisi) **Walk** (*Cammino di Francesco*), is an 80-kilometre pilgrimage trail where pilgrims can walk, cycle or drive in the footsteps of St Francis. Pilgrims receive a St Francis walk passport which can be stamped at the various stops along the way. The pilgrimage area is known as the Sacred Valley, a region north-east of Rome which was much loved by the saint. Stops are made at churches and sanctuaries and at a spectacular shrine on the peak of Monte Terminillo near the town of Rieti.

❧ **The Sanctuary of Fonte Colombo**, on the outskirts of Rieti, is part of the Sacred Valley and a stopping point on the St Francis Walk. St Francis lived for a time at the Fonte Colombo Hermitage and the Cappella della Maddalena, a tiny, cave-like chapel where St Francis often celebrated Mass can be visited.

❧ Monasteries and churches surround the cave in **Subiaco** (70 kilometres east of Rome) where St Benedict of Nursia, founder of the great Benedictine religious order, lived as a hermit for 3 years. The cave is known as the 'sacred grotto' (*Santuario Sacro Speco*) and is a revered pilgrimage site within the **Basilica of St Benedict**.

♱ Sunday Mass 0900, 1000 & 1100

❧ With her twin's help, St Benedict's sister, St Scholastica, established the **Abbey of St Scholastica** close to St Benedict's Monastery in Subiaco.

♱ Sunday Mass 1000 & 1630

Abruzzo

¶ The **Santuario del Miracolo Eucaristico** (*Sanctuary of the Eucharistic Miracle*) in Lanciano in the province of Chieti is where a Eucharistic Miracle (the consecrated Bread and Wine changing into real flesh and blood) is said to have occurred during a Mass celebrated there during the 8th century. The relics are kept inside the sanctuary. The flesh and the blood are of blood type AB which is the same as the blood found on the **Shroud of Turin**, believed to be the cloth covering the body of Christ when he was buried.

¶ Situated in Isola del Gran Sasso, **The Sanctuary of St Gabriele** is one of Italy's most visited pilgrimage sites. Thousands of pilgrims spend time at the sanctuary each year to worship before the miraculous tomb of St Gabriele, a young saint and Patron of the Italian Catholic Youth Movement who died aged 24 in the year 1824.

¶ **The Staircase of Divine Forgiveness**, a staircase similar to the stairs which Jesus climbed in Jerusalem on his way to be sentenced by Pontius Pilate, is located next to the Church of St Paul (*Paolo*) in the town of Campli, near the Adriatic coast in the province of Teramo. All 28 steps must be climbed on the knees as an act of penance and to receive a plenary indulgence granted by Pope Clement XIV in 1772.

¶ Situated in Manoppello, in the Pescara province, **The Sanctuary of the Holy Image** is a much venerated pilgrimage destination. An image said to be of the face of Jesus Christ, similar to that found on the Shroud of Turin, can be seen on a piece of cloth on display in the sanctuary. Pilgrims visiting the sanctuary gain a plenary indulgence (forgiveness of all sins) granted by Pope Clement XI in 1718.

Liguria

¶ **The Route of the Sanctuaries** is a 12-kilometre walking trail leading from the village of Riomaggiore, one of the Cinque Terre Ports in Liguria, to wayside sanctuaries in Montenero, Volastra, San Bernadino, Reggio Madonna and Vernazza ending at the **Sanctuary of Our Lady of Soviore** near the town of Monterosso al Mare.

Marche

❡ **The House of the Holy Family** is believed to be the dwelling that Jesus, Mary and Joseph lived in while in Nazareth. The 'Holy House' is enclosed within a specially constructed church, the **Basilica di Santa Casa**, in the town of Loreto in the Marche region of Italy. According to the legend the house was miraculously transferred by angels from Nazareth to Loreto.

Piedmont

❡ **The Sacred Mountain of Varallo** is one of the nine 'Sacri Monti' (*Sacred Mountains*) in Northern Italy. The Sacred Mountains are carefully placed groupings of tiny chapels of various design, established in some of the most naturally beautiful areas of Italy. The chapels were built to encourage Catholics of the 16th and 17th centuries to worship outside their local church. The Varallo site is an arrangement of over 40 chapels and monuments and hundreds of religious icons and objects and is a world heritage-listed site. Other *Sacri Monti* in the Piedmont region can be found at Allesandria, Novara, Turin and Vercelli and at Biella, Como, Varese and Verbania in Lombardy.

Puglia

❡ **St Pio of Pietrelcina**, commonly referred to as Padre Pio, was a member of the Order of Minor Capuchin Friars, and was a recipient of the Stigmata 50 years before his death. Padre Pio was canonized by the late Pope John Paul II in 1999. He is buried in the pilgrim **Church of Our Lady of Grace** in the town of San Giovanni Rotondo. The tomb of St Pio, who died in 1968, is a much visited place of pilgrimage and attracts thousands of visitors each year. The local Capuchin order have established a **Via Crucis** (*Way of the Cross*) for pilgrims which leads from the Church of Our Lady of Grace to the last Station of the Cross on the peak of nearby Monte Castellano.

⛪ Sunday Mass 0600, 0700, 0800, 0900, 1000, 1100, 1200, 1600, 1730 & 1900

❡ The town of **Monte Sant'Angelo** on the summit of Monte Gargano is 25 kilometres east of San Giovanni Rotondo and a place of pilgrimage to the **Sanctuary of San Michele**. It is said the Archangel Michael appeared in the Grotto within the Basilica of St Michele during the 5th and 17th centuries.

Tuscany

❡ **The Sanctuary of Madonna delle Grazie del Sasso** is a place of pilgrimage near the village of Santa Brigida on the scenic outskirts of Fiesole. The Virgin Mary is said to have appeared to two shepherd girls around 1480 instructing them to build a church in her name. The rock on which Mary is said to have stood is under the altar of the sanctuary church in Sasso, which is built on the site of her appearances.

❡ **The Via Francigena pilgrimage trail** from Canterbury in England, through France and Switzerland to the burial place of St Peter, in the Vatican in Rome, passes through Piedmont and Lombardy down to the Tuscan towns of Pontremoli, Lucca, San Gimignano, Poggibonsi, Colle Val d'Elsa, Monteriggioni, Siena and Arezzo. The trail crosses to Umbria and on to Assisi, and continues on down through the Lazio province and finally to Rome.

Umbria

❡ **The Via Slavica** is an ancient pilgrimage route from Vienna which enters Italy at the old Roman port of Aquileia in the north of the country and passes through Venice, Bologna and Assisi to the Vatican in Rome. The route is currently being formally reinstated. St Francis of Assisi spent times of silence and solitude in the **Monastery of La Verna**, a stop on the pilgrimage trail near the village of Chiusi della Verna. It was at La Verna in 1223 where Francis received the Stigmata (*the Wounds of Christ*). The road leading to the monastery is a well trodden pilgrimage trail for followers of St Francis.

❡ Pilgrims travel to a tiny chapel in the **Hermitage at Montesiepi**, near Siena, to pray at the shrine of 'the sword in the stone' which is said to have been driven into a rock by St Galgano in 1180 to mark his rejection of worldly pleasures. The sword forms the shape of a cross.

❡ In a long-standing tradition a **Good Friday Procession** is held in Grassina, 10 kilometres south of Florence where hundreds of villagers re-enact the Passion of Christ (tickets required).

❡ On the outskirts of the town of Assisi, the **Basilica of St Francis** is the burial place of St Francis of Assisi who was born in the town c1181.

† Sunday Mass

0730, 0900, 1030, 1200, 1700 & 1830

The Veneto

❡ In the town itself stands the **Basilica of St Clare**, founder of the Catholic religious order The Poor Clares and the Patron Saint of Television. The sainthood was bestowed upon her by Pope Pius XII in 1958. Towards the end of her life, when Clare was too ill to attend Mass, it is said that images of the Mass would appear on the walls of her cell (room). St Clare's incorrupt body lies in the crypt in the basilica which carries her name.

† Daily Mass 0715, 0900 & Summer: 1730

  Winter: 1630

❡ A Crucifix which once stood in the Church of San Damiano, on the southern outskirts of Assisi and from where Jesus is said to have spoken to St Francis asking him to repair the dilapidated church, now hangs in the **Chapel of the Crucifix** inside the Basilica of St Clare.

✉ Church of San Damiano

† Sunday Mass 0730 & 0930

❡ Part of an ancient church once used by St Francis, **The Shrine of Porziuncola** is now enclosed within the **Basilica of Santa Maria degli Angeli** in the town of Santa Maria degli Angeli (*St Mary of the Angels*), 5 kilometres from Assisi.

† Sunday Mass

  0700, 0800, 0900, 1000, 1130, 1700 & 1800

❡ Pilgrims arrive by the hundreds each day to pray before a shrine in the **Basilica of San Antonio in Padua** (*Padova*) which contains the relics of St Anthony, the Patron Saint of Travellers.

† Daily Mass 0600, 0700, 0800, 0900, 1000,

  1100, 1215, 1700 & 1900

❡ **The Via Slavica** pilgrimage trail from Vienna passes through Venice and the region of Emilia Romagna, and continues on down to the Lazio province and on to the Vatican in Rome.

**Additional
Accommodation**

Lazio &
Rome

☩ BOLSENA

**ⓣ Convento Santa Maria
del Giglio**

✉ Via Madonna del Giglio, 49
01023 Bolsena (VT)
☏ +39 (0) **761 79 90 66**
✉ *puntidivista@pelagus.it*
♨ Open to both men and women

☩ MONTECASSINO

**ⓢ Abbazia di
Montecassino**

✉ Via Montecassino
03043 Montecassino (RM)

☏ +39 (0) **776 31 15 29**
☏ +39 (0) **776 31 16 43**

✉ *info@montecassino.it*

♨ Open to both men and women

☩ RIETI

**ⓢ Santuario Francescano
di Fonte Colombo**

✉ 02100 Fonte Colombo Rieti
(RM)

☏ +39 (0) **746 21 01 25**
♨ Open to both men and women

**ⓢ Oasi Francescana San
Antonio al Monte**

✉ Via Fonte Cottorella, 24a
02199 Rieti (RM)

☏ +39 (0) **746 20 06 90**
☏ +39 (0) **746 20 06 90**

♨ Open to both men and women

☩ ROME

**ⓣ Casa Per Ferie Suore
Carmelitane**

✉ Via Trionfale, 6157
00135 Rome (RM)

☏ +39 (0) **6 35 40 641**
☏ +39 (0) **6 35 49 77 36**

✉ *info@villamontemario.com*

♨ Open to both men and women

ⓣ Casa San Gabriele

✉ Via Trionfale, 12840
00135 Rome (RM)

☏ +39 (0) **6 30 35 90 406**
☏ +39 (0) **6 30 35 90 406**

✉ *sgcsg@stgabrielinst.org*

♨ Open to both men and women

ⓣ Casa San Tommaso

✉ Viale Romania, 7
00197 Rome (RM)

☏ +39 (0) **6 80 70 274**
☏ +39 (0) **6 80 70 246**

✉ *villanova@casasantommaso.it*

♨ Open to both men and women

ⓣ Hotel Carisma

✉ Viale Guglielmo Marconi, 700
00146 Rome (RM)

☏ +39 (0) **6 54 22 57 88**
☏ +39 (0) **6 54 22 58 56**

✉ *hotelcarisma@tin.it*

♨ Open to both men and women

ⓣ Hotel Domus Aurelia

✉ Via Aurelia, 218
00165 Rome (RM)

☏ +39 (0) **6 39 36 59** (5 lines)
☏ +39 (0) **6 39 37 64 80**

✉ *info@domusaurelia.com*

♨ Open to both men and women

ⓣ Hotel Ponte Sisto

✉ Via dei Pettinari, 64
00186 Rome (RM)

☏ +39 (0) **6 68 63 10**
☏ +39 (0) **6 68 30 17 12**

✉ *info@hotelpontesisto.it*

♨ Open to both men and women

ⓣ Hotel Villa Rosa

✉ Via Giovanni Prati, 1
00152 Rome (RM)

☏ +39 (0) **6 58 10 243**
☏ +39 (0) **6 58 80 254**

✉ *info@villarosa-hotel.it*

♨ Open to both men and women

ⓣ Istituto Cavanis

✉ Via Casilina, 600
00177 Rome (RM)

☏ +39 (0) **6 24 19 336**
☏ +39 (0) **6 24 19 336**

✉ *cavanisroma@fastwebnet.it*

♨ Open to both men and women

**ⓣ Istituto Maria
Santissima Bambina**

✉ Via Paolo VI, 21
00120 Rome (RM)

☏ +39 (0) **6 69 89 35 11**
☏ +39 (0) **6 69 89 35 40**

✉ *imbspietro@mariabambina.va*

♨ Open to both men and women

ⓣ Istituto Santa Sofia

✉ Piazza Madonna dei Monti, 3
00184 Rome (RM)

☏ +39 (0) **6 48 57 78**
☏ +39 (0) **6 48 71 064**

✉ *santasofia@tiscalinet.it*

♨ Open to both men and women

ⓣ Pensionato San Paolo

✉ Viale Ferdinando Baldelli, 41
00146 Rome (RM)

☏ +39 (0) **6 54 10 287**
☏ +39 (0) **6 54 03 073**

✉ *pensanpaolo@libero.it*

♨ Open to both men and women

T Residenza Madre Pie

✉ Via Alcide De Gasperi, 4
00165 Rome (RM)

☎ +39 (0) 6 63 19 67
📠 +39 (0) 6 63 19 89

✉ info@residenzamadripie.it

⛪ Open to both men and women

T Residenza Paolo VI

✉ Via Paolo VI, 29
00193 Rome (RM)

☎ +39 (0) 6 68 48 75 00
📠 +39 (0) 6 68 13 62 44

✉ reservations.paolovi@email.it

⛪ Open to both men and women

**T Suore di Sant'Anna
della Providenza**

✉ Via Giusti, 5
00185 Rome (RM)

☎ +39 (0) 6 70 45 34 62
📠 +39 (0) 6 70 45 35 13

✉ s.annagiusti@tiscali.it

⛪ Open to both men and women

**T Suore di Santa
Elisabetta**

✉ Via dell'Olmata, 9
00184 Rome (RM)

☎ +39 (0) 6 48 88 271
📠 +39 (0) 6 48 84 066

✉ ist.it.s.elisabetta@libero.it

⛪ Open to both men and women

T Suore Teatine

✉ Salita Monte del Gallo 25
00165 Rome (RM)

☎ +39 (0) 6 63 74 65 3
📠 +39 (0) 6 39 37 90 50

✉ suoreteatine@inwind.it

⛪ Open to both men and women

**T Suore Mercedarie della
Carita**

✉ Via Iberia, 8
11083 Rome (RM)

☎ +39 (0) 6 77 26 90 00
📠 +39 (0) 6 77 26 90 92

✉ mcresiden@tin.it

⛪ Open to both men and women

T Villa Aurelia

✉ Via Leone XII, 459
00165 Rome (RM)

☎ +39 (0) 6 66 01 74 58
📠 +39 (0) 6 66 04 49 467

✉ info@villaaurelia.net

⛪ Open to both men and women

T Villa Lante

✉ Istituto Sacro Cuore
Via San Francesco di Sales, 18
00165 Rome (RM)

☎ +39 (0) 6 68 80 60 32
📠 +39 (0) 6 68 93 848

✉ villalante@libero.it

⛪ Open to both men and women

☙ SUBIACO

**S Convento San
Francesco**

✉ Piazza San Francesco
00028 Subiaco (RM)

☎ +39 (0) 774 85 542
📠 +39 (0) 774 85 600

⛪ Open to both men and women

**T Monastero Santa
Scolastica**

✉ Piazzale Santa Scolastica
00028 Subiaco (RM)

☎ +39 (0) 774 85 569
📠 +39 (0) 774 82 28 62

✉ foresteria@benedettini-subiaco.it

⛪ Open to both men and women

☙ SUTRI

**T Casa Suore
Francescane**

✉ Via delle Viole, 15
01015 Fontevivola (VT)

☎ +39 (0) 761 65 91 75
📠 +39 (0) 761 65 91 75

⛪ Open to both men and women

☙ TERMINILLO

**S Rifugio di Angelo
Sebastiani**

✉ 02010 Terminillo (RM)

☎ +39 (0) 746 26 11 84
✉ rifugioangelosebastiani@
virgilio.it

⛪ Open to both men and women

**Additional
Accommodation**

Abruzzo

✦ ISOLA DEL GRAN SASSO

**🄣 Centro di Spiritualità
San Gabriele**

✉ Località San Gabriele, 187
64048 Isola del Gran Sasso
(TE)

☎ +39 (0) 861 97 72 101
📠 +39 (0) 861 97 72 506

✉ oasisangabriele@libero.it

🕮 Open to both men and women

✦ LANCIANO

🄢 Casa San Francesco

✉ Via Monsignor Tesauri
66034 Lanciano (CH)

☎ +39 (0) 872 40 432
📠 +39 (0) 872 40 432

✉ info@casasanfrancesco.com

🕮 Open to both men and women

✦ MANOPPELLO

**🄢 Sanctuary of the Holy
Image**

✉ Via del Santuario
65024 Manoppello (PE)

☎ +39 (0) 85 85 91 18
📠 +39 (0) 85 85 90 041

✉ info@voltosanto.it

🕮 Open to both men and women

Campania

✦ CASTELLAMMARE DI STABIA

**🄣 Hotel Istituto Salesiano
San Michele**

✉ Via Salario, 12
80053 Castellammare di
Stabia (NA)

☎ +39 (0) 81 87 17 114
📠 +39 (0) 81 87 15 260

🕮 Open to both men and women

**🄣 Casa per Ferie di
Christo Re**

✉ Via Panoramica, 66
80053 Castellammare di
Stabia (NA)

☎ +39 (0) 81 80 26 897
📠 +39 (0) 81 80 26 897

✉ info@piccoleancelle.it

🕮 Open to both men and women

✦ NAPLES

**🄢 Casa Di Nostra Signora
del Cenacolo**

✉ Via Manzoni, 131
80123 Naples (NA)

☎ +39 (0) 81 76 92 093
📠 +39 (0) 81 76 92 723

✉ cenacolonapoli@libero.it

🕮 Open to both men and women

🄣 Eremo ss. Salvatore

✉ Via dell'Eremo 87
80131 Camaldoli (NA)

☎ +39 (0) 81 58 72 519
📠 +39 (0) 81 58 76 819

✉ eremo.camaldoli@libero.it

🕮 Open to both men and women

✦ PIANO DI SORRENTO

**🄣 Casa per Ferie Suore
Elisabettine**

✉ Via Madonna di Rosella, 120
80063 Piano di Sorrento (NA)

☎ +39 (0) 81 87 86 090

🕮 Open to both men and women

✦ POMPEII

**🄣 Hostel Casa del
Pellegrino**

✉ Via Duca d'Aosta, 4
80045 Pompeii (NA)

☎ +39 (0) 81 85 08 644
📠 +39 (0) 81 85 08 644

✉ ostellopompei@virgilio.it

🕮 Open to both men and women

✦ SORRENTO

**🄣 Convento Oasi Madre
Della Pace**

✉ Via Parise, 22
80067 Località Priora
Sorrento (NA)

☎ +39 (0) 81 87 81 924
📠 +39 (0) 81 87 81 924

✉ info@oasimadredellapace.com

🕮 Open to both men and women

Liguria

🕏 LA SPEZIA

🅣 Casa di Soggiorno

✉ Piazzale Giovanni XXIII, 1
19121 La Spezia (SP)

📞 +39 (0) 187 24 322
📠 +39 (0) 187 20 349

✍ madripiespezia1@infinito.it

🎎 Open to both men and women

🕏 MONTEROSSO AL MARE

🅣 Hotel Villa Adriana

✉ Via IV Novembre, 23
19016 Monterosso al Mare
(SP)

📞 +39 (0) 187 81 81 09
📠 +39 (0) 187 81 81 28

✍ info@villaadriana.info

🎎 Open to both men and women

🕏 SPOTORNO

🅣 Hotel Acqua Novella

✉ Via Acquanovella, 1
17028 Spotorno (SV)

📞 +39 (0) 19 74 16 65
📠 +39 (0) 19 74 16 61 55

✍ info@acquanovella.it

🎎 Open to both men and women

🅣 CASA STELLA MARIS

✉ Via Maremma, 12
17028 Spotorno (SV)

📞 +39 (0) 19 74 51 56
📠 +39 (0) 19 74 1314

✍ stellamariss@libero.it

🎎 Open to both men and women

🕏 VERNAZZA

🅢 Santuario di Reggio

✉ Via di Reggio, 2
19018 Vernazza (SP)

📞 +39 (0) 187 81 22 46

🎎 Open to both men and women

Lombardy

🕏 BERGAMO

🅢 Monastero San Benedetto

✉ Via Sant'Alessandro, 51
24122 Bergamo (BG)

📞 +39 (0) 35 24 74 61
📠 +39 (0) 30 065 24 74 61

✍ monsanben.bg@tiscali.it

🎎 Open to both men and women

🕏 BRESCIA

🅢 Centro Mater Divinae Gratiae

✉ Via San Emiliano, 30
25127 Brescia (BS)

📞 +39 (0) 30 38 47 212 210
📠 +39 (0) 30 38 47 297

✍ info@materdivinaegratiae.it

🎎 Open to both men and women

🕏 COMO

🅣 Istituto Santa Croce

✉ Via Tommaso Grosso, 50
22100 Como (CO)

📞 +39 (0) 31 30 53 00

🎎 Open to both men and women

🕏 MILAN

🅣 Casa del Clero san Tomaso

✉ Via San Tomaso, 2
20144 Milan (MI)

📞 +39 (0) 2 86 92 705

🎎 Open to both men and women

🅣 Centro Paolo VI

✉ Via Andrea Verga, 9
20144 Milan (MI)

📞 +39 (0) 2 49 96 31

🎎 Open to both men and women

🕏 VARESE

🅢 Villa Mater Dei

✉ Via Casati Confalonieri, 12
21100 Varese (VA)

📞 +39 (0) 332 31 25 55
📠 +39 (0) 332 32 04 20

🎎 Open to both men and women

**Additional
Accommodation**

Marche

⚜ LORETO

🆃 Casa del Clero

✉ Asdrubali, 104
60025 Loreto (AN)

📞 +39 (0) 71 97 47 218

✉ delegpontificia@libero.it

🕮 Open to both men and women

🆃 Casa San Francesco

✉ Via San Francesco, 15
60025 Loreto (AN)

📞 +39 (0) 71 97 71 28
📠 +39 (0) 71 97 82 37

✉ albergo@casasanfrancesco.it

🕮 Open to both men and women

🆃 Hotel Giardinetto

✉ Corso Boccalini, 10
60025 Loreto (AN)

📞 +39 (0) 71 97 71 35
📠 +39 (0) 71 97 00 67

✉ info@hotelgiardinetto.it

🕮 Open to both men and women

🆃 Suore Della Sacra Famiglia di Nazareth

✉ Via Maccari, 7
60025 Loreto (AN)

📞 +39 (0) 71 97 01 81
📠 +39 (0) 71 75 04 604

✉ c.sfn@tiscali.it

🕮 Open to both men and women

⚜ MONTEFORTINO

🆃 ALBERGO DELL'AMBRO

✉ 63044 Montefortino (AP)

📞 +39 (0) 736 85 91 70

✉ serafic@tin.it

🕮 Open to both men and women

⚜ PESARO

🆃 Oasi San Nicola

✉ Via San Nicola, 8
61100 Pesaro (PU)

📞 +39 (0) 721 50 849
📠 +39 (0) 721 39 04 28

✉ info@oasisannicola.it

🕮 Open to both men and women

Piedmont

⚜ NOVALESA

🆂 Abbazia di Novalesa

✉ San Pietro, 4
10050 Novalesa (TO)

📞 +39 (0) 122 65 32 10
📠 +39 (0) 122 65 32 10

✉ info@abbazianovalesa.org

🕮 Open to both men and women

⚜ NOVARA

🆂 Fraternità Domenicana

✉ Agognate, 1
28100 Novara (NO)

📞 +39 (0) 321 62 33 37

✉ ennio.staid@poste.it

🕮 Open to both men and women

⚜ SAN AMBROGIO

🆂 Sacra di San Michele

✉ Via alla Sacra, 14
10057 San Ambrogio (TO)

📞 +39 (0) 119 39 130
📠 +39 (0) 119 39 706

✉ info@sacradisanmichele.com

🕮 Open to both men and women

⚜ SUSA

🆂 Convento San Francesco

✉ Piazza San Francesco, 3
10059 Susa (TO)

📞 +39 (0) 122 62 25 48
📠 +39 (0) 122 62 25 48

✉ info@ichiostri.it

🕮 Open to both men and women

Puglia

⚜ TURIN

⑤ Casa Mamma Margherita

✉ Via Marie Ausiliatrice, 32
10152 Turin (TO)

📞 +39 (0) 11 52 24 253
📠 +39 (0) 11 52 24 262

✉ m.ausiliatrice@tiscali.it

♻ Open to both men and women

⑦ Istituto Giovanna d'Arco

✉ Via Giuseppe Pomba, 21
10123 Turin (TO)

📞 +39 (0) 11 55 40 411
📠 +39 (0) 11 55 40 463

✉ istituto@giovanna-d-arco.it

♻ Open to both men and women

⑦ Villa San Giuseppe

✉ Corso Giuseppe Lanza, 3
10131 Turin (TO)

📞 +39 (0) 11 819 33 23
📠 +39 (0) 11 819 32 19

✉ direttore@villasangiuseppe.it

♻ Open to both men and women

⚜ VARALLO

⑦ Albergo Casa del Pellegrino

✉ Sacro Monte
13019 Varallo (VC)

📞 +39 (0) 163 56 44 58
📠 +39 (0) 163 56 43 71

✉ info@
albergocasadelpellegrino.com

♻ Open to both men and women

⑤ Albergo Sacro Monte

✉ Sacro Monte 14
13019 Varallo (VC)

📞 +39 (0) 163 54 254
📠 +39 (0) 163 51 189

✉ info@sacromontealbergo.it

♻ Open to both men and women

⚜ VERBANIA

⑦ Hotel Il Chiostro

✉ Via Fratelli Cervi, 14
28921 Verbania Intra (VB)
Lago Maggiore

📞 +39 (0) 323 40 40 77
📠 +39 (0) 323 40 12 31

✉ chiostrovb@chiostrovb.it

♻ Open to both men and women

⚜ MONTE SANT'ANGELO

⑦ Casa del Santuario di San Michele

✉ Via Carlo d'Angiò
71037 Monte Sant'Angelo (FG)

📞 +39 (0) 884 56 11 50
📠 +39 (0) 884 56 11 50
📠 +39 (0) 884 56 23 96

✉ santuariosanmichele@interfree.it

♻ Open to both men and women

⚜ SAN GIOVANNI ROTONDO

⑦ Casa Pace e Bene

✉ Corso Roma, 83
San Giovanni Rotondo (FG)

📞 +39 (0) 882 45 78 35
📠 +39 (0) 882 45 78 35

✉ info@casapaceebene.it

♻ Open to both men and women

⑤ Centro di Spiritualità Padre Pio

✉ Via Anna Frank
71013 San Giovanni Rotondo
(FG)

📞 +39 (0) 882 41 80 94
📠 +39 (0) 882 41 80 87

✉ info@centrospiritualepadrepio.it

♻ Open to both men and women

Additional Accommodation

Sicily

⚜ BELVEDERE DI SIRACUSA

🅣 Villa Mater Dei

✉ Via delle Carmelitane
96010 Belvedere di Siracusa
(SR)

☎ +39 (0) 931 74 40 44
📠 +39 (0) 931 74 50 14

✉ info@villamaterdei.it

⚭ Open to both men and women

⚜ CATANIA

🅣 Villa Mater

✉ Via Vittorio Bottego, 10
951325 Catania (CT)

☎ +39 (0) 95 58 00 32
📠 +39 (0) 95 58 00 32

✉ info@villamater.com

⚭ Open to both men and women

⚜ PALERMO

🅣 Casa Diocesana Oasi Baida

✉ Piazza Baida, 1
90136 Palermo (PA)

☎ +39 (0) 91 22 38 93
📠 +39 (0) 91 22 38 93

⚭ Open to both men and women

🅣 Convent of Cefalù

✉ 90136 Palermo (PA)

☎ +39 (0) 329 14 11 371
📠 +39 (0) 178 27 19 909

✉ collegiodimaria@conventisicilia.it

⚭ Open to both men and women

⚜ SICULIANA MARINA

🅣 Casa per Ferie Don Giustino

✉ Via Principe di Piemonte, 1
92010 Siciliana Marina (AG)

☎ +39 (0) 922 81 52 10
📠 +39 (0) 922 81 74 84

✉ info@casaperferiedongiustino.it

⚭ Open to both men and women

⚜ SIRACUSE

🅣 Hotel del Santuario

✉ Via del Santaurio, 1
96100 Siracuse (SR)

☎ +39 (0) 931 46 56 56
📠 +39 (0) 931 46 55 65

✉ info@hoteldelsantuario.it

⚭ Open to both men and women

Tuscany

⚜ AREZZO

🅣 Foresteria San Pier Piccolo

✉ Via della Bicchieraria, 32
52100 Arezzo (AR)

☎ +39 (0) 575 37 04 74

✉ info@foresteriasanpierpiccolo.it

⚭ Open to both men and women

⚜ CORTONA

🅢 Casa Francescana

✉ Piazzale Santa Margherita, 1
52044 Cortona (AR)

☎ +39 (0) 575 60 50 69
📠 +39 (0) 575 60 31 16

✉ smargheritacortona@interfree.it

⚭ Open to both men and women

🅢 Eremo Le Celle

✉ Celle, 73, 52044 Cortona (AR)

☎ +39 (0) 575 60 33 62
📠 +39 (0) 575 60 33 62

✉ eremo@lecelle.it

⚭ Open to both men and women

🅣 Hotel Oasi

✉ Via delle Contesse, 1
52044 Cortona (AR)

☎ +39 (0) 575 63 03 54
📠 +39 (0) 575 63 04 77

✉ hoteloasineumann@servizire.it

⚭ Open to both men and women

⚜ FLORENCE

🅣 Casa Per Ferie Madonna del Rosario

✉ Via Capo di Mondo, 44
50136 Florence (FI)

☎ +39 (0) 55 67 96 21
📠 +39 (0) 55 67 71 33

✉ info@madonnadelrosario.it

⚭ Open to both men and women

ⓣ Conservatorio Santa Maria deglo Angeli

✉ Via della Colonna, 34
50151 Florence (FI)

☎ +39 (0) 55 24 78 051

✉ angeli.fi@tiscali.it

⚥ Open to both men and women

ⓣ Istituto Santa Zita

✉ Via Nazionale, 8
50123 Florence (FI)

☎ +39 (0) 55 23 98 202

⚥ Open to both men and women

ⓣ Monastero Benedettino di Santa Marta

✉ Via Santa Marta, 7
50139 Florence (FI)

☎ +39 (0) 55 48 90 89

⚥ Open to both men and women

ⓣ Oasi Sacro Cuore

✉ Via della Piazzola, 4
50133 Florence (FI)

☎ +39 (0) 55 577 75 88
☎ +39 (0) 30 055 57 48 87

⚥ Open to both men and women

ⓣ Villa I Cancelli

✉ Via Incontri, 21
50139 Florence (FI)

☎ +39 (0) 55 42 26 001

✉ villa.i.cancelli@virgilio.it

⚥ Open to both men and women

⚜ LUCCA

ⓣ Casa Enrico Bartoletti

✉ Via della Chiesa 427
55050 Lucca (LU)

☎ +39 (0) 583 32 60 00
☎ +39 (0) 583 36 86 91

✉ lucca_casabartoletti@libero.it

⚥ Open to both men and women

⚜ PISA

ⓣ Hotel Santa Croce

✉ Piazza Santa Croce
56125 Pisa (PI)

☎ +39 (0) 50 97 09 11
☎ +39 (0) 50 97 11 044

✉ info@fossabanda.it

⚥ Open to both men and women

⚜ PONTREMOLI

ⓢ Casa Padre Pio Da Pietrelcina

✉ Via Cappuccini, 1
54027 Pontremoli (MS)

☎ +39 (0) 187 83 03 95

⚥ Open to both men and women

⚜ PRATO

ⓢ Villa San Leonardo

✉ Via del Palco, 228
59100 Prato (PO)

☎ +39 (0) 574 24 727

⚥ Open to both men and women

⚜ SAN GIMIGNANO

ⓣ Monastero di San Girolamo

✉ Via Folgore, 30
53037 San Gimignano (SI)

☎ +39 (0) 577 94 05 73

✉ vallombrosane@virgilio.it

⚥ Open to both men and women

⚜ SANTA BRIGIDA

ⓣ Casa del Pellegrino Santuario Madonna del Sasso

✉ Via del Sasso
50060 Santa Brigida (FI)

☎ +39 (0) 55 83 00 013
☎ +39 (0) 55 83 00 013

⚥ Open to both men and women

⚜ SANT'ANNA IN CAMPRENA

ⓣ Monastero di Sant'Anna in Camprena

✉ Via Don Flori
53026 Sant'Anna in Camprena (SI)

☎ +39 (0) 578 74 80 37
☎ +39 (0) 578 74 80 37

✉ camprena@ diocesimontepulciano.it

⚥ Open to both men and women

⚜ SIENA

ⓣ Casa Betania

✉ Via Montarioso, 35
53100 Siena (SI)

☎ +39 (0) 577 58 70 11
☎ +39 (0) 577 58 70 39

⚥ Open to both men and women

ⓣ Casa dei Ritiri Santa Regina

✉ Via Bianca Piccolomini Clementini, 6
53100 Siena (SI)

☎ +39 (0) 577 22 01 43
☎ +39 (0) 577 22 12 43

⚥ Open to both men and women

⚜ VALLOMBROSA

ⓣ Abbazia di Vallombrosa

✉ Via San Benedetto, 115
50060 Vallombrosa (FI)

☎ +39 (0) 55 86 20 74
☎ +39 (0) 55 86 20 36

✉ info@vallombrosa.it

⚥ Open to both men and women

Additional
Accommodation

Umbria

❀ ASSISI

ⓣ Albergo Ancajani

✉ Via Ancajani, 16
06081 Assisi (PG)

☎ +39 (0) 75 81 51 28
📠 +39 (0) 75 81 51 29

✎ albergoancajani@libero.it

⚥ Open to both men and women

ⓢ Casa Madonna della Pace

✉ Via Bernardo da
Quintavalle, 16
06081 Assisi (PG)

☎ +39 (0) 75 81 23 37
📠 +39 (0) 75 81 68 51

✎ alcantapace@alcantarine.org

⚥ Open to both men and women

ⓣ Casa di Santa Brigida

✉ Via Moiano, 1
06081 Assisi (PG)

☎ +39 (0) 75 81 26 93
📠 +39 (0) 75 81 32 16

✎ s.brigida.assisi@libero.it

⚥ Open to both men and women

ⓣ Casa Rogazionisti

✉ Via Petrosa, 2
06081 Assisi (PG)

☎ +39 (0) 75 81 67 35
📠 +39 (0) 75 81 68 56

✎ info@eraonline.org

⚥ Open to both men and women

ⓣ Cittadella Ospitalita

✉ Via Ancajani,1
06081 Assisi (PG)

☎ +39 (0) 75 81 32 31
📠 +39 (0) 75 81 24 45

✎ ospitalita@cittadella.org

⚥ Open to both men and women

ⓣ Hotel Giotto

✉ Via Fontebella, 41
06082 Assisi (PG)

☎ +39 (0) 75 81 22 09
📠 +39 (0) 75 81 64 79

✎ htlgiotto@tin.it

⚥ Open to both men and women

ⓣ Hotel San Francesco

✉ Via San Francesco, 48
06081 Assisi (PG)

☎ +39 (0) 75 81 22 81
📠 +39 (0) 75 81 62 37

✎ info@hotelsanfrancescoassisi.it

⚥ Open to both men and women

ⓣ St Anthony's Guest House

✉ Via Galeazzo Alessi, 10
06081 Assisi (PG)

☎ +39 (0) 75 81 25 42
📠 +39 (0) 71 81 37 23

✎ atoneassisi@tiscalinet.it

⚥ Open to both men and women

❀ PERUGIA

ⓣ Casa del Sacro Cuore

✉ Strada Vicinale del Brozzo, 12
06126 Perugia (PG)

☎ +39 (0) 75 33 141
📠 +39 (0) 75 36 452

✎ info@hotelsacrocuore.it

⚥ Open to both men and women

ⓢ Convento di San Francesco del Monte

✉ Via Monteripido, 8
06125 Perugia (PG)

☎ +39 (0) 75 40 679

⚥ Open to both men and women

❀ SANTA MARIA DEGLI ANGELI

ⓣ Casa Maria Immacolata

✉ Viale Patrona d'Italia, 5
06088 Santa Maria delgi
Angeli (PG)

☎ +39 (0) 75 80 41 145
📠 +39 (0) 75 80 44 517

✎ acc.giov.fmgb@libero.it

⚥ Open to both men and women

The Veneto

🏠 BELLUNO

🅣 Istituto Salesiano Agosti

✉ Piazza San Giovanni Bosco, 12
32100 Belluno (BL)

☎ +39 (0) **437 34 815**
📠 +39 (0) **437 32 704**

📧 belluno@salesianinordest.it

👥 Open to both men and women

🏠 PADOVA (*PADUA*)

🅣 Hotel Casa del Pellegrino

✉ Via Mario Cesarotti, 21
35123 Padua (PD)

☎ +39 (0) **49 82 39 711**
📠 +39 (0) **49 82 39 780**

📧 info@casadelpellegrino.com

👥 Open to both men and women

🏠 VENICE

🅣 Casa Santa Maria della Pietà

✉ Calle della Pietà 3701
30122 Castello (VE)

☎ +39 (0) **41 52 22 171**
📠 +39 (0) **41 52 04 431**

📧 info@pietavenezia.org

👥 Open to both men and women

🅣 Casa Sant'Andrea

✉ Santa Croce 495B
30135 Venice (VE)

☎ +39 (0) **41 27 70 945**
📠 +39 (0) **41 27 76 429**

📧 info@casasantandrea.it

👥 Open to both men and women

🅣 Centro Don Orione Artigianelli

✉ Zattere Dorsoduro 909A
30123 Venice (VE)

☎ +39 (0) **41 52 24 077**
📠 +39 (0) **41 52 86 214**

📧 info@donorione-venezia.it

👥 Open to both men and women

🅣 Domus Ciliota

✉ Calle delle Muneghe, San Marco, 2976
Venice 30124 (VE)

☎ +39 (0) **41 52 04 888**
📠 +39 (0) **41 52 12 730**

📧 info@ciliota.it

👥 Open to both men and women

🅣 Istituto Canossiano

✉ Ponte piccolo
Giudecca, 428
30133 Venice (VE)

☎ +39 (0) **41 52 22 157**
📠 +39 (0) **41 52 22 157**

👤 Women only

🆂 Istituto Buon Pastore

✉ Castello, 77
30122 Venice (VE)

☎ +39 (0) **41 52 22 689**
📠 +39 (0) **41 52 22 353**

📧 sede@buonpastore.org

👥 Open to both men and women

🅣 Istituto Canossiano Maria Immacolata

✉ Fondamenta de le Romite
Dorsoduro, 1323
30123 Venice (VE)

☎ +39 (0) **41 24 09 711**
📠 +39 (0) **41 24 09 712**

📧 cvenezia@fdcc.org

👥 Open to both men and women

🏠 VERONA

🅣 Centro Monsignor Carraro

✉ Lungadige Attiraglio, 45
37124 Verona (VR)

☎ +39 (0) **45 91 58 77**
📠 +39 (0) **45 83 01 929**

📧 info@centrocarraro.it

👥 Open to both men and women

Rôti di dinde
à la Normande
Roast Normandy Turkey

Serves	4
Preparation time	20 minutes
Cooking time	2 hours
Oven	210°C

- 1 small turkey
- 1kg of Calvados (or cooking) apples
- 500g onions
- juice of half a lemon butter
- olive oil
- salt and pepper

Slice the onions and place in a pan with some gently heated olive oil. Cover pan and keep onions on low heat for 20 minutes, tossing occasionally.

❧ Peel and cut apples into quarters. Place the half the apples, lemon juice and butter in a separate pan and cook gently until apples become barely soft. Add salt and pepper to taste. Mix well.

❧ Combine the apple mix with the onions and stuff the turkey with the mixture. Brush the turkey with olive oil and melted butter. Place the turkey in a baking dish and cook in a moderate oven for 2 hours. Baste frequently to stop the turkey from drying out.

❧ Add water to the pan if the turkey appears dry or cover in foil. Remove foil 20 minutes before turkey is cooked to allow it to brown.

❧ When the turkey is almost ready to serve add butter to a pan and gently toss the remainder of the apples until they become soft. Serve on the side with slices of turkey.

❧ *Bon appétit!*